Anthony Howard is a distinguished political commentator who has been editor of both the *Listener* and the *New Statesman* and has written for the *Guardian*, the *Sunday Times* and the *Observer* (where he was deputy editor).

From 1999 to 2005 he wrote a weekly political column for *The Times* and is well known to viewers of *Channel 4 News* and *Newsnight*. He has also edited *The Crossman Diaries: Selections from the Diaries of a Cabinet Minister*, and is the author of the acclaimed biographies *Rab: The Life of R.A. Butler* and *Crossman: The Pursuit of Power*.

In 1997 he was appointed CBE and ~~~~~~~~~~~ is wife in London and Shropshire

Praise for *Basil Hume*:

'Delightfully written . . . ~~~~~~~~~~~ ~raphy, an invaluable resource and an inspiration~~ read' *The Times*

'Captures the man to perfection . . . Howard, one of the great political journalists of his generation, is such a fluent and economical writer' *Sunday Telegraph*

'Illuminating . . . an elegant tribute to the man' *Spectator*

'A delight to read' *Observer*

'Erudite and eminently readable' *Independent on Sunday*

'A Rolls-Royce of a Biography' *The Tablet*

'A vivid and moving biography' *Catholic Herald*

BASIL HUME
The Monk Cardinal

Anthony Howard

headline

First published in 2005
by HEADLINE BOOK PUBLISHING

First published in paperback in 2006
by HEADLINE BOOK PUBLISHING

1

ISBN 0 7553 1248 1

Typeset in Scala by Palimpsest Book Production Limited,
Polmont, Stirlingshire

Text design by Palimpsest Book Production Limited,
Polmont, Stirlingshire

Printed and bound in Great Britain by
Mackays of Chatham plc, Chatham, Kent

Headline's policy is to use papers that are natural, renewable
and recyclable products and made from wood grown in sustainable forests.
The logging and manufacturing processes are expected to conform to
the environmental regulations of the country of origin.

HEADLINE BOOK PUBLISHING LTD
A division of Hodder Headline
338 Euston Road
London NW1 3BH

www.headline.co.uk
www.hodderheadline.com

In memory of WGH and JRH

CONTENTS

FOREWORD

A NYONE READING A BIOGRAPHY OF THIS KIND HAS THE right to know something of the author's own attitude towards religion. The British are notoriously reticent in such matters, but, if I had to define my own position, it would have to be that of a 'wistful agnostic'.

In choosing that particular phrase (first, I think, coined by an Anglican bishop to describe his own beliefs, or lack of them) I fully accept that some will feel that by itself it disqualifies me from seeking to understand – let alone actually to write about – one of the great Christian leaders of the twentieth century. On the other hand, I draw comfort from the fact that this does not seem to have been a view endorsed by Basil Hume's own literary executors.

When, some three years ago, Liam Kelly and Charles Wookey – together with the then Abbot of Ampleforth, Timothy Wright – asked me to write the late Cardinal's life, they did so armed with the knowledge of the ambivalence of my own theological standpoint. Indeed, they went further and were generous enough to suggest that my very role as 'an outsider' might turn out to be an advantage rather than a liability.

It is just possible that they may even have been right – at least in the sense that I came to the task with no ideological baggage and very few preconceived notions. That was also true of any impressions left by personal acquaintanceship. Although once or twice we were in the same room together, I was never formally introduced to the Cardinal and held no conversation with him of any sort. Again, however, that could be argued to have proved less of a limitation than an asset.

It has certainly meant that this book – in sharp contrast to the two political biographies I have previously written – has represented very much a voyage of discovery and exploration. Getting to know my subject and beginning to have some feeling for the world in which he moved soon became for me easily the most rewarding aspect of the whole exercise.

Not that the terrain I found myself contemplating was entirely new or wholly unfamiliar. As the (often wayward) son of an Anglican clergyman, I spent the first twenty years of my life living in a succession of vicarages and rectories. That inevitably meant that I learned something of the strains and demands made on the life of a priest. I saw singularly little, however, of how that (necessarily celibate) way of life was led within a Roman Catholic presbytery, still less in a monastery. Congregationalist divines, Methodist ministers, even the occasional rabbi, may all from time to time have come to our house to be closeted behind the doors of my father's study; but, to the best of my recollection, no Roman Catholic priest ever crossed the threshold.

In fact, such was the strength of antagonism between the Catholic Church and the Church of England at that time that if – by some piece of ill-fortune – the local Catholic parish priest and my father should find themselves in danger of bumping into each other, while going about their respective pastoral duties in the same street, one of them would always cross the road in order to avoid the embarrassment of having to acknowledge the other's existence.

Looking back, I remain amazed at the speed with which such things have changed over the past forty years. The main agent of that change, at least in Britain, was undoubtedly the subject of this book. By the time Basil Hume became Archbishop of Westminster, I happened to be editor of the *New Statesman* and I have never forgotten the aura he brought to his very first encounter with the press on the day his appointment was announced in February 1976.

I had gone to the initial news conference, in what was then the London Press Club just off High Holborn, planning to ask what seemed to me a perfectly legitimate question: in what way did the Archbishop-Elect feel that his many years at Ampleforth – at least partially spent helping to bring up the sons of the middle and professional classes to the greater glory of their parents – had prepared him for being leader of the country's five million predominantly working-class Catholics? I never got round to putting the point – not because I was prevented from doing so, but simply because there was an air of calmness and simplicity about him that even I, as a brash, young, left-wing journalist, felt reluctant to disturb.

In part, no doubt, this was the product of his Benedictine background – the message that this former Abbot consistently transmitted was that his purpose lay not in promoting any particular brand of faith but rather in talking about God (something that, in contrast to many prominent churchmen, he was never shy of doing). The first duty of a monk has always lain in the praising of God and throughout the twenty-three years of his extra-monastic life Basil Hume somehow served as a reminder of that. It was a quality – the perception that he was a pilgrim on a journey whose destination he knew but about whose course he did not have to be totally explicit – that lent him his unique authority. Probably it is best called 'spirituality', and it was this attribute above any other that Basil Hume for nearly twenty-five years brought to the service of both his Church and the nation. It is something far easier to recognise than to describe – and, if it fails to come across fully in the pages that follow, then I can only plead that as a quality it needs to be experienced and cannot always be explained. The number of religious leaders who possess it – and it is by no means solely the property of Christians – is remarkably few but, at least when it does surface, it reaches across rival creeds and can be appreciated by those of all faiths, or of none.

I

A NEWCASTLE BOYHOOD

No 4 ELLISON PLACE STANDS IN THE CENTRE OF NEWCASTLE upon Tyne in what used to be known as 'Doctors' Row'. A four-storey, Georgian terraced house that has seen better days – it now houses part of Northumbria University's administration – its exterior nevertheless proudly displays a blue plaque, recording the fact that it was here that the future Cardinal Basil Hume was born on 2 March 1923.

In those days the address was home to a professional middle-class family. When George Haliburton Hume came into the world – Basil was his monastic name, adopted only on entering into his novitiate as a Benedictine monk in 1941 – it was to join a second generation medical household. Already forty-three when his first son was born, William Errington Hume was himself the son of a doctor and had been brought up in this self-same house. A tall, distinguished heart specialist, who passed on his height, his Roman nose and his piercing blue eyes to his first son, he was a man of conventional habits who had done only one truly rash thing in his life.

As an RAMC officer serving in France during the First World War he had met and fallen in love with the eighteen-year-old daughter of the French family who happened to be living next door to the house in the Pas-de-Calais in which he was billeted. The first encounter between him and his future wife was thus the product of pure chance. Her family originally came from Lille and found themselves living in the vicinity of the handsome British Army major only because her mother, in order to get away from the advancing German Army, had taken herself and her children to the seaside resort of Wimereux, the village from which the already 35-year-old William Hume commuted every day to the British military hospital in Boulogne where he worked.

From the moment the austere Border Scots doctor set eyes on Marie Elizabeth Tisseyre (her father, then on active service, was a colonel in the French Army) he appears to have made up his mind. He and 'Mimi' – as she had been known from child-hood within her own family – were very soon engaged and were married in the same month that the Armistice was signed – November 1918.

It was in many ways an improbable match. The Tisseyres were devout Catholics (the wedding eventually took place in the Pyrenees because the bride's father was serving at the time as a military attaché at the court of King Alfonso XIII of Spain) while their daughter's suitor, though nominally a Protestant, had long since abandoned much interest in, or sympathy with, organised religion. That, however, may have been providential: at least it removed any entrenched grounds for argument over in whose faith any children resulting from the union should be brought up.

Yet for the by now 21-year-old Mimi Hume, her marriage still involved a heavy price. It necessarily meant her removal from the gentle landscape of northern France to the industrial bustle of Tyneside. A preliminary trip to meet her prospective in-laws there in August 1918 had scarcely proved wholly encouraging:

even well into old age – she lived to see her son awarded his red hat – Mimi would recall that she could still hear the shuddering tones in which her mother observed to her as they both first emerged from Newcastle Station into driving rain: '*Mon pauvre enfant* . . . my poor child, to think that you are to be buried in this awful place.'

However, Mimi, despite being swiftly abandoned by the French cook she brought across the Channel with her, managed to cope pretty well. She looked after her husband, ran the house and within six years had produced four children – initially two daughters, Madeleine and Christine, then in 1923 George, a year later a third daughter, Frances, and four years after that a second son, John. When he was born in 1928, Mimi was only just thirty-one.

She had certainly established her credentials as a model Catholic mother – and, within the limits of her class and background, that was what she was. Talking to her children (except when their father was present) she always insisted on speaking only in French – the sole opportunity she got, once the French cook had departed, of using her own native tongue. For that reason alone, it was probably just as well that the nursery filled up as quickly as it did. So little gap was there between the first three children that, when George was born in 1923, his father decreed that, since 'no woman can be expected to look after three children' (which was presumably not intended to refer to his wife), an under-nurse must instantly be engaged to assist the already established nanny with the task of caring for the three infants in her charge.

No 4 Ellison Place may not exactly have been a *Forsyte* household – the staff were not, for example, addressed by their surnames – but it was still very much the product of its time. The children, who slept in the attics and spent their waking hours in the third-floor nursery, generally saw their mother only once a day. They would be brought down to the first-floor drawing-room by their nanny at tea-time. It was a slightly formal ceremony, but Mimi saw it as a vital part of the day's routine and insisted it took place every afternoon without fail. By today's standards she may not have been an outstandingly demonstrative or even affectionate parent, but at least she was a dependable and reliable one who always raised her children to the highest standards.

Among her children George was probably the one of whom most was expected and, indeed, the one upon whom the greatest attention was lavished. There was a rather touching reason for this. Before George was born Mimi had, at the suggestion of her confessor, prayed that her next child would be a boy and, when that turned out to be the case, she felt honour-bound to keep her simultaneous promise to God that, if her prayers were answered, she would do her best to see that he became a priest.

In George's early days all that, however, must have seemed distinctly remote. In inter-faith matters a *modus vivendi* was maintained within the Hume household by an unspoken concordat. Every Sunday mother and children would go to Mass while, almost equally dedicatedly, their father (no Calvinist in this respect) would set off to play golf. In fact, so much of a sceptic was William Hume about formal religious observance that, having attended the Catholic baptism of his first-born daughter Madeleine (in the absence of his wife who was recovering from her confinement) he never darkened the doors of a Catholic church again.*

For her part, Mimi did her best to play by her husband's

---

* Here his older son followed in his father's footsteps, if in the reverse direction. The first Anglican service Basil ever attended was his father's funeral held in Newcastle upon Tyne in January 1960. Thereafter, first as Abbot and then as Archbishop, he became something of an *habitué* at ecumenical services.

Erastian rules. No religious insignia were imported into the house, priests were rarely, if ever, invited to visit, and no form of grace was said at meals. All this was, no doubt, done in deference to her husband's secular (rather than Protestant) susceptibilities* – the product perhaps, as with many ex-soldiers, of William Hume's experience of the horrors of the First World War. Yet the tactful way in which religious conflict was avoided prompted at least one exasperated local Catholic priest to remark that it provided 'altogether too peaceful an advertisement for a mixed marriage'.

There was one area, though, that William Hume could neither inhibit nor influence – and that was the nursery. There re-enactments of the Mass regularly took place, Mimi having supplied the candles, with George acting as celebrant and his three sisters, all in their dressing-gowns, being required to play the parts of servers or acolytes. (There was nothing sacrilegious about this – it was merely a case of the children performing for themselves the one piece of drama or ritual that they regularly witnessed.)

The Hume household of the 1920s and the early 1930s (the family moved out of Ellison Place about the time George first went away to school) could claim, in fact, to be a thoroughly normal one, at least given its place in the then far more rigid class structure of life and society. The factor that most distinguished it from equivalent professional homes in the modern world was probably the presence of domestic staff. Although, unlike many of the grander specialists working in Harley Street or Wimpole Street in London, William Hume never employed a butler, he did normally have living under his roof a cook, a

---

* William Hume went on, however, to number an Anglican clergyman among his friends. He was Harry Bates who, after the Second World War, became the Evangelical vicar of nearby Jesmond. He would occasionally take Communion to his old friend (by now Sir William) as he lay dying.

parlour maid and a housemaid, to say nothing of the nanny and the under-nurse. In addition, since the house was as much a workplace as it was a home, there were a (male) secretary and chauffeur who both came in each day and a washerwoman who arrived twice a week to do the laundry. From 1925 onwards, there was also a governess, although she did not live in and gave most of her lessons in the house next-door, which belonged to another medical family who had more room as they had only a single daughter. Named Ann Drummond, this little girl – although a Protestant – became a lifelong friend of both the elder Hume girls.

The five-year-old George joined the classes held for Madeleine and Christine, together with their neighbour and friend, around Easter 1928. He would sit at the back of the schoolroom and it is doubtful if he benefited much from any of the tuition. The governess, a Miss Conway, was already fairly elderly and most of her teaching was based on books – *Little Arthur's History of England, Lamb's Tales from Shakespeare, Reading without Tears* – that she herself had been brought up on as a small child in the mid-Victorian era. When Miss Conway died in 1930, the experiment of having George taught at home was not long maintained, though he and his youngest sister Frances did for a time share a replacement governess (the older girls already having gone to a day school).

In a family so dominated by girls – Mimi's last child and second son, John, was not born until 1928 – the temptation obviously was for George to be spoilt. He tended to be endlessly indulged, especially by the succession of youngish under-nurses who came to work in the Hume household. One of them always remembered taking him to visit her own grandmother who lived on one of the bleaker outskirts of the city. His first words on being greeted by his hostess – who had put on a starched apron in honour of the occasion – displayed, if not a pampered existence, then at least a rather sheltered upbringing. Delivered in a piping voice, they were: 'Are you the cook?' – a question to which in the modest setting of an artisan's cottage there was no easy or obvious way of replying.

To be fair, though, every effort was made to remind the Hume children of how fortunate they were. The 1920s and the 1930s were not easy decades for an industrial, shipbuilding city such as Newcastle and their father's regular work at the Royal Infirmary, where he was a consultant, brought him into constant contact with the meaning of deprivation and poverty. The children would accompany him every Christmas Day as he carved the turkey and they handed out the Christmas dinners to the patients – but as they got older they grew less and less deceived by the spirit of this sort of Saturnalia. For George, in particular, much more influential in terms of his political education were his increasingly frequent visits to the Priory of St Dominic's, not the family's regular place of worship but a large Dominican church in the poorest part of the city, where a dynamic Dominican priest, Father Alfred Pike, gradually took him under his wing. It was on one of Father Pike's pastoral visits to Newcastle's slums that George at the age of ten was introduced to a Catholic family of twelve, all subsisting together in one room. He was many years later to say that what he saw of real poverty on that occasion played a crucial part in his own spiritual development – 'I believe it was that childhood experience that determined me one day to become a priest.'

Little, if any, evidence survives of the political outlook and social ethos that prevailed within No 4 Ellison Place – although the head of the household William Hume (twice mentioned in despatches and, unusually, appointed CMG for his wartime service) bore all the superficial marks of being a thoroughly conventional figure. Certainly, the fact that he served as medical adviser to the Northumberland and Durham Coalowners'

Association scarcely suggests that he can have been of any radical disposition. Doctors in the pre-NHS era were seldom anything but conservative by instinct and George's father, too, owed a large part of his professional success to the early patronage of Sir Bertrand Dawson (later, as Lord Dawson of Penn, Physician-in-Ordinary to King George V) – something, again, which hardly raises any suspicion of revolutionary inclinations. Everything, in fact, that can be gathered about Sir William Hume (as he became in 1952, for his services to medicine) conveys the impression of a slightly aloof, conformist pillar of the community who played a much less formative role in the upbringing of the children than did their mother.

Mimi was, of course, if only by reason of her French background, a much more exotic presence – and she, predictably, was responsible for most of the excitement in her children's lives. It was under her aegis, for example, that there took place every summer a seven-week holiday with their French grandparents – who had elected to stay on in Wimereux, just north of Boulogne, after the ending of the First World War. There they would spend most of the time with their Continental cousins – the three children of their mother's sister – and it was largely from them that they learnt to speak French both colloquially and fluently. (Although their mother still insisted on their speaking French at home, their conversations with her necessarily had a certain stiffness.)

These yearly visitations to the French seaside came to possess in retrospect all the associations of a family idyll, damaged but not shattered when Mimi's sister got divorced. They took place each summer for the first fourteen years of George's life, coming to an end only (under the threat of a new war) in 1938. George's French male cousin, Philippe, was roughly his own age and having him to play with must have come as something of a relief to a boy accustomed to living in a home dominated by girls and women. This aspect of his elder son's development seems to have been a minor source of anxiety to his father. To counteract the domestic petticoat influence William Hume tried to do two things: first, taking his son on winter Saturday afternoons to watch Newcastle United's home fixtures at St James's Park (a success); and, second, hiring a carpenter to give him carpentry lessons at home (an abject failure – 'George,' according to one sisterly comment, 'was always hopeless with his hands.')

The summer visits to France were not the only break in routine the children enjoyed. Every Easter they would be taken by their nanny or the under-nurse to stay with their father's unmarried sister, Aunt Betty (a great breeder of Dandy Dimonts), at her hilltop home at Alston in Cumberland. There they always enjoyed much greater freedom than they could expect surrounded by the disciplined routine of a doctor's household in the city centre of Newcastle. They also sometimes were taken to stay at a modest hotel in Wooler in Northumberland, which ran its own farm. So there, too, they had the opportunity of learning about rural, as opposed to urban, life.

However, very much at the centre of George's existence there remained religion. Even before his encounter with the Catholic family of twelve in the slums, he had betrayed the occasional sign that his mind was veering towards a clerical destiny. Living around the corner – at No 10 Ellison Place – was another doctor with a family of grown-up unmarried sons and daughters. They became, in effect, an additional regiment of uncles and aunts to the Hume children, their favourite among them being the youngest, Aunt 'Jossie'. She formed a particular attachment to George and vice versa – indeed, he had more than once declared that he intended to make her his wife once he grew up, but then, at least according to Hume family folklore, the day dawned when he suddenly and solemnly announced to her: 'I'm afraid I won't be able to marry you, after all. You see, I'm going to be a priest.' He is then supposed to have added, as if by way of consolation: 'But, if you like, I'll bring you Communion on your deathbed instead.'

The afterthought, in particular, has all the flavour of an apocryphal family legend – but what remains true is that George took on board the prospect of becoming a Catholic priest from a relatively early age.* His oldest sister, for example, recalls how upset he was when, at the age of eight, having for the first time on one of their holidays in France made his confession in French, he found himself rebuked by the priest for having got too many words wrong. He felt, she says, as if it had been God Himself who had humiliated him, but today consoles herself with the reflection that the undoubted hurt caused by the episode may have had a lasting and beneficial effect. It taught her brother, she argues, to be extremely careful about the way in which he handled people in future years and always to exercise his priestly duties with tact and restraint.

Going to school, which he first did at the age of seven, increased George's consciousness of his Catholicism. He first went with Frances, the sister who was nearest to him in age, to the kindergarten department of Newcastle Central High School, where his two elder sisters had already been admitted to places in the main school.†

Yet within a year George found himself being moved – perhaps again to put him under more direct male influence –

---

* In his book *Footsteps of the Northern Saints* (Darton, Longman and Todd, 1996) Basil Hume states that the idea of becoming a priest came to him 'about the age of 11' but other family evidence – including the re-enactments of the Mass held in the nursery – suggests that it may have been an intention half-formed well before that.

† All three girls subsequently went away as boarders to St Mary's, Ascot, a smart Catholic convent school in the south of England run by nuns of what was then the Institute of the Blessed Virgin Mary.

to the all-boys Newcastle Preparatory School which, at least in his father's eyes, had the advantage of being run by a friend of his as well as being his own alma mater. These, however, turned out to be about the only advantages it possessed. George was one of only two or three Catholic pupils in the entire school and, as such, found himself excluded – along with the Jewish boys – from both scripture lessons and the daily morning school prayers. (The experience taught him, he was later to say, what 'it felt like to be a member of a minority'.) It was also while at Newcastle Preparatory School that he first stubbed his toes against the realities of class conflict. All the boys in the school were required to wear Eton collars and these, combined with a distinctive black cap ringed with gold, made them an inevitable target for the rougher elements of the neighbour-hood. The boys at the local state schools would ambush and attack 'the ringworms' (as their caps led to the prep school boys being called) on their journeys home. Although Newcastle Preparatory School was only a short distance from Ellison Place, George soon decided that discretion was the better part of valour and took to coming home each evening in the safety of a Corporation tram.

Despite the fact that it gave him the opportunity of playing rugby for the first time – with the headmaster reporting encour-agingly to his father on his aptitude for the game – George was not happy at Newcastle Prep School. How much his own feel-ings had to do with his father's – or, more likely, his mother's – decision to remove him after a mere two years and send him to the nearest Catholic boarding school can only be a matter for conjecture. What is established as a matter of record is that in mid-September 1933 G. H. Hume joined fifteen other new boys at Gilling Castle, the preparatory school for Ampleforth, standing just across the Holbeck Valley from the college and the monastery.

A ten-year-old schoolboy can hardly be expected to foresee his future – but this slightly gaunt setting on the edge of the Yorkshire Moors was, in fact, to provide him with his physical base and spiritual home for the next forty-three years.

II

THE HONOURABLE SCHOOLBOY

THE AMPLEFORTH COLLEGE AT WHICH GEORGE HUME first arrived in September 1933 was very different from the celebrated Catholic public school that exists today. Established on its present site as long ago as 1803, it was essentially an inexpensive educational institution with a limited (predominantly Yorkshire and Lancashire) catchment area. No one in those days would have dreamt of describing it as 'the Eton of the North' – though its geographical location had meant from the beginning that it also numbered among its pupils a fair smattering of Scottish Catholic aristocrats, including representatives of the Kerr, the Fraser, the Stirling and the McEwen clans.

Ampleforth, however, in the 1930s was not considered anything like as grand as its southern counterpart in Somerset run by the Benedictine monks at Downside. Nor was that the sole example of the pull of social geography. While two Thames Valley Catholic public schools annually held a cricket match at Lord's,*

---

* The two schools were Beaumont and Oratory, the first now defunct. This Lord's Catholic fixture was discontinued in 1965, although the annual Eton v. Harrow match still goes on.

the high-point of Ampleforth's own sporting calendar lay in its regular 'local Derby' rugby fixture against its Protestant rival, Sedbergh (this was a match taken much more seriously than that against any other school, not excluding the Jesuit foundation of Stonyhurst across the Pennines).

Apart from being the product of 'a mixed marriage' – his father had gone to the muscular Anglican public school of Repton – George Hume was very much the typical Ampleforth pupil of his time. From a comfortable, though scarcely affluent, background, he was unusual perhaps only in having come from a day rather than a boarding preparatory school. His year at Gilling soon, though, made up for that. He spent only a year there because at that time Ampleforth followed the slightly odd practice of maintaining two separate introductory stages for younger boys – Gilling, across the valley in what was known as 'the castle', for those up to the age of eleven, and then, as part of the main school complex, Junior House for all boys of eleven up to the normal Common Entrance and scholarship exam age of thirteen.

Towards the end of his time in Junior House, George sat the Ampleforth scholarship examination but failed to win any award. Yet there does not seem to have been any question of his not progressing into the main school – or 'Shac' as, for reasons that are lost in the mists of time, it has been known to successive generations of Ampleforth boys.[*] The young Hume loved Ampleforth from the moment he arrived and he already displayed considerable promise on the rugby field. (Once he joined the school proper he almost immediately – in 1937 – began playing for the under-sixteens' Colts XV becoming its captain in 1938, the next year entering the 1st XV, and in 1940

---

[*] Some maintain that 'Shac' is simply an acronym for 'Senior House Ampleforth College', an echo of the time when the senior half of the school was housed in a single building.

becoming its captain, too.) Nor was the issue of having to pay the full school fees a crucial one for his father, by now prosperously established as a consultant in Newcastle and with a second salary coming in from holding a chair of medicine at King's College in the same city.

So the autumn of 1936 saw G. H. Hume by now a fully-fledged Ampleforth schoolboy as virtually a founder member of a new house, St Dunstan's, launched the previous year by a young monk, Father Oswald Vanheems. Here it may be worth noting that the teenage George Hume was lucky enough to enter Ampleforth at a time of confidence and expansion. The senior school in 1936 may have numbered only some 300 boys but no one seems to have been in any doubt that it was set to grow and develop both in size and standing. This was largely due to the inspiration of one man – Father Paul Nevill, its headmaster since 1924. (He was eventually to hold the job for thirty years and, as the shaper and moulder of a modern public school, ranks in every sense as the equal of Arnold of Rugby, Thring of Uppingham or Percival of Clifton.)

A tall, imposing figure, Father Paul – known universally as 'Posh' – owed his success partly to being a bit of a showman. Each morning he would impress his personality on the boys by appearing god-like on the top of the stairs at Assembly, looking down on the boys in 'Big Passage', with the long corridor linking the college to the monastery immediately on his right. Everyone seems to agree that he had an intimidating presence, but he never ruled by fear or physical force. Whatever may have been true of the schools run at the time by the Irish Christian Brothers,* Ampleforth – as befitted the gentler spirit of the

---

* A teaching order of lay Brothers, founded in Ireland in 1802 by a Waterford businessman. By the twentieth century, particularly strong in places such as Liverpool, it viewed the strap as an indispensable instrument of education.

Benedictine Order – was a notably civilised place. Here Father Paul himself set the pattern. In relative old age (he died still in harness at the age of seventy-two in 1954) he liked to recall that he had beaten only two boys in his life and that he had come to regret both occasions. The ferula – the piece of whalebone with its widened end for hitting boys painfully on the hand – may have played its part in maintaining discipline both at Gilling and in Junior House, but the senior school at Ampleforth appears to have had a more enlightened attitude towards corporal punishment, whether administered by monks or monitors, than most other educational institutions of its day.*

Part of the reason for this may, of course, have lain with the attitude and character of the type of pupil who came to Ampleforth in the first place. Without going as far as Queen Victoria, who at the age of eighteen immortally declared 'I will be good', the boys of Ampleforth in the 1930s do seem to have possessed at least an aspiration towards religion and piety.

In this respect the young George Hume was certainly no exception. When, for example, a local branch of the Catholic workers' organisation of Christ the King was formed within the school – rather derivatively since as a public school innovation it had already been pioneered at Downside – the sixteen-year-old Hume immediately took his place within it. As a member of the local 'cell' (also known opaquely as 'the thing') he and his colleagues set out to improve and intensify the whole religious ethos (and, indeed, the teaching of religion) within the school. It is by no means certain that the headmaster felt sympathetic to this development: indeed Father Paul is said to have reacted with relief when – thanks partly to his refusal to get

---

* When he became a housemaster, Hume himself did not, however, eschew the occasional use of the ferula – though he would normally offer its victims a cup of coffee afterwards.

worked up about it – 'the thing' eventually withered and died the year after George left the school.

His close involvement in so self-conscious an initiative came as something of a surprise to his contemporaries since in general he did not have much of a reputation for being a 'joiner'. Coincidentally or not, his main mentor at this stage of his life was a young lay member of the Ampleforth staff who had come to teach at the College after converting to Catholicism at Cambridge, where he had also won a rugby Blue. His name was Hugh Dinwiddy and, as coach to the Colts XV, he necessarily saw a good deal of his young captain. Dinwiddy detected very early on a seriousness of purpose in Hume's make-up and character that was not always immediately apparent in the case even of much older boys. In later life Hume himself was modestly inclined to put this down to the fact that, unlike most boys in the school, he had already made up his mind as to what he wanted to do. He was thus operating on more of a fixed compass than they were. Yet the decision to be a priest was one thing; the choice of the means to go about it was quite another – and that debate appears to have continued well into his schooldays.

The earliest letter of his to survive is a formal communication sent by him at the age of sixteen to the Father Provincial of the Dominican Order in England and Wales. Written from Ampleforth on 9 September 1939 (that is, within a week of the Second World War breaking out), its principal interest lies in the revelation that the young Hume had already established contact with the Dominicans at a much higher level than the purely parochial one. As was indicated in the previous chapter, Father Alfred Pike of St Dominic's Priory in Newcastle had already played an influential part in his spiritual and political development, but this letter suggests that contacts with the Dominicans had taken place on an altogether different plane and, for that reason, is worth quoting in full:

Ampleforth College,   9/9/39

Very Reverend and dear Father Provincial,

I want to apologise for not having written sooner. I have been sent back to Ampleforth* and so I am afraid I could not come down to London but I suppose you could not have seen me as you are probably very busy.

The monks are in retreat, which is being given by Father Keogh, OP. I had a word with him and he advised me to write to Father Moncrief and to keep in touch with him. Father Keogh advised about the sort of work I ought to do and gave me general advice about it, which was very useful.

I must apologise again for the delay and any trouble I may have given you.

I remain your obedient servant,

George Hume

As luck would have it, the letter was preserved – presumably originally in the Dominican Order's archives – along with the scribbled comments of 'Fr B' (Bernard Delaney, the English Dominican Father Provincial) on what was plainly regarded as an application to join the Order. His note ran:

I forget whether I have already told you about this postulant George Hume – aged 16 at Ampleforth & a parishioner of St Dominic's, Ncle-on-Tyne: mother French, father a doctor (non-Catholic but very well disposed). George seems a very fine type, manly and very pious with a great

---

* This could be a reference to the emergency precautions taken at the outbreak of war. Newcastle, being an industrial, shipbuilding city, was seen as a natural target for German bombers.

zeal to do apostolic work – average in intellectual direction but plenty of character. If he writes, you will be able to encourage him.

Fr B

So far as can be established, George Hume did not write again, though it remains possible that at Ampleforth alarm bells had begun to ring and that active steps may even have been taken to prevent matters going any further. (One contemporary even retains a suspicion that a letter may have been intercepted.) Hugh Dinwiddy, who was very much George's confidant, was by no means himself entirely certain as to what choice should be made by the young sixteen-year-old he had taken under his wing. On the one hand, he fully appreciated that George's temperament chimed in very well with the restrained Benedictine style but, on the other, found he could not entirely get rid of the feeling that his protégé's intellect might benefit from the more rigorous academic challenge posed by the Dominicans. In the end, in true Benedictine fashion, the question seems to have been settled by the games master, Father Anthony Ainscough, who insisted to his new captain of the 1st XV that the Benedictines were quite capable of supplying all the intellectual stimulus he could take.

For what it is worth, though, the Father Provincial of the Dominican Order probably got about right his estimate of the academic capabilities of the schoolboy who came to see him. At Ampleforth, Hume may have shone on the sports field – he was a star on the athletics track (where he won the long jump and came second in the 100 yards) as well as at rugby – but he did not initially bring anything like the same energy or enthusiasm to the classroom. In his early years he was, at best, middling – coming in eighth, ninth or tenth in most subjects – or, in his own words, 'at the bottom end of the top lot'. As he got older, his performance tended to improve – he achieved, for example, six credits in the old School Certificate (though two of these were in French, and the subjects he took, revealingly or not, did not include Latin, Greek or even Maths). He passed History and French in what was then the Higher Certificate, and the best guess probably is that, had he been required to seek Oxbridge entrance in the normal way, he would – in the climate of those more relaxed times – probably have gained a place, although almost certainly not a scholarship or exhibition.

Perhaps more to the point, so far as Hume's future was concerned, he started towards the end of his school career to make a name for himself in the school debating society, where – along with his co-chairman, a boy called O. O. Lamb – he was reported in the *Ampleforth Journal* of May 1941 as having kept up 'throughout the term a flow of eloquence fully worthy of any predecessors, and which considerably surpassed the rest of the House'. Nor was that merely an isolated Indian summer flowering. In the previous number of the school journal he had been described as 'a confident and able speaker who, by his clear delivery and persuasive arguments, repeatedly succeeded in winning the support of the House'.

Yet his true triumphs remained on the sports field, where in his initial year of representing the school the 1st XV won ten out of its eleven matches and then, with a war on, in the next season when he was captain, seven out of nine. Nor should it be overlooked that in his last term the by now eighteen-year-old George managed jointly to win the Ampleforth doubles' tennis championship. (Tennis was later to make way for squash, a game he played energetically until almost into his sixties.)

What everyone seems to have been agreed upon is that he was a very popular boy. There is even an Ampleforth legend that he was known throughout the school not by his surname but always by his Christian name of George. (This, however, given the suspicion of homosexuality that the use of Christian names provoked in any public school of that era, is probably best regarded as a piece of folklore.) The quality that was universally ascribed to him was kindness. The writer Neville Braybrooke remembered to the end of his days the generosity that Hume displayed to him when they found themselves together in the college infirmary suffering, along with a number of other boys, from mumps. To help pass the time a game of mock cricket was arranged with a chair as the wicket, a rolled-up pair of socks as the ball and a table tennis racquet as the bat. It fell to Braybrooke, who was only thirteen, to open the innings for his side – and, to his mortification, he was out first ball. Even before he could ceremonially hand over the bat, there came a command from Hume, the captain of the opposing team: 'Go on, you can have another try.' Braybrooke duly did (with rather more success) and generosity saw to it that self-respect was preserved.

There is no record of Hume playing cricket proper, at least once he was in the main school: apparently he suffered from an astigmatism in one eye that made it too dangerous a game for him to risk taking part in. He played, though, a full role in the Junior Training Corps – where, from being the player of the big drum in the band, he eventually rose to being a Company Sergeant Major. It was, in fact, his leadership qualities – in his last year he was also a school monitor and deputy head of his house – that tended to make the greatest impact upon his contemporaries. If it was at rugby that he excelled, then the informed judgment always was that, while he was a highly competent player, he was a quite outstanding captain. Interestingly, he had already started to develop a proprietary attitude towards anything with which he was closely associated: his invariable habit of referring to the Ampleforth 1st XV as '*my* team' provoked some innocent amusement among both monks and boys.

This readiness to throw himself into any endeavour in which

he was engaged reached well beyond the realm of sport. In the summer of 1940, for instance, he was one of a group of sixth formers who came together to form a travelling concert party.* They gave performances up and down the country – in places as far afield as East Bergholt in Suffolk or Benson in Oxfordshire – in an effort to collect funds for wartime charities. (At this they did rather well – raising a total of £70, a not inconsiderable sum at the time.) George's speciality in the show was his impersonation of a gawky schoolgirl – a feat he brought off so successfully that once, after a performance in an army camp, two of the soldiers in the audience insisted (to his great embarrassment) on showering him with kisses afterwards.

By the time of George's last year at school the war, of course, was an ever-present reality. Ampleforth had gone through the second half of the 1930s rather averting its gaze from the Spanish Civil War – if the monks were on anyone's side then it had to be on Franco's, but it was, to say the least, embarrassing that this meant also supporting Hitler as well as Mussolini. The Second World War, however, posed no such moral dilemmas and monks and senior boys alike soon rallied to the colours of the Home Guard (or the Local Defence Volunteers as recruits to that *Dad's Army* were originally called). As a school monitor and a CSM in the Corps, George – armed with a Lee Enfield rifle and three rounds of ammunition – frequently found himself keeping watch over Ampleforth at night and supposedly protecting both the monastery and the school from possible attack by German parachutists.

It does not appear to have been a duty that he took particularly seriously, although conscience was certainly not behind

---

* The efforts of this group are now commemorated in a stained glass window in the Holy Cross Chapel of the Ampleforth Abbey Church. It was unveiled by Abbot Timothy Wright in May 2004.

any scepticism he felt as to the likely effect of his or anyone else's efforts. The Fall of France in June 1940 may well have come as a heavier blow to the Hume household than it did to most British families, if only because of the clear French orientation of both George's mother and all five of her children. There was even a contemporary theory that, with France defeated, Mimi Hume, who had always been something of a pessimist, took the view that Britain by herself could not conceivably prevail and that this downbeat outlook on her part affected her older son. It is certainly the case that many years later, in an interview with *The Times* in March 1976, Hume himself admitted that one motive for his wanting to become a monk derived from his romantic desire to share the lot of ordinary people 'living in a bombed-out or even enemy-occupied Britain'.* His close friend and contemporary in the sixth form, Brendan Smith, also recalls that they were both convinced that there was little or no hope of victory.

Whatever the truth of that, it is probably too easy to magnify the mystery of far and away the most controversial decision that Hume made as a young man – his entering the monastery in September 1941 rather than joining the Armed Forces of the Crown. To understand how it all came about it is necessary to paint in a little of the background history. Under the National Service (Armed Forces) Act of 1938 'ministers of religion' were expressly exempted from the call-up, though it remained, of course, perfectly possible for them – with the permission or encouragement of the relevant ecclesiastical authorities – to volunteer for service as chaplains. No sooner, however, had this general policy been formulated than Whitehall began to realise

---

* Two years later in a Thames TV profile of him he went further: 'I had this kind of boyish idea that we would be invaded and that all priests and people like me would be strung up on lamp-posts.'

that, unwittingly, it had stumbled into a mare's nest. Vicars, parish priests, Free Church ministers, rabbis and all the rest might not be too difficult to cover by legislation; but what about all those on the fringe of the regular ministry, such as theological college students, lay brothers in the various Religious Orders, to say nothing of the novices already being trained in monasteries or even the prospective postulants about to enter them? There were clearly a number of 'grey areas' and, for once, plain British common sense – rather than the letter of the law – was allowed to provide the answer.

At least from the time Ernest Bevin took over as Minister of Labour and National Service in Churchill's War Cabinet in May 1940 an informal understanding existed between the Government and the Religious Orders whereby call-up papers would go out in the normal way to all intending monks of the relevant age: these call-up papers, would, however, be withdrawn on certification by the Superior or Provincial of whatever Order was involved that the man in question was a *bona fide* future monk with a genuine vocation.

In the case of the Benedictines this meant in practice that some intimation needed to have been given before the outbreak of war that the candidate concerned was seriously contemplating a monastic future; only if he had, as it were, put his name down as a potential postulant before 3 September 1939 could he escape the provisions of the National Service Acts (the intention here obviously being to forestall any efforts to use a claimed monastic vocation as an easier alternative to having to appear before a Conscientious Objector's Tribunal).

As a working compromise between the separate needs of Church and State, this wholly unofficial arrangement had a good deal to recommend it. From Bevin's point of view it certainly involved no sacrifice of principle, as that old trade union boss underlined by grimly remarking at the time: 'We know where these men are. If we need to bring them in, we can easily get them out.' And from the perspective of the monasteries, it at least demonstrated that the Government was prepared to give them its trust, and to permit them to use their discretion, albeit in severely circumscribed circumstances.

If the scheme had a snag, it lay in the weight of responsibility it necessarily threw on the shoulders of a small group of young men who attained their eighteenth birthdays in and around 1940 or 1941. It was not a responsibility they could renounce. By definition they were bound to be confronted by the school authorities with the choice they had to make. What is more, in the nature of things, the decision had to be taken in relative solitude, with few, if any, of their contemporaries having the remotest idea what was going on.

That was certainly true in the case of George Hume. Having been made aware of the option open to him, he decided in February 1941, along with Brendan Smith, not to withdraw his application to join the monastery (which had been in place ever since his flirtation with the Dominicans in the autumn of 1939). At first nothing at all was said, although four or five other Ampleforth sixth formers were making the identical decision at roughly the same time, and between 1939 and 1941 a total of fourteen Ampleforth boys went straight from school to enrol in the Benedictine novitiate and, even more exceptionally, every one of them stayed the course.

In the gloomy first half of 1941, when Britain stood alone against the Axis powers, all that, however, was far in the future, and the immediate reaction at the time, once the secret was out, was far from complimentary. For George himself the moment of truth probably came when he found himself being asked by a contemporary with whom he had always got on – and who had just been offered a wartime commission in the Grenadier Guards – what regiment *he* would be joining. When he replied that he wasn't, but instead would be going straight into the monastery, the response was perhaps predictable. He found himself being told he was 'a bloody coward' and, to add insult to injury, once the war was over in 1945, received a message from the same critic informing him: 'You can come out now – it's quite safe.'*

That is the kind of experience that tends to leave some scars on the back of even the most honourable schoolboy. It, no doubt, goes some way to explaining why much later in life, as Cardinal Archbishop of Westminster, Hume would sometimes take to saying wistfully: 'It was a terrible choice. If it happened again, I think I'd have gone into the Army.' Significantly or not, in all the years he lived at Archbishop's House he never once appeared as a formal participant at the annual Remembrance Sunday ceremony held at the Cenotaph in Whitehall, preferring to hide himself in an old mackintosh as an ordinary onlooker in the crowd.

---

* The author of the message and the source of the original remark was the former Comptroller in the Lord Chamberlain's Office, Lieutenant-Colonel Sir John Johnston who, to both their credits, became a lifelong friend.

III

NOVICE
AND MONK

I F THE GUARDS BRIGADE'S METHODS OF BASIC TRAINING
are notoriously tough, then the initiation period endured by
a novice in a monastery is probably even more so. For one
thing, it lasts much longer – two years as opposed to ten weeks.
For another, it tends to leave much deeper marks upon the character. Whoever first said 'A novitiate ties you up in knots and
it takes the rest of your monastic life to untie yourself' was not
entirely joking.

The approach to monastic training shares, though, at least
some things in common with military practice. The guiding
principle in the mind of any novice master (who, like the drill
sergeant, is the most important figure in the life of any new
recruit) has always been that, in order to build, you have first
of all to put down fresh foundations. In the case of the training
officer of a monastery this means getting rid of the old Adam
and raising up a new man in his place. Being subjected to such
a process is bound to be particularly hard on anyone entering
a novitiate immediately following a sparkling and successful
school career. In the autumn of 1941 the newly-named Basil
Hume (taking a fresh monastic name in place of the former

Christian one chosen by your parents is one of the first things that happens to a novice) faced a daunting spiritual journey.

He had embarked upon it, of course with his eyes wide open. Nobody could have been at Ampleforth for as long as he had – eight years in all – without having a general idea of what life in a monastic community was all about. Most boys may have had direct dealings only with those monks who taught them in class; but at another level the school was part of a worshipping community. Every morning in term time there would be early calls for those older pupils eager to assist the Fathers individually celebrating Mass at the altars in the Abbey crypt (the rest would daily cluster at the feet of their housemaster as he said Mass in the House Chapel), and on Sundays the entire school would join with the monks at both High Mass and Vespers.

However, that did not imply that even a novice recruited straight from the school knew everything that lay in wait for him. Coming as he did from a closely-knit family, Basil encountered one shock in particular. The Rule of St Benedict, he discovered, lays down in Chapter 69 that no monk shall take under his protection another 'even though they be united by blood relationship'. This meant that, if Basil encountered his younger brother John (now in the school), somewhere out-and-about in the Abbey grounds, he was required to ignore him or, at best, pretend not to see him – with, as the Rule recommends, 'his head bowed and his eyes toward the ground'.

The Rule, composed by an Italian Abbot who lived in the fifth and sixth centuries, is a truly remarkable document which, like the Bible or the Koran, has acquired an immortality all of its own. Consisting half of spiritual guidance and half of administrative regulation, it represents the lode-star in any Benedictine's existence. Instructing aspirant monks in the content of its seventy-three Chapters – and drawing out the contemporary relevance of its various directions and injunctions

– is perhaps the greatest responsibility that rests on the shoulders of any novice master. For, though much of it may superficially appear concerned with arcane and out-of-date detail – its preoccupations range from 'How Monks Should Sleep' to 'The Clothes and Shoes of the Brethren' – it does, in fact, contain what is, in effect, a guide to living. Perhaps the most famous phrase in it is contained in the injunction to an Abbot that he must always 'so temper all things that the strong have something to strive after, and the weak may not fall back in dismay' (in itself a summation of the whole Benedictine outlook). For any Benedictine monk the Rule rapidly becomes the yardstick of the success or failure of his own spiritual life – and St Benedict, for all his wisdom and gentleness, certainly never attempts to make out that the way for those who seek God will be in any way an easy one.

Basil and his half-dozen colleagues in 1941, none of whom were to see their parents more than once in the next four years, soon found that out for themselves. They started with an eight-day retreat, after which they were 'clothed', meaning that the Abbot clothed them in their black habits at a solemn service attended by the whole Community in the Abbey. After that, they became subject to what are known as 'perseverances' – reports at three-monthly intervals made on each novice's progress to the Abbot's Council by the novice master. Provided these were satisfactory, and the Abbot and his senior colleagues agreed with what the novice master had to say, the aspirant monk could expect to take his 'simple vows', binding him for the next three years, at the end of the first year of his novitiate. (The 'solemn vows', binding for life, normally came at the completion of 'simple vows'.)

The daily regime for novices must also have come as something of a shock. It was altogether more rigorous than anything that was followed within the school. Where the boys got up at

7 a.m. and were considered to have done their religious duty by attending, or serving at, Mass at 7.25 a.m. before going into breakfast, the novices had to observe a much more austere time-table. They were required to rise at 5 a.m. (when they attended the first of the six daily Offices), devoted their mornings to listening to lectures (delivered by the novice master, along with the monks responsible for plainsong and the liturgy), and dedi-cated their afternoons not to sport but to manual labour (work in the fields or simply cleaning up their own quarters) before retiring to bed exhausted at 9.30 with lights out at 10 p.m. Their life, too, was far more claustrophobic than that in the school. At least for the first year they lived together in a kind of bubble; the only people they were permitted to talk to were the other novices – including the members of the intake of the previous year as well as their own – the novice master and their confessor. (In addition on major feast days, such as Christmas and Easter, and during the short monastic 'holidays', they were allowed to take their place alongside the rest of the Community.)

For someone as naturally gregarious as the new Brother Basil, who at school as rugby captain had been accustomed to going in and out of other boys' houses all the time, this deliberate policy of seclusion merely added to an initial mood of depres-sion. Nor can this have been alleviated by the diminished oppor-tunity for playing games or even taking physical exercise. In term time the novices were allowed out once a week for a run and, though in the school holidays they could kick a ball around outside their quarters, no organised sport was permitted until they took their simple vows and got into the second year of their novitiate. (Unhealthily, or so it must seem today, it was also at this stage that the tobacco ration was increased from three to seven cigarettes a day.)

There was another aspect of what was essentially seminary life that appears to have bewildered and burdened this particular postulant. One of the stranger aspects of Catholic monastic training remains to this day that all the aspirant members of an Order are required to present themselves to the world outside just as if they are already ordained priests (complete with dog collars). The nineteen-year-old Brother Basil clearly found this irksome and, when he had to go on some expedition outside the monastery, took to changing into what was deemed the proper clerical dress only at the last possible moment. He was undeterred even when a fellow novice following the same practice got into terrible trouble. On a visit by bicycle to see his dentist in York, Kentigern Devlin, who had joined the monastery at the same time as Basil, was spotted hiding his working clothes under a hedge and putting on the dark suit and dog collar of a priest. In the wartime climate of 1942 he was immediately assumed to be a German spy. Only when his dentist obligingly proved prepared to vouch for him was arrest and incarceration avoided.

Episodes of that kind – and there was later another more deliberately comic one when a much made-up Basil and an equally impish colleague masqueraded as being a colonel and his wife giving Ampleforth the once-over with a view to sending their son to the college* – doubtless did something to lighten what must at other times have seemed an oppressively serious and solitary existence. Part of the discipline of the novitiate, at least in those days, lay in leaving each aspirant monk to spend a good deal of time alone – 'in the desert', as Basil himself was later to put it, rather than 'in the market-place'. The motivation here clearly was the belief that solitary prayer and contemplation offered one of the most direct routes to what every monk is supposed to seek – 'union with God'.

---

* They were exposed when the steam from the tea served in the guest quarters made Basil's false moustache fall off and the Guest Master was able to deliver the immortal line, 'All right you two, the game's up.'

At this stage of his spiritual odyssey, it was not something that came at all easily to Basil. Indeed, according to his contemporaries, there were moments in his early days in the monastery when he was on the verge of despair. There is a technical term for the condition of the soul which afflicted the young Brother Basil as he sought to follow the life of a religious. It is known as 'aridity', meaning dryness, joylessness, a sense of God being absent. In no way a reflection on the person suffering from it, rather is it the label given to a certain sort of spiritual desolation. It was to be Basil Hume's fate to be attacked by it at various stages in his life, including well after he had been elevated to the Ampleforth abbacy. However, this first bout, if only because it was at that stage wholly novel to him, was a particularly bad one. For a time his friends felt it was a matter of touch-and-go whether he would remain in the monastery at all.

One factor that perhaps made it all the more difficult to shake off lay in a certain lack of rapport between the young novice and his novice master. The latter was an experienced monk named Father David Ogilvie Forbes. A Scotsman of great conscientiousness – who had been Basil's confessor when he was a schoolboy – Father David tended to believe that the right reaction to anyone undergoing spiritual difficulties was to convince them that all they needed to do was to try harder in order to overcome them. That was never going to be the solution to Basil's problem. By now, in addition to aridity, he was being badly undermined by 'scruples'. This is another theological term which, in its specialist usage, has little or nothing to do with the meaning the outside public would normally associate with it. Within a religious community it does not so much connote the reservations resulting from a highly developed sense of right and wrong as an obsession with small things that do not matter or are of little consequence. A victim of aridity is thus highly susceptible to being overcome by scruples as well. Unable to come to terms with one big, important thing, he or she slides easily into worrying excessively about trivial or superficial issues instead.

This appears to have been the trouble that plagued Basil in the early stages of his novitiate, and his novice master's 'brace up' approach did singularly little to help him. Fortunately, some of his fellow novices showed themselves to be more sensitive and, one way or another, he managed to struggle on.

As a means of reassurance, individual incidents came to count for a lot. There was the occasion, for example, when – having confided to his new confessor his intention to depart – he was persuaded not to put it into effect until that particular monk returned from hospital. The priest, who was much sicker than he knew, never did return – and Basil, his tongue slightly in his cheek, explained to his contemporaries that clearly God didn't want him to leave.

On another later moment of crisis similar uncovenanted support came from perhaps his closest friend among the novices, Martin Haigh, who had entered the monastery just nine months ahead of him. Talking to him in the library after supper, a despondent Basil had said enough thoroughly to alarm his almost exact contemporary (they had even played together in the school rugby XV). Brother Martin was shrewd enough to realise that the best way he could help was simply to listen – but then the 9 p.m. bell went for the *Summum Silentium*, meaning that complete silence had to be maintained until the morning.

Although himself only twenty-one, Brother Martin knew that things could not be left where they were. 'So I went up to my room not knowing what I should do. And I knelt down by my bed, and my Bible was there and I did something I'd never done before and I don't think I've ever done again. I said a little prayer, opened the Bible at random and my finger landed immediately on a particular passage. It was the words of Our Lord about Lazarus: "This sickness is not unto death, it is for God's glory and through it the Son of Man will be glorified." So I wrote the text down on a postcard, explained what had happened and put it under his door.' This episode made a deep impression on Basil, and some light appears to have entered into what had threatened to become a long, dark night of the soul.

The decisive break in the clouds came, however, in 1944 when Basil, together with three other members of his original novitiate, found themselves, at the end of the third year of their profession of simple vows, dispatched to pursue their studies at Oxford University. Basil's solemn vows might still be a year away – he finally took them in the Long Vacation of 1945 – but at least he now had the comfort of knowing that nothing was likely to disturb his hopes of becoming a full member of the Ampleforth community.

Not that then, or indeed today, religious communities took any undue risks with those whom they selected to round off their education with a university degree. All such undergraduates were expected to follow a monastic routine, being attached to one of the three 'houses' that were maintained for this purpose in Oxford: Greyfriars for the Franciscans, Campion Hall for the Jesuits and St Benet's Hall, founded by Ampleforth, for Benedictines. The last of these, sited at 38 St Giles since 1922 but in existence since 1903, had not changed all that much in the intervening years. Run at that time on a tight rein by a distinguished Benedictine monastic scholar, Father Justin McCann, it had made few concessions to a changing world. Its ambience in 1944 was still very much that of brown linoleum and waxed floor polish; the furniture looked as if it had once belonged to a rundown railway hotel; and women were firmly discouraged from ever crossing its threshold. Its male inmates were expected to subsist on pocket money of ten shillings a term and, while attending lectures and going to tutorials, were simultaneously required to observe the usual devotional rhythm of the monastic life.

This ruled out any full participation in university-wide activities. No member of St Benet's Hall, where an early evening curfew was in operation to enable attendance at Compline, could expect to take an active part in the Union, in the Oxford University Dramatic Society or even in helping to run the various student publications. At this awkward interface between undergraduate and spiritual life it was at the time necessary to obtain a special dispensation even to be allowed to sing with the Bach Choir. If the rules for sport seemed a little less rigorous, this was only because games tended to be an after-lunch affair, and even St Benet's Hall students were allowed their afternoons to themselves. Along with Brendan Smith, Basil managed to turn out for the Oxford Greyhounds (in effect the university second rugby XV) and the two of them together with Martin Haigh, a member of the Oxford XV, also played from time to time in a 'Cuppers' scratch side which St Benet's Hall combined with the home students' St Catherine's Society and the Jesuits' Campion Hall to enter for the annual college competition. But even this level of active participation was achieved only with great difficulty. Justin McCann was not prepared to grant leave of absence before 2.15 p.m. (even on a Saturday) and this meant that, while home matches were feasible, all away fixtures were ruled out.

However, having been directed by his monastic superiors to read Modern History and not, as might have been expected (given his strength in French), Modern Languages, Basil seems to have been content to concentrate on his studies. The Oxford version of Modern History does not mean quite what its title might suggest and, although his special subject was the French Revolution of 1789, most of his time was taken up with studying medieval monastic chronicles (one of his tutors was William Pantin, a Fellow of Oriel and an eminent authority in this field).

Basil does not seem to have found the analysis of documents as rewarding an occupation as he had hoped and, in all the circumstances, probably did well to emerge in 1947 with a second-class degree in a subject that, as the main focus of his interest, was rapidly losing out to theology.

There was never any question of Basil reading theology at Oxford – if only because the Anglican-dominated theological faculty was at the time highly suspect to Catholics – but this was, in fact, the discipline that was next to claim his attention. In 1947 Basil and two of those who had been his contemporaries both in the monastery and at St Benet's Hall, Kentigern Devlin and Edmund Hatton, embarked on an even greater adventure: enrolment in the Dominican-controlled theological school of the Catholic University of Fribourg in Switzerland. If anything, Basil was probably the least nervous among them: not only did he have a complete command of French, he also possessed a smattering of German and could claim already to have acquainted himself with the Continent before the war. In a diary he briefly kept at the time, he went out of his way to record that Sunday 19 October 1947 – the day he boarded the Calais Channel steamer at Folkestone – represented 'the 35th time I have made the crossing'. There were not many young Englishmen of twenty-four who could make that sort of boast in the immediate postwar world; Basil owed his ability to do so entirely to the French holidays at Wimereux of his boyhood (though the ferry on those occasions, as he reluctantly conceded in that same day's diary entry, would normally have been the one from Folkestone to Boulogne.)

Cosmopolitan though he may have felt, Basil was not entirely spared all the indignities that can befall a Continental traveller. At first all went well. Both the boat train from Victoria and the steamer he and his two companions embarked upon at Folkestone in the afternoon were, according to his diary, 'remarkably empty' (not perhaps surprising for 1947, just two years after the end of the war). The same went for the Calais–Berne express they boarded on the Sunday evening – but it was there that their troubles started. It was all a question of luggage: one of the trio (Kentigern Devlin) had made the mistake of booking his trunk through to their ultimate destination of Fribourg, where there were no customs officers to examine it, rather than to Berne, where such facilities existed. This led to endless complications – compounded when, on the Monday evening at the very end of the journey, Basil actually succeeded in leaving his own suitcase on the pavement as he climbed into their shared taxi outside Fribourg station. Fortunately a swiftly said prayer to St Anthony (invoked as a finder of lost articles) had the desired effect and the case was still there when Basil ran all the way down from the seminary to reclaim it. The only price paid for the episode was a second taxi fare back up the hill – no laughing matter when the allowance for the whole year was 85 Swiss francs.*

As part of the university, the seminary was housed in a vast, rather forbidding building known as the Salesianum. Edmund Hatton subsequently described it as being 'full of aspidistras', but that was not, in fact, the most off-putting thing about it. How far they had been warned about it in advance is not wholly clear, but the three young Ampleforth monks soon learnt that not only the lectures they listened to but even the exam papers they eventually wrote would, by custom and tradition, be in Latin. At first even Basil – who, with his command of French, was not usually intimidated by the need to learn another tongue – felt distinctly discouraged. Of their opening day on the course he wrote in his diary:

---

* The sum was not as much as it may sound. In 1947 there were 17 Swiss francs to the pound.

Our first experience of Latin lectures. We made little of them. The first by Fr Hacfele, OP, on Fundamental Theology led me to suppose that perhaps it would not be too long before I would be able to understand but my false hopes were soon dashed to the ground by Fr Hoffman, the Dogma man, who spoke at great speed with a German accent. He made impressive gestures with his hands and I really got more out of watching him than from listening. However, we have been told not to be disheartened by the language problem since most people acquire the technique quite soon.

Fortunately in Basil's case this ultimately proved to be true. It may have taken him six months to master Latin (during which period, he years later recalled, he cried himself to sleep every night), but in his contemporary diary he did his best to put a brave face on things. Thus even by the end of his second week he can be found reporting that he was 'understanding more of what was being said'. However, that note of optimism may have been struck in the light of developments elsewhere.

At first the Ampleforth contingent understandably felt pretty lonely, but it did not take them long to found a Britannia Society incorporating the ten or so English faculty members or students in the university. Each week, on a Thursday afternoon, this group would meet at a tea-shop in the town, and, in the words of Brother Edmund: 'It was something we looked forward to tremendously.' What also struck Edmund was how good Basil was at getting on with everyone, regardless of nationality: 'He was a great mixer, he got on fearfully well with all the non-Swiss students and even a few of the Swiss, the three or four who related to us.'

It was all the more formidable an achievement since it was

in no way explicable in terms of sporting prowess. After less than a week in Fribourg, Basil was to be found lamenting in his diary: 'These chaps never take exercise and I can't do without it.' But where there was a will – as he was soon to demonstrate – there could be a way. It was not long before the three Ampleforth monks were joining each other after lunch every day for a run. Initially, they tended to be a little clandestine about it – stealing out of the Salesianum in their habits with their running kit concealed underneath. The only snag, as Basil ruefully noted, was that – since they were permitted only one bath a week (originally it had been one a month) – there was always the risk of being a bit sweaty afterwards.

There can be little doubt, however, that in Basil's eyes Fribourg, even given its restrictions, proved much more fulfilling an experience than Oxford had ever been. This was largely because he increasingly found himself excited by his studies. In his diary he even managed to record the moment at which his enthusiasm first became genuinely engaged. It occurred in his first week during a lecture on Church history (one of the rare subjects that was not taught in Latin):

The French lecture on Church history by Père Vicair was a joy. He has a gracious manner and a wonderful fluency. He said that Church history was an essential part of a priest's training and that it should lead a man to a greater love of God and give him the spirit of an Apostle. In seven lectures he is going to discuss the nature of Church history and why we study it. This is precisely what I want since my three years at Oxford have made me conscious that all such study must be a means of reaching God.

Whatever divine consciousness may have been awakened in Basil's mind by his time at Oxford, his view of the objective of study can hardly have represented anything but an unfashionable outlook in a university dominated at the time by the logical positivists, but at Fribourg things were very different. Here, in an academic setting in which his own assumptions were generally shared, he found his intellectual milieu.

Basil was lucky, too, in the moment that he arrived there. The postwar stirrings that were to lead eventually to Vatican II* had begun to make themselves felt by the late 1940s and the theological faculty at Fribourg – being a Dominican-led school – was very closely involved with the movement for change. That did not mean that the teaching there had ceased to be Thomist in flavour: the Dominican friars on the faculty still sought to reconcile faith with reason, but that in itself made them susceptible to contemporary influences. Indeed, it was in his four years at Fribourg that Basil was able to drench himself in the work and thought not just of St Thomas Aquinas but of modern philosophers too – with results from which successive generations of Ampleforth monks were later to benefit. He would always afterwards cite St Thomas Aquinas's *Summa Theologica* – a vast synthesis of the moral and political sciences brought within a theological framework – as the book that had most influenced him as a young man, and he was never shy either of acknowledging his debt to the prominent Thomist scholars at whose feet he had sat.

Being of the temperament that he was, Basil could never, though, completely abandon his role as action man. Father Edmund Hatton still recalls an episode in their second summer

---

* Pope John XXIII announced the Second Vatican Council, within three months of his taking office, in January 1959. It was only the second General Council to be summoned in ninety years, its predecessor having been held under Pope Pius IX in 1870. On 11 October 1962 some 2,400 bishops of the worldwide Catholic Church assembled in Rome with the twin declared purposes of promoting Christian unity and bringing about pastoral renewal.

together at Fribourg. It was the Feast of Pentecost – or what used in the Church of England to be called Whit Sunday – and as the two of them were going down to the refectory for lunch they heard a phone bell insistently ringing. As soon as they had finished lunch they learned why. The Regent, the priest who presided over the seminary, announced that two young Englishmen who had been staying at the Salesianum had gone out the previous morning on an expedition from Gruyère on the other side of the Swiss Alps and had not been seen since. He asked for everyone's prayers.

For a time there seemed nothing to do except pray and hope for the best, but by teatime – when a further message came through that no trace of the two Englishmen had yet been found – this essentially passive posture seemed altogether too much for Basil to bear. Somehow he laid his hands on a car, drove off to Gruyère and took general charge of the search. It was not until another three days had gone by that any news came. Then it was very mixed. Two men had been sighted on the other side of the Alps, but only one was alive. It was Basil who organised the rescue operation and took care of everything. He arranged the funeral for the man who had died – a priest from Birmingham – and saw to it that the other, who eventually became a professor of philosophy at Cambridge, got safely back to England. Nor did he forget the villagers who had helped both with the search and the rescue. They all were given cigarettes. The whole performance was a remarkable achievement for a 26-year-old theology student, and from that time on Edmund Hatton never doubted that somewhere in his friend's character there lurked genuine leadership potential.

In another sense, Basil's conduct in this crisis could be said to have vindicated a Benedictine practice. It was never the policy of the monastic authorities at Ampleforth to encourage those members of the community sent abroad for study to make more than one summer trip home each year. In the other vacations they were expected to take advantage of the opportunity with which they had been presented: to absorb and learn about the local culture in which they found themselves, to become familiar with other Benedictine monasteries nearby and, if at all possible, to deploy what slender funds they were given to make their first pilgrimage to Rome.

Between 1947 and 1951 – his last summer vacation in 1950 coincided with his being ordained priest in Ampleforth Abbey – Basil Hume contrived to do all of these things. He thus turned himself into a good 'European' rather ahead of his time, even if there were aspects of the traditional Continental Church with which he was never quite at ease – from the moment of his first visit at Eastertide in 1949 he never, for example, felt entirely at home in Rome, seeing it from the start as a hotbed of ecclesiastical intrigue.* What could not be denied, however, was that by 1951 he already possessed a deeper and wider knowledge of the religious life of Europe – and, indeed, of the habits of Continental thought and action – than most other priests or monks of his generation.

It is hard, in fact, to resist the conclusion that it was to Fribourg, rather than to Oxford, that the young monk who had flown the nest at Ampleforth at the age of twenty-one owed his coming to maturity. It had been a stern test, but he had come through it with flying colours: of the colleagues who either came out with him or, as in the case of Brendan Smith, followed him to Fribourg, he was the only one to stay the course and emerge

---

* Even many years later, as Archbishop of Westminster, Basil once told the leading Dominican Father Timothy Radcliffe, then Master of the Order of Preachers and as such resident in Rome, that he tried to keep his own visits to the Eternal City to a strict limit of two a year.

at the end with a Licentiate in Theology (which he was awarded *magna cum laude*, only one notch below the top *summa cum laude*). To say that from that moment on he was a marked man may be to claim too much – but he had certainly singled himself out from most of the other members of the Ampleforth monastic community.

IV

THE APPRENTICE
SCHOOLMASTER

O NE OF THE THREE 'SOLEMN VOWS' THAT ANY BENEDICTINE
monk takes goes under the slightly improbable name of
'stability'. What it signifies is that on enrolling in the
Order any new monk also commits himself to a specific monastic
community. Thus an English Benedictine will in common
parlance refer to himself as 'a monk of Ampleforth', 'a monk
of Downside' (or whatever the mother house may be) rather
than as merely a member of the Benedictine Order. Since the
Benedictines are essentially a confederation, a Benedictine
monk's primary loyalty remains to the monastery he joins, not
– as with, say, the Jesuits – to the Society to which he belongs.

This aspect of a Benedictine outlook shone through Basil
Hume's early career. By the time he left Fribourg at the age of
twenty-eight in 1951 he had spent most of the previous seven
years – first at Oxford and then in Switzerland – away from
the Community settled on the borders of the Moors in North
Yorkshire; yet the main focus of his allegiance remained the
monastery at Ampleforth which he had first joined as a novice
almost a decade earlier. So much is obvious from the correspondence he maintained with Edmund Hatton who had

returned home in 1949. Of course, a proportion of the letters
Basil Hume wrote to Hatton (amiably addressed under his
schoolboy nickname of Stooge) merely imparted information
about what was going on at the Salesianum where they had
both lived for two years, but when it came to questions, the
young Basil's thirst for knowledge always centred on Ampleforth
itself – how the 1st XV was doing, the likely reaction of either
the Abbot or the Prior to the idea of having a Continental
colleague to stay, even (a clear case of a *cri de coeur*) what sum
it would be appropriate to spend on the printing of an ordination card.

It is hard, therefore, not to feel that it was with a measure of
relief that Basil returned to Ampleforth in the summer of 1951.
However, after his academic success, the first job he was given
could hardly be counted as recognition of his achievement at
Fribourg. Instead of filling some responsible post in the school,
he found himself appointed curate in the local village of
Ampleforth – scarcely one of the teeming industrial parishes
that the monastery ran in urban centres as far apart as Liverpool
and Cardiff, but rather a rural cure which, while having a Catholic
village life of its own, served essentially as a chapel-of-ease for
those working on the Abbey farm or otherwise employed on the
Ampleforth estate.

Probably his posting to so modest a task – the village already
had its long-serving parish priest in the person of a formidable
Irish monk called Hubert Stephenson – represented a typical
Benedictine response to someone who might be thought in
danger of getting above himself; and, having taken the vow of
obedience, the freshly minted licentiate in theology was hardly
in a position to grumble or (as the Benedictine phrase rather
more vividly has it) to 'murmur' about the decision. Instead,
the young priest, who was much later to confess that he would
never have joined the community at Ampleforth at all had it

not been for its work with its parishes,* embarked with enthu-siasm on what was to prove his one-and-only piece of parochial experience.

One group he took very much under his wing consisted of the young men who served at Mass. It remains a remarkable tribute to the impact he made that nearly fifty years later his personality should still be recalled as vividly as it is within the parish, and six of the young men who had been his servers – all from one local Catholic family – bore his coffin at his funeral, held in Westminster Cathedral on 25 June 1999.

Nor did it take long for other responsibilities to come his way. He began teaching in the school shortly after his return and fortunately – since Ampleforth in those days had a rather haphazard practice of plunging young monks into the class-room – soon discovered that he had a real talent for it. At Oxford he had, of course, read history but, though he taught it to the fifth and sixth forms, it was languages – and especially French – that he specialised in teaching to the broad mass of Ampleforth boys. If he had a favourite class, it did not consist of the high-flyers – the sort of pupils who might end up winning univer-sity scholarships – but rather the more solid types of the Upper Fifth. One of the subjects he taught at this level was Modern European History, but he was probably most renowned for getting those who had failed French in their O-levels through the exam at their second attempt. Here legend has it that he possessed an almost 100-per-cent record of success, achieved not so much by communicating the beauties of the French language as by artfully anticipating the kind of questions the examiners were likely to ask.

---

* Perhaps harking back to his youthful flirtation with the Dominicans, Basil Hume made this admission in one of the 'chapters' he delivered as Abbot at Ampleforth: see *Searching for God* (Ampleforth Abbey Press, 1977) p. 114.

He was always a most conscientious marker and corrector of his pupils' work, wielding his red ball-point pen without restraint or inhibition. Sometimes he would go to the length of rewriting an entire essay himself in order to show how it should have been done. Nor was he above rubbing salt into the wound by adding a little note recording the time at which this self-imposed task had been completed – as in the message delivered to a fifteen-year-old Andrew Knight,* a future head monitor of the school, saying simply 'My own effort at 10.40 p.m!' Most of those who were taught by him probably appreciated only many years afterwards the exceptional trouble that he took. He was conscientious to a fault, especially given all the other calls upon his time. Within a couple of years of coming back to Ampleforth he had already been made coach to the 1st XV, as well as being appointed Head of Modern Languages for the entire school. In academic terms he may not have been quite the racehorse trainer that some of the lay masters were – notably Tom Charles-Edwards, the Head of History, and Philip Smiley, the Senior Classics Master (both of whom at this time were getting excellent results in terms of Oxbridge scholarships); but what no one doubted was that Basil had the flair and dedication of the born teacher. It helped, of course, that he remained as a schoolmaster what he had been as a schoolboy, an accomplished devotee of both rugby and athletics. (The 1st XV did notably well, even on occasion beating the school's great rival, Sedbergh, during the decade that he coached it). But what was also noticed about him was his total lack of pretension and the simple way he was content to live his Christian faith.

One illustration of this was his devotion to Our Lady and, therefore, to Lourdes (something he inherited from his mother).

---

* Editor, *The Economist* (1974–86); Chief Executive, the *Daily Telegraph* (1986–89); Chairman, News International (1990–94).

For many years only a small group of monks, boys and parents had gone to Lourdes from Ampleforth, joining a large pilgrimage made up of five dioceses. However, in 1955 Basil and his near contemporary on the staff, Martin Haigh, went on holiday together, beginning with a week in Lourdes. They were overwhelmed and left with great reluctance, but with a promise they made to each other that the following year they would start an independent Ampleforth pilgrimage.

The first, with about forty pilgrims, was an immense success, despite running into one of the worst general strikes France has ever had. There were no trains and the only way out of Lourdes was by bus. The bus ride began at 5 a.m. and finally ended at 11 p.m. A French colonel – part of the company and said to have been in the Resistance during the war – managed, after much telephoning, to find rooms for the more elderly ladies, while the rest of the party slept in the bus. Only a year later was it revealed that the reason why there were rooms to spare was because they were in a house of ill-repute whose normal rather younger inmates were all on holiday in the south of France.

Basil took a particular pride in having instituted this pilgrimage – it became an annual event – and he never lost sight of its spiritual value and unique character. However, as fresh responsibilities were thrust upon him, the burden of organisation fell more and more on the shoulders of the pilgrimage's joint founder, Father Martin, who saw the numbers taking part – not just boys in the school but mothers, fathers and a cross-section of families and friends – increase over a decade to something like 300.

The development, of course, that changed Basil's life most as a schoolmaster was his appointment as housemaster of St Bede's in 1955. At thirty-two, he was young to be offered the job – for a time he was the youngest housemaster in the school – but the death at the beginning of that year of Ampleforth's long-serving headmaster, Paul Nevill, meant that, from the Abbot downwards, there was now a general realisation that the school needed to look to the future. The first sign that a mood of looking forward had surfaced came with the appointment of probably the ablest monk teaching in the school – the highly intellectual but sternly austere Patrick Barry (known to the boys as 'Black Molasses') – to succeed William Price, the newly chosen headmaster, in his former post as housemaster of St Wilfrid's.

Patrick Barry, who appears as the faintly forbidding housemaster, Father Timothy, in Piers Paul Read's early novel, *Monk Dawson*, was only thirty-seven, and the selection six months later of Basil to take over at St Bede's at thirty-two was seen as completing a classic double: certainly, the two of them were generally perceived, in the slightly transitional era that followed, as effectively running the school. Almost from the start there appears to have been a tacit acceptance that somehow – through the combined, if contrasting, talents of these two very different men – the future not just of the college but of the whole community would be secured. Minds were inevitably moving in this direction, if only because it was not merely the late headmaster who had been well into his seventies. So also, if only on the fringe of them, was the Abbot – a formidable figure of great authority called Herbert Byrne* who had first been elected to the office as long ago as 1939 and had since then been re-elected twice. Basil had a high regard for Byrne – he was the only Abbot he had ever really known – and in later life always carried his photograph with him wherever he went. However, no amount

---

* Something of a legend in his own lifetime, Abbot Byrne acquired a certain renown from his encounter with a young monk who had come to see him in order to announce that he felt he needed 'wider horizons'. The response he got was both brief and to the point: 'What's her name?'

of hero worship could conceal the fact that by the mid-1950s both the school and the monastery were, by the nature of things, in the charge of figures who necessarily represented the *ancien régime*.

Being given responsibility for a house of some sixty boys was not the only mark of recognition to fall on Basil in the course of 1955. That summer he was both elected to the Abbot's Council (effectively the Abbot's Cabinet) and personally chosen by the Abbot to be the new Professor of Dogmatic Theology. For all the grandeur of its title, the duties attached to this post consisted of instructing the younger monks in the latest developments in theological thinking.

The choice of Basil reflected Abbot Byrne's awareness of his training in Thomist theology at Fribourg, but it may also have done something else. The seventy-year-old Abbot had more than once hinted at his belief that Basil might well end up one day with 'a chain around his neck' (meaning wearing the pectoral cross of an Abbot); and this key post, simply through the contact it would bring him with all the younger monks, might well have struck Byrne as one way of ensuring that result.

It is questionable, however, if Basil himself immediately welcomed the appointment. He was never anything but a conscientious exponent of the principles and propositions he was supposed to elucidate – and many of his young, pre-Vatican II pupils found his interpretation of Thomist theology an invaluable source of support when the time came for the traditional works of authority no longer to command automatic assent. But the truth was that Basil always lacked the natural dedication of the born theologian. Having to prepare his lectures – normally inconveniently timed for 10 a.m. – four days a week was more often than not a chore or, at best, a distraction from his already full life as a schoolmaster. Nevertheless, the Abbot's bet paid off: when in 1957 a vacancy occurred for a delegate to be elected to the Chapter of the English Benedictine Congregation, the body that brings together fourteen separate Benedictine Houses in the United Kingdom and the United States, it was not filled by any senior Ampleforth monk but rather by the youngest of the housemasters who, unlike the other candidates, had his feet firmly planted in both the monastery and the school. That same year he was also elected (and re-elected in 1962) to be the *Magister Scholarum* of the English Congregation or, in effect, the monk responsible for maintaining academic standards throughout the various Benedictine monasteries in the British Isles.

If Basil showed a certain impatience as these additional obligations crowded in upon him, it was understandable enough. As housemaster of St Bede's he had discovered total fulfilment – he would always afterwards say that the eight years he spent running a house were the happiest of his life. There was a very human reason for that. To his friends Basil never made any secret of the fact that for him the greatest of all the sacrifices involved in keeping the vow of celibacy lay in the necessary forgoing of all the normal joys and frustrations of family life.* Now, miraculously, in his early thirties he suddenly found that gap filled. Living very much at the heart of his house he was, in effect, the single parent to a large, varied and demanding family.

Here it is probably worth saying something about the rather special role of a monk-housemaster at Ampleforth. In contrast to the way these things are normally arranged in a conventional Anglican public school, the monk running a house at Ampleforth has no domestic domain of his own or anything approaching

---

* As the newly appointed Archbishop of Westminster in 1976, Basil Hume was asked by Canon Colin Semper during a radio interview on the BBC World Service whether he would like to have been married. 'Yes, I think I would,' came the reply. Did he often think about it? 'Yes,' he answered, rather to his clerical interviewer's surprise, 'every day.'

it. (No green baize door divides the communal parts of the house from the generally more civilised quarters occupied by the house-master, his wife and family.) Indeed, the monk-housemaster – and all housemasters were monks at least until the end of the 1980s – exists cheek-by-jowl alongside the boys under his charge. On the ground floor, his study (generally sited next door to the chapel) serves as a kind of common room, the sort of place where boys would congregate to listen to a favourite radio programme or even browse books, newspapers or magazines.*

Nor did the housemaster enjoy much comfort or seclusion even in his own bedroom. Normally tactically positioned next door to the junior dormitory, it was neither much grander nor much larger than the study-bedrooms occupied by house moni-tors. It was also completely without what nowadays would be called *en suite* facilities (any housemaster was expected to make use of the same ablutions arrangements as the boys in his house).

It was not a way of adult living, even in the 1950s, that would have appealed to everyone, but for Basil it presented no prob-lems. Always completely without side, and possessor of a natural, outgoing disposition, he did not want any artificial walls set up between himself and those to whom he was *in loco parentis*. In a very few years he saw to it that St Bede's – especially after it moved out of the main school building onto the nearby Aumit Hill, a site it shared with another house – gained renown within the school as very much a community in its own right.

No doubt, the more traditionalist elements feared that the atmosphere that Basil created was altogether too lax. He certainly

---

* The part current affairs played in the curriculum at Ampleforth should not be overestimated. The late Chairman of the Scott Trust, Hugo Young, Basil's first head of house and also captain of the school, always insisted that in his time no newspapers were even taken at St Bede's. He used to recall how he would trek all the way to the school library to get a glimpse of either *The Times* or the *Manchester Guardian*.

was not a disciplinarian of the rigid kind – one of his characteristic observations was that he always rather liked rogues because they tended at least never to be conceited – and he ran his house on a pretty light rein. He believed that the art of looking after boys lay in enabling them to find their own fulfilment and he developed something of a Nelson touch in turning a blind eye towards routine peccadilloes. On the other hand, if he felt spiritual or ethical standards were slipping, he would not hesitate to move in, and the boys in his care grew accustomed to having to expect at least one such moral blitz a term.

Every house at Ampleforth (interestingly it was only Paul Nevill who had introduced the house system into the school, which had previously been run on the same 'vertical' principle as the various Jesuit foundations) operated as a miniature city-state, and under Basil, St Bede's – especially after it had won its geographic independence – was no exception. With its house-master often absent, accompanying the 1st XV on its away matches, it became almost a self-governing democratic dominion. Basil himself used to like telling the story of the young boy who, having claimed the house captain's authority for something he should not have done, was entirely unfazed by having the demand put to him by his housemaster: 'Who do you think runs this house, me or him?' The reflective reply, which came only after a pause, was: 'Well, sir, that's a very good question – I'd need a bit of time to think about it.'

There was one area, though, where Basil never tried to delegate. Although the whole school would attend High Mass in the Abbey on Sundays and (until the 1960s) Vespers on Sunday evenings as well, weekday religious observance was a matter for the individual houses, each of which had its own chapel. Accordingly, once a week Basil would deliver a talk (or, as it is vulgarly known, 'a jaw'). Unfortunately, no scripts of these talks survive. It remains, however, a reasonable supposition that they provided the opportunity for the young housemaster to hone and perfect the strikingly informal technique that he later as Abbot brought to the service of the monastery through the 'chapters' and addresses that he regularly gave to the whole community.

Of course, at that stage, only the most romantic of prophets would have envisaged the youngest and most junior of the ten housemasters becoming the next occupant of the Abbot's chair. Nevertheless, one advantage of an abbatial election over a papal one is that – since any Abbot is elected only for a fixed term – a contest for the succession can at least be anticipated and foreseen well in advance. So, as the 24th anniversary of Abbot Byrne's original election approached, it was not perhaps surprising that a sense gradually took hold of a crucial decision being about to be required of the members of the community.

Under the benign, if scarcely radical, guidance of Cardinal Griffin (from 1943 to 1956) and of Cardinal Godfrey (1956–63) the Catholic Church in England and Wales was a solidly conservative institution. However, by the beginning of 1963 it was already four years since John XXIII had been elected Pope and the early sessions of Vatican II (see page 44) had taken place. It was only to be expected, therefore, that the rustle of a reforming breeze would begin to make itself felt even within monastic institutions. As it had already done with the election of John F. Kennedy in America in November 1960 – incidentally, the first Catholic ever to be elected President of the United States – that breeze initially found its expression in the demand that the torch of leadership should pass to a new generation.

The existence of such a feeling does not seem to have been taken into account by Abbot Herbert Byrne who, even at seventy-eight, appears initially to have taken the view that, having done three terms, there was really no reason why he should not do a fourth. In fact, the rules for a Benedictine election do not allow an incumbent Abbot to withdraw, so it would not have made much difference whatever Abbot Herbert had decided (unless, that is, he had resolved to resign in advance of the election thereby precipitating the calling of one). Yet, despite his hopes of remaining in office, the immediate field was soon effectively reduced to two – the choice in the minds of most monks lying between the strongest personalities in both the monastery and the school: Patrick Barry who had been serving as housemaster of St Wilfrid's and Second Master since 1955, and Basil Hume who, though younger by five years, had been housemaster of St Bede's for almost the same length of time. The general consensus was that one of them was bound to end up being elected Abbot and that the other would then automatically succeed to the headmastership once it became vacant.

That, in the event, was the way things worked out, though not without an element of stress, especially for Abbot Byrne, along the way. One of the characteristics of an abbatial election is that any monk can propose the name of any other member of the community, with any candidates so nominated having to withdraw while their names are being discussed (or, to use the technical term, while their claims come under the 'scrutiny' of their colleagues). This meant that during the actual process – officially known as a *tractatus* – one figure was always for a time left in virtual solitude; on the first day of the election this nominee, following the principle of alphabetical order, turned out to be Patrick Barry and on the next morning, when the decision was finally reached, Basil Hume. (There are even some eye-witness accounts which maintain that in the course of the intervening evening Hume who, together with Barry, had been invited in for a drink with a friendly housemaster, spent some time seeking to strengthen the resolve of the rival he was to defeat the next day.)

How much of a shock was Hume's election to him? Everyone

seems to recollect his 'shrinking visibly in size' when the news was formally broken to him (in Latin) and he also appears to have been temporarily overcome by tears (causing the more hard-boiled of his colleagues to 'murmur' about their new Abbot's 'Gallic temperament').

In fact, however, he must have known that such an outcome was on the cards – or, if he did not, his removal from the *tractatus* going on in the school library on the second morning must have awoken him to what by then was a real and present danger. Yet what may have allayed his fears was a genuine feeling on his part that Patrick Barry's claims on the office were superior to his own. Not only was Barry older and more experienced – as a schoolboy he had left Ampleforth the term before Basil arrived – he was also, by general consent, the more intellectually formidable of the two. But in the world of John XXIII of the spring of 1963, an outstanding intellectual was not necessarily the type of figure the monks of Ampleforth were looking for. The die was probably cast when early in the *tractatus* one of the older monks, Father Raphael Williams, said in a very brief speech: 'The decision is a simple one – do you want the mind or the heart?' He had crystallised what for most of those present was the central issue, and by formulating it in the way he did virtually ensured what the eventual answer would be. Within the school Father Raphael taught philosophy: on this occasion he also proved to be something of a prophet – but then so also did the young Ampleforth schoolboy who, departing for the Easter holidays, somewhat brazenly remarked that the boys all hoped that the monks, in the school's absence, would manage to make the right decision. On being asked whom that might mean, he airily replied: 'Oh, Basil of course – he's the man.'

V

THE
YOUTHFUL ABBOT

I N THE BRITAIN OF THE SWINGING SIXTIES, THE ELECTION
of a Roman Catholic Abbot scarcely ranked as an event
of great popular appeal. Even in the world of public life,
monastic communities were not always favourably regarded
– witness Harold Wilson's remark in a radio interview in 1963
that, if he became Prime Minister, he would seek to turn No
10 into 'a power house not a monastery'. So it was hardly
surprising that, apart from a few lines on the Court and Social
pages of *The Times* and the *Daily Telegraph*, Basil Hume's
emergence as leader of the Ampleforth monks at the age of
just forty should have been greeted with a marked lack of
media interest.

Within Ampleforth itself, however, the election was rightly
seen as marking a turning-point. Nothing like it had happened
in nearly twenty-five years. A reigning Abbot of almost eighty
had made way for a successor barely half his age, who would
now become only the fourth head to be chosen by the
Community since the turn of the century.

As if to mark an historic event, on the afternoon of 17 April
1963, there sallied forth out of the school library – the boys were

still on holiday – an impressive array of monks all singing the *Te Deum*. At the front of the procession were the novices and the juniors in simple vows who had not been permitted to take any part in the election. They were followed by the ranks of solemnly professed monks, their number swollen to 114 by those serving outside the monastery in the twenty or so inner city parishes which Ampleforth at that time still maintained. (On this exceptional occasion they were also joined by a representative from the recently founded daughter house in St Louis, Missouri.) Finally, in the place of honour bringing up the rear, came the new Abbot flanked on one side by Christopher Butler, the Abbot of Downside and President of the English Benedictine Congregation, and on the other by Father Anthony Ainscough, the Ampleforth Prior and, therefore, the number two figure within the Community. Once everyone was safely within the Abbey Church, the 135 monks present (including the novices and those in simple vows) took it in turns to kiss the new Abbot's ring, as a token of their obedience to the man they had just elected to lead them.

For Basil – younger by far than most of those who now knelt before him – it must have been a highly emotional moment. Although he managed to get through this first service of thanksgiving without losing his composure, the very next day, while celebrating High Mass, he once again broke down (just as he had done at the end of the *tractatus* in the school library) and had to be rescued in saying the Lord's Prayer by his loyal friend and supporter Martin Haigh. Less than helpful, too, was the fact that the ceremonies turned out to be very protracted, and it was another two months before the formal service of blessing by the local diocesan from Middlesbrough – an abbot while in office is entitled to wear a mitre but does not have the rank of a bishop – eventually took place. Once again, Abbot Christopher Butler, the titular head of the English Benedictines, was present and so was Basil's predecessor, Abbot Herbert Byrne. At the reception held afterwards the old Abbot deftly took the opportunity of replying to the modest and highly diffident address that Basil had delivered at the service itself. His words could hardly have been more chivalrous:

> I want to tell you, Father Abbot, that for the first and last time in your career you are slightly out of touch with the Community. We are very pleased and satisfied with what we have done – you are not. But be assured that, with the blessing of God and the help of our obedience and prayers, you will not find the task intolerable and that the Community gives you wholeheartedly its entire confidence and support.

Little wonder, though, if the young Abbot did shrink from the responsibilities that had been thrust upon him. As the Rule of St Benedict makes all too clear, the abbot is the focal figure in any monastic community, answerable not just to the brethren but to God himself for any failures or shortcomings that may affect its running.

Nor was it true that guiding the fortunes of Ampleforth was essentially a quiet, sheltered occupation. Overnight a monk who up to that moment had had no greater administrative experience than that represented by caring for some sixty boys in a boarding house found himself accountable for a variety of important projects. These included being responsible for the running and staffing of a score of industrial parishes, having overall charge of a major public school, and carrying the ultimate authority for a residential house of studies in Oxford, to say nothing of being expected to guide the destinies not just of Ampleforth itself but of a monastic daughter house some 4,000 miles away in the United States. It was an alarming combination of different portfolios and wholly understandable that Basil's first resolve should have been that he would do nothing precipitate.*

Curiously enough, what later came to be seen as the most formidable challenge to confront him was not one that initially seemed to pose any threat to the Community's peace of mind. Vatican II – which, as a mere Abbot without being an Abbot-President, Basil did not attend – eventually brought a host of problems in its wake; but monasteries tend to be conservative institutions and at first there does not appear to have been any awareness at Ampleforth of just how far-reaching the changes introduced by Vatican II (particularly in the case of the liturgy) would prove to be. That lack of foreboding, as it happened, fitted in well with the mood of the new Abbot: what he believed the Community most needed – especially after the upheaval of his own election – was a period of reassurance and consolidation, and this is what he set out to provide.

He did not even force the pace of change in the school. William Price, who from the beginning had been seen very much as an interim headmaster, was allowed to complete ten years running Ampleforth College before in September 1964 making way for Patrick Barry. However, even so key a move on the chess board as the appointment of a new headmaster – with typical self-sacrifice the 68-year-old Price agreed, after a year's sabbatical, to take on responsibility for Gilling (the prep school for Ampleforth) – did not imply any allegiance on Basil's part to change for change's sake. Simultaneously, and as if to balance change with stability, the longest-serving housemaster of all was left securely *en poste*. Father Oswald Vanheems had been Basil's

---

* He did, however, cause some consternation by early on insisting that every member of the Community, whether old or young, must be able to drive a car (something, incidentally, he was very bad at himself).

own housemaster at St Dunstan's when he was a schoolboy, and imperturbably continued in the same role now that the thirteen-year-old who had arrived in his house in 1936 had become Abbot. That was not the only symbol of things being left in place, however. Prudently, Basil prevailed on the highly traditionalist Anthony Ainscough, to continue to serve under him as Prior, just as he had done under Herbert Byrne. As for the previous Abbot, he behaved impeccably by taking himself off to the industrial parish of Leyland, just outside Preston, where he faithfully served as assistant to the parish priest until his death in 1978.

Basil's father, Sir William Hume, had died in 1960 while his son was still running St Bede's, so it was only his formidable French mother who was there to see him installed as Abbot (she even made his mitre). His new grandeur was not, however, allowed to alter in any way the relationship that had always existed between them. Even when 'Georges', as she continued to call him, was living in the Abbot's Gallery in the new wing of the main monastery building she would frequently turn up unannounced and expect her son to come scurrying down to greet her. His reward as often as not was some imperious instruction such as that his hair was too long and that he needed to get it cut. If this kind of treatment shocked the more conventional brethren and fathers, it at least had the effect of emphasising the lack of grandeur of their new Abbot in the eyes of the less inhibited members of the community.

Nor did it in any way undermine his position. The acquisition of authority, despite the obvious contrast in terms of age and experience with his predecessor, soon proved to be the least of the new Abbot's problems. It came to him naturally – not merely because most of the Community liked him but, rather more pertinently, because over the years there had come to be an increasing regard for his spirituality. This authority did not manifest itself in any obvious form. Basil may have been blessed with a distinctive, medieval face but he never quite managed to muster the natural dignity of a sacerdotal figure. The mitre that on high days he was now expected to wear would seldom be set straight; in a procession he loped rather than glided; and there was always somehow the apprehension that he was about to trip up. None of this mattered, however, compared with his striking ability at what was perhaps his most important duty. This lay in delivering weekly 'conferences' (as such talks were known) to the monks on Tuesday evenings, or the more formal 'chapters' with which at special moments the Abbot was supposed to address his colleagues. These moments usually had reference to a particular stage of the spiritual journey some of the listeners were undergoing – novices about to take their vows, postulants on the point of being 'clothed', or whatever it might be.

At this kind of personal talk – possibly because of the years of practice he had had as a housemaster – Basil was a natural. There would normally be some surprisingly informal word or phrase towards the beginning in order, as it were, to break the ice; there would never be any diffidence about drawing from personal experience or, indeed, over sharing difficulties or doubts; and, above all, there would be a total readiness to admit that in any life dedicated to the search for God there were bound to be moments of discouragement, not to say of despair. Within the Community these talks offered the key to the position of spiritual leadership that the young Abbot very soon came to occupy – and beyond the walls of Ampleforth they probably still provide the best testimony to the exceptional qualities that even a secular nation gradually came to recognise in him.*

* They were published the year after he became Archbishop of Westminster in Basil Hume's first – and best – book, *Searching for God* (Ampleforth Abbey Press, 1977).

What is interesting about them is that they do not really depend for their power on the context in which they were first delivered. Thus one year's intake of novices found themselves being told that, while they had acquired a good understanding of the theory of monasticism, they had not been anything like as good at acquiring monastic instincts. They would need, according to their Abbot (here the informal touch), 'to put a spurt on', something he was sure they could and must do. Put pithily like that, it no doubt risks sounding much like any other pep talk, but, if it does not come across in that way on the printed page, it is because Basil possessed the very rare gift of making even arcane situations relate to the outside world. If his own early years within the Community had been altogether cheerful and easy, it is at least arguable that he would never have made the sensitive and intuitive Abbot that he eventually became.

Inevitably, there were criticisms – and they tended to come from those monks (predominantly the traditionalists) who wanted more of the smack of firm government than their new Abbot was prepared to provide. It was not so much that Basil had a dread of confrontation (though he never much liked it); rather was it that he genuinely believed that conflict was best avoided if it humanly could be – whatever disputes took place, they all had, after all, to go on living together in one community. He had almost an aversion to thrashing matters out, and it was wholly characteristic of his approach that during his first term as Abbot, when the various decrees of Vatican II were gradually being brought into effect, there was never once a full discussion of them on the Abbot's Council. Instead, he preferred to go for the informal approach – as when he casually announced one Ember Week (when there would normally have been four or five separate readings, all in Latin): 'I think we'll have the readings in English today. Just let me know what people think.' Although inevitably there was some criticism, it was probably as good a way as any of riding the first wave of Vatican II liturgical reform.

There were some decisions, though, that could not be finessed. An early one concerned the future of Ampleforth's daughter house, the Priory at St Louis, Missouri, with its accompanying day school. Already in existence for eight years when Basil became Abbot in 1963, it had had its fair share of problems. For instance, far too many of the postulants brought over from the United States to train at Ampleforth failed to stay the course. (No one seems to have foreseen how daunting the damp and misty Yorkshire climate would prove to be for young Americans.) Basil's first instinct was to close the project down, but on visiting St Louis he allowed himself to be talked round by his Ampleforth contemporary and old friend, Father Luke Rigby, who had been at the Priory since its foundation in 1955. Instead, together they worked out a scheme whereby the Priory in future would be responsible for training its own novices, and help from the mother house would be confined to the sending out of occasional experienced monks to assist with the teaching and generally to lend an administrative hand. The strategy eventually worked:* the last monks arrived from Ampleforth early in the 1970s, the Priory became fully independent in 1973 and had its status promoted to that of an Abbey in 1989.

What undoubtedly helped the new Abbot in this kind of decision-making was the role he allowed to confidants. The commitment to the future of St Louis came about, for example, as the result of a weekend he and Luke Rigby spent together on a local ranch, and it was in these one-to-one discussions that

---

* It was not, however, undertaken without pain, involving as it did, the return to Ampleforth of the then Prior (and founding father) of St Louis, Father Columba Cary-Elwes, a magnetic, if slightly chaotic, figure.

Basil always felt most at home. This sometimes, of course, could serve as a limitation. It became something of a standing joke within the Community that the Abbot could persuade himself that collective decisions had been made when all that had taken place had been a conversation *à deux*. (The abbatial shorthand for meeting this situation was the phrase 'As, I think, you all know, dear Fathers . . .' which, roughly translated, meant 'I'm terribly sorry but I entirely forgot to get this matter cleared . . .')

It was not perhaps surprising that one of the more familiar criticisms made of Basil was that he displayed a natural hesitation in facing up to difficulties and preferred, where possible, to avoid the provoking of division or, worse, the giving of offence. If such traits existed, they were at least understandable. Unlike a bishop, an abbot has to live day-by-day with the human consequences of the decisions he makes. There is no escaping the baleful glare in the cloisters, the wounded look from the choir stalls or even the averted gaze in the calefactory – this last being the nearest equivalent within a monastery to what in schools or colleges would be known as the common room.

However, if that was the vulnerable point of a particular leadership style, it had its compensating aspects as well. There is no doubt that what Basil *was* good at was not merely listening to other people's ideas, but often taking them on board and adopting them for an entirely new purpose of his own. On his first visit to America, for example – when he went to sort out the problems at St Louis – he came back brimming with notions of how, even in the saying of the Daily Offices, changes might be introduced to make each act of worship more meaningful. Not all his proposals commended themselves to the Community as a whole, but at least he got a dialogue going and eventually, in 1972, a Liturgy Committee was established under the chairmanship of one of his eventual successors, Timothy Wright. The committee laboured for four years, then in 1976, just after

Basil, who had commissioned the process, left for Westminster, it produced an agreed new Ampleforth breviary, which remains in use to this day.

How much of a reformer was he? He himself always liked to say that, while his head was progressive, his heart was conservative – and it was interesting that he should have put things that way round, since it is normally the emotional tugs of the heart that prevail in the end. At Ampleforth the latter was certainly the case with Vespers which (much to the relief of the traditionalists) he ruled should go on being sung in Latin. It seems unlikely that this was primarily an aesthetic decision – his own grip on the complexities of plainsong being notoriously less than certain. Throughout, his fundamental concern remained with unity: what he was determined should not be allowed to happen – at least within his own monastery – was that anyone should find himself being pushed beyond the limits of endurance. Hence all the trouble he took to make sure that the traditionalists never felt that they were being forced to the wall.

It was, and had to be, a highly delicate balancing act, but Basil carried it off with sufficient tact and sensitivity for Ampleforth to fare much better than did most equivalent monastic communities. It lost, at most, 10 per cent of its members in the decade that followed Vatican II. Most of those departures may today have about them the flavour of ancient, musty controversies, but for a monastery any enforced changes or alterations (especially to the liturgy) were bound to go to the very heart of day-to-day existence. The established rhythm of praise and worship within the Abbey Church was the focal point of all the monks' lives, and an assault upon that was bound to seem to some like an attack on the faith itself.

It was the care and compassion that Basil brought to handling the susceptibilities of those who felt their whole way of life betrayed by Vatican II that ensured that there was so little outright opposition and so few defections. Always he would try to offer loopholes or provide for legitimate exceptions – for example, meeting halfway the elderly, traditionalist monk for whom the solitary daily celebration of Mass was the cornerstone of his religious life. If he could not change other people's minds, he could at least allow for their consciences, and, in a typically tolerant Benedictine manner, this was what he proceeded to do. Latin and English were interleaved in the daily saying and singing of the various Offices (at all except Vespers, which survived in an exclusively traditionalist form); Gregorian plainchant was carefully preserved; and permission was never withheld from any monk who insisted on his right to say Mass alone, supported only by a server. In the context of a diocese such dispensations might well have suggested a disorderly muddle; within the normally stricter confines of a monastery they offered probably the only way of living together in peace.

Yet, as Basil always had the wisdom to realise, such outward and visible changes in form could not be treated in isolation. Inevitably, they reflected deeper and more fundamental shifts going on underneath. If the Abbot had a greater understanding of this than some of his Ampleforth colleagues, it was partly the result of his month-long experience at the Abbots' Conference held in Rome in 1967. Here, at the Benedictine monastery of San Anselmo, Basil found himself put in the next-door room to a leading American liberal theologian, Rembert Weakland.* The two of them became allies and friends, with Weakland – who at the end of the conference was elected Abbot Primate of the Benedictines (a post that could certainly have been Basil's had he wanted it) – acting for the next decade as

---

* Then Archabbot of St Vincent Archabbey, Latrobe, and later (1997–2002) Archbishop of Milwaukee.

very much the radical pace-maker to his more cautious English colleague.

No doubt partly in recognition of Basil's resolve to commit himself exclusively to the service of his own monastery, he went on in April 1971 to be effortlessly re-elected to a second term as Abbot of Ampleforth. He won the requisite two-thirds majority on the first ballot or 'scrutiny'. Since he was still only forty-eight, it would have been a shock if he had not prevailed – though, if only for his own peace of mind, it was important that he should be seen to have done so conclusively.

There were those among his colleagues who thought that Basil was unduly nervous in advance of the election. Certainly the speed and efficiency with which it was all wrapped up hardly suggests that he had any cause to feel apprehensive. In a sense, however, things would never be quite the same again once he had been re-elected. Inevitably, he had ceased to be the fresh, exciting figure that he had been when he was first chosen in 1963. The monks had got used to him and he had got used to them. That did not mean that either side valued the other any less. It simply reflected the fact that the curiosity, not to say the novelty, had gone out of the relationship, and it may be that Basil (with his always highly tuned antennae) was more aware of this than were the monks themselves.

After his re-election had been safely secured, Basil tended to follow rather a different course from the Ampleforth-centred one he had done before. He did a good deal of outside travelling and took on special troubleshooting assignments for his friend, the Abbot Primate of the Benedictines. On Rembert Weakland's behalf he would conduct 'visitations' of various Continental monasteries and thus came to have – as he had already done as a young man – a wider and deeper knowledge of the problems besetting European Catholicism than most of his contemporaries.

The truth was that it was a time of upheaval for all monastic communities. At least one of the Vatican II decrees – *Perfectae Caritatis* (1965) – had been concerned with the renewal of the Religious Life in the general framework of the Church, so there was really no escape from a course of re-examination being undertaken from within, and whatever slim chance there might have been of avoiding such an outcome was effectively blocked off by a second Vatican document on the renewal of monastic life: *Renovationis Causam*, published in 1969.

In some ways the timing here was unfortunate. While the original reforming waters emanating from Vatican II had lapped gently enough against the already changing ways of English Benedictine monasticism, the situation was much less peaceful by the end of the 1960s. The upholding by Pope Paul VI of the Church's ban on artificial contraception in his 1968 encyclical *Humanae Vitae* – despite a majority of the expert papal commission advising the other way – did more to raise the flag of revolt among both priests and laity than any conciliar decree flowing from the General Council opened by Pope John XXIII in 1962.

Yet the birth control dispute, increasingly bitter though it became, was not the only development to put pressure on traditional Catholic attitudes. The Church, whether it likes it or not, has to live in the world, and it was never a realistic prospect that it would manage to emerge unscathed from the whole social and political convulsion that accompanied the *événements* of 1968. Behind the walls of monastic foundations the questions that tended to be asked may not have been exactly the same as those posed rhetorically on the barricades, but there was little doubt that a new sceptical attitude towards both deference and dogma had come into being.

For Ampleforth this meant that some tough questions had to be faced. By the beginning of the 1970s a group of young monks had already emerged, prepared to ask whether it was compatible with God's will that the efforts of the Community should be so exclusively devoted to the teaching and training of the sons of the prosperous and the well-to-do.* Ampleforth might have been founded as a monastery, but it was as a public school that it was now famous. Had the position been reached where the tail was wagging the dog? And would not one way of solving the problem be for the monastery simply to split – those who liked the somewhat grand life of an English public school carrying on with running the college, while the rest embraced a more conventional monastic existence of devotion, solitude and prayer?

Nor in the mood of the times did the questions necessarily stop there. What was the relevance of staffing so many outside parishes to the aims and purpose of a monastery? Apart from historical accident, what was the justification for so many monks doing what was essentially the job of the secular clergy (that is, clergy not bound by monastic rules)? And if they were to go on being required to do so, should they not at least try to fulfil their obligations to the Rule by working together rather than leading separate lives in different presbyteries, even when situated in the same town?

Such fundamental questions about the true purpose of being a Benedictine increasingly troubled Basil as he moved into his fifties. He was by no means certain he had the answers to all of them and, though he was always ready to explore possibilities, it sometimes seemed to his colleagues that, with his essentially cautious instincts, he was nothing like so keen to put plans into practice. Thus, while one Ampleforth monk was permitted

* This question was made more pointed by the abolition at around this time of the Direct Grant grammar schools and the more or less simultaneous collapse of a number of minor Catholic public schools.

to go off and live by himself as a hermit – something expressly allowed for under the Rule of St Benedict – a more complex scheme for three or four monks to form a commune, living and praying together, had to wait until Basil's departure to take any practical shape.

The suspicion has to be that, in his last two or three years as Abbot, much the same difficulties and doubts that had plagued him as a novice returned to haunt Basil. It led to a certain paralysis, even to a feeling that he was no longer in control and that things were getting on top of him. Probably only his closest friends noticed that anything was wrong; to them he would occasionally confide that he felt he had lost his way.

Superficially, he continued to lead a very energetic, active life – he was a member, and eventually became chairman of, the Benedictine Confederation's Commission on Monastic Renewal, as well as chairing the same Confederation's Ecumenical Commission – but he saw such tasks as essentially administrative distractions. What worried him was his sense that he should be contributing more to the future life of Ampleforth and the feeling that he was falling short. (It was entirely typical of him in this respect that he probably got more satisfaction out of forming from the ranks of local clergy and ministers what was first known as 'the Abbot's Group' and later as the Ryedale Christian Council than he did out of the four years he spent chairing his own Order's Ecumenical Commission.) Back at the monastery some questions even began to assume the preoccupying character of his old 'scruples'. The housekeeping agenda, in particular, seemed endless: always there would be questions of building, planning or fundraising to be resolved, to say nothing of more mundane matters such as the collapse of a new church just two days before it was due to open its doors, or the need to modernise the monastery's own sewage plant.

It was all made harder for Basil as what he really wanted to do was to attend to the spiritual needs of the monks under his charge. Even here, of course, there were inevitably defeats and disappointments – as when he had to announce to the members of the Community the departure of one of their colleagues.* On such occasions he never tried to sugar the pill, opening one of his 'chapters' with the bleak statement: 'I have to give you, I am afraid, Fathers, bad news and probably the Community a bit of a shock . . . You will not expect me to tell you the reasons which led this particular Brother to leave us. I can best sum it up, I think, by saying that the heart had gone out of his vocation. And, once that happens and a man becomes unsettled to the degree where the strain is too much, it seems only prudent to release him.'

What made such moments particularly unsettling for Basil was the knowledge that he had to hold himself answerable for what had occurred. The Rule of St Benedict is quite explicit about that – 'Let the Abbot be aware that any loss of profit the Master of the House may find in the sheep will be laid at his door.' Of course, as we have seen, Ampleforth in the post-Vatican II world could claim a better record than many similar communities, but it was wholly characteristic of Basil that he should describe this as 'cold comfort'.

How discouraged did he get? It is important not to exaggerate (though he did tell his predecessor early in 1973 that he was 'finding the job a burden and, for the moment, joyless'). Yet to most of the Community he simply appeared tired and tense – as he certainly looks in the official portrait of him as Abbot painted by Derek Clarke later in 1973, and which now

* Basil always found this an ordeal. He used to recall how on his very first night as Abbot a monk came to him and announced his decision to leave, a sharp reminder of the burden that thenceforward would be his.

hangs in the Ampleforth Monks' Refectory. To those who knew him best, however, it was as if he was undergoing much the same trial of faith as that which he had endured all those years ago in 1941, when he had first enrolled in the monastery as a novice.

VI

THE MOVE
TO WESTMINSTER

B Y THE AUTUMN OF 1975 THE SEVENTY-YEAR-OLD CARDINAL John Heenan had already been Archbishop of Westminster for a dozen years. He had suffered successive heart attacks in 1973 and 1974 and, although he had not officially announced his retirement, he had in September 1975 placed his resignation in the hands of Pope Paul VI. In fact, he had done more than that. In an effort to smooth the path for his successor he had already circulated a letter around the clergy and laity of his archdiocese. In it he encouraged his flock to make known their views as to whom they would like to have as their next archbishop ('If you have any names to suggest, write to the Apostolic Delegate').

If it was a slightly unorthodox way of proceeding – Heenan was to die in harness on 7 November 1975 before any formal arrangements had been put in place – it at least reflected a democratic shift that had taken place within the Church in the wake of Vatican II. No longer, even by such a conservative as Heenan, was a *diktat* from Rome thought sufficient to provide an indigenous church with its leadership: to be effective a new archbishop must command widespread support from both priests and people – and that meant proper consultation before any name was announced.

The extent of the preliminary soundings conducted before Heenan's death remains obscure, though the Apostolic Delegate, Archbishop Bruno Heim, did subsequently disclose that he found himself confronted with a total of ninety-five names. From these he was expected to draw up a short list of three which, in what is known as a *terna*, he was required to submit to Rome. Most of the consultation process appears, however, to have gone on below the surface – until, that is, an article appeared in the *Sunday Times* on 28 September 1975.

Written by the well-informed Catholic journalist, Muriel Bowen, it not only surveyed the field of potential candidates for Westminster, but also went on to provide photographs and potted biographies of six of them. Among the half-dozen contenders specially selected for this treatment was the name of the Abbot of Ampleforth, Basil Hume.

That fact is not an unimportant one, since it undermines the theory of the ninth Archbishop of Westminster (the English Hierarchy was restored only in 1850) being mysteriously conjured out of the mists surrounding the Yorkshire Moors. The article in the *Sunday Times* was undoubtedly an influential one and could be said to have defined the parameters of the contest.

The familiar and expected names were all there: Bishop Derek Worlock, Bishop of Portsmouth since 1965 and before that for 18 years private secretary to three successive Archbishops of Westminster; George Patrick Dwyer, Archbishop of Birmingham; Alan Clark, Auxiliary Bishop of Northampton; to say nothing of the only Benedictine and leading intellectual in the Bishops' Conference, Christopher Butler, former Abbot of Downside and now Auxiliary Bishop of Westminster. In addition, two dark horse candidates got mentioned. They were

Michael Hollings, a former Guards officer now in charge of a very successful multi-ethnic parish in Southall, and Basil Hume whose choice as Abbot of Ampleforth at the age of forty was said by Miss Bowen to have 'marked him out as a high-flyer'.

What was Basil's reaction to seeing himself propelled into such prominence? It turned out to be engagingly human – he rang his elderly mother in Newcastle in order to alert her to what the *Sunday Times* was saying. To his slight chagrin, her only response was to roar with laughter.

Plainly, therefore, the notion of seeing his own hat thrown publicly into the ring was not at that stage wholly repugnant to him, even if – like his mother – he probably did not take it seriously. More disturbing was a private development that took place a month later. On or around the date of Cardinal Heenan's death Basil Hume got a letter from Donald Coggan, the Archbishop of Canterbury, whom he had first got to know when the latter was Archbishop of York, living only some twenty miles away from Ampleforth. Dated 3 November 1975, it was a brief note mainly concerned with thanking the Abbot for a message he had sent in support of the Archbishop's ill-fated 'Call to the Nation' revivalist campaign of 1975, but it concluded on a distinctly prophetic (and for Basil probably unsettling) note:

I see a fair bit of John Heenan. He is far from well. How we would delight in having you as our neighbour across the river. But I should not wish such a fate upon you! *Dominus dirigat te.*
Jean [his wife] joins me in affectionate greeting.

Yours ever,

+Donald Cantuar

Press comment might be easily brushed aside, but it is hard to think that a letter of that kind – arriving, as it did, just when the vacancy at Westminster was being officially declared – failed to make an impact.

In any event, Basil had now to reckon with what was virtually a campaign being waged on his behalf. Some of it was deliberately subterranean. There were, for example, dark rumours of some leading Catholics (the names of Norman St John-Stevas, Shirley Williams and William Rees-Mogg were the ones most frequently mentioned) seeking to circumvent the official channel, symbolised in the person of the Apostolic Delegate, by establishing their own direct line to the Vatican. There were also suspicions of the role being played by the Irish Ambassador in London, Donal O'Sullivan, whose imposing embassy and residence on the corner of Grosvenor Place was claimed to have been the venue for a number of candidates (including Basil Hume) being invited for meals to meet Archbishop Heim.

In fact, though, Hume had first met the Apostolic Delegate when the latter paid a visit to Ampleforth shortly after he arrived in England in 1973 – and Heim always insisted in later life that from that first moment he had been 'very impressed with him'. Probably even more decisive, however, was the sheer coincidence that just after Heenan died an Italian priest, Father Giovanni Tonucci – who served as private secretary (or, more grandly, counsellor) at the Apostolic Delegation in Wimbledon – happened to be attending an Advent Retreat held at Ampleforth. He is said to have come back to London feeling 'very hot for Hume' – a conclusion that he, no doubt, pressed upon his boss (who had, in any case, already been strongly influenced in Basil's favour by Gordon Wheeler, the Bishop of Leeds, who remained until his retirement in 1985 closer to Basil than any other member of the Hierarchy).

Any resentments at such worldly manoeuvrings can, no doubt,

safely be relegated to what the Benedictines call 'murmurings' – though, if there was a single decisive moment, it probably came at a private meeting of prominent Catholics held in a London flat. It was then that the leading Catholic layman of the day, the 17th Duke of Norfolk, realised that his own original candidate, Father Michael Hollings from Southall, was unlikely to prevail. He, therefore, transferred his allegiance to Basil Hume. By then, whether the Abbot of Ampleforth knew it or not, some fairly formidable lobbying was being undertaken on his behalf. Representatives of the patrician, recusant strain in English Catholicism joined forces, for once, with the more liberal, intellectual elements within the Church.

They were united in not wanting to have imposed upon them some old-style Catholic prelate typical of the past. For them, the sheer novelty of a monastic choice was part of its attraction, and the whole English demeanour of the Ampleforth Abbot merely added to his appeal.

Nowhere was the case for Basil argued more persuasively than in the columns of *The Economist*. Edited at the time by a former Ampleforth head boy, Andrew Knight, it had first promoted his cause in the wake of the original, defining *Sunday Times* article published at the end of September. *The Economist* of 11 October 1975 included an item in its 'In Britain' section entitled 'Bishops' Move'. Having run through the leading contenders – whom it took to be Archbishop Dwyer of Birmingham and Bishop Worlock of Portsmouth – it reserved its punch for its final paragraph. The two outsiders, it adjudicated, were Father Michael Hollings of Southall and Abbot Basil Hume of Ampleforth. Having disposed of Father Hollings ('Fireworks may be very well in multi-ethnic parishes; they might be less easy to accommodate at the top'), it finally declared its hand with an encomium for its candidate that could hardly have been bettered by a PR agency:

Much the most attractive dark horse is Abbot Basil Hume of Ampleforth, a man of great firmness and wisdom (and, incidentally, a good linguist), he manages to entrance everybody who comes into contact with him at his Abbey and outside.

The Economist, however, was not content to leave matters there. Four weeks later it was at it again. This time, having added Bishop Alan Clark to its list of serious contenders, it still struck the same note at the end:

The laity would undoubtedly welcome a progressive of ecumenical bent and with talents for public life but it is not going to be easy for the Pope to find such a paragon – unless he were to opt bravely for Abbot Basil Hume of Ampleforth.

None of the other candidates enjoyed that kind of press support – probably all the more effective for the wistful tone in which it was expressed. To claim that *The Economist* tipped the balance (still less that it determined the result) would obviously be absurd; but the endorsement of what, even in those days, was pre-eminently an international weekly, with a readership even within the Vatican, can hardly have done Basil's chances any harm.

More to the point, however, was the effect that such supportive speculation must have had at Ampleforth and not least on Basil himself. Certainly, the picture that was later to emerge of the Abbot of Ampleforth blinking his way into the sunlight from pottering around in a herb garden is difficult to sustain. Monasteries are notorious hotbeds of gossip and it simply is not conceivable that the Community at Ampleforth avoided all mention of a prospect that was now firmly in the public domain. It was, after all, their future that was at stake as well as Basil's.

It is possible, in fact, to detect some inkling of that period of uncomfortable uncertainty in an article that appeared in the *Ampleforth Journal* of Summer 1976. Having paid full tribute to the achievements of Basil's first term as Abbot, Brendan Smith, the newly appointed Ampleforth Prior who contributed the piece, went on to remark rather more bleakly: 'But his second term of office was only half spent when the call to Westminster came and the fulfilment of his hopes and ours is left to his successor.' Given the formal farewell context in which that observation surfaces, it would appear to reflect at least a measure of frustration at the way in which things had eventually worked out.

In fact, the last few months that Basil spent at Ampleforth were particularly difficult. In the first place he was himself, as has been noted, in a rather depressed frame of mind, and this period of uncertainty as to the future cannot have helped his equanimity. Yet if it was hard for the Abbot to concentrate on the tasks in hand, it equally was not easy for members of the Community to dismiss from their minds an awareness that events were going on elsewhere that might well disrupt any plans they might want to make.

Fortunately, Archbishop Bruno Heim – conscious perhaps that there were two key episcopal vacancies to be filled (the 71-year-old George Beck, Archbishop of Liverpool, had announced his retirement a month before Cardinal Heenan's death) – moved relatively quickly. Although no one can know for certain, the external evidence suggests that he was in a position to present his *terna* for both archdioceses by the end of November. The vital decisions were probably taken at a three-cornered meeting between himself, the Pope and Cardinal Sebastiano Baggio (Prefect of the Congregation of Bishops) held on 4 December 1975. Thereafter the Vatican apparently felt the need to seek reassurance from a score of leading English lay people, who found themselves presented with a kind of questionnaire as to the qualities they would hope to see reflected in the choices made, and how they matched up with the more obvious potential candidates. This led to rumours that there had been a hiccup along the way but none, in fact, had occurred. With his well-known regard for the important and the powerful, Bruno Heim sometimes liked afterwards to claim that the choice for Westminster was clinched for him when he went to see the Archbishop of Canterbury at Lambeth Palace. That morning – and it must have been the first such meeting between an Apostolic Delegate and the Primate of All England since before the Reformation – Donald Coggan apparently said he had only one candidate to propose, and that was the Abbot of Ampleforth.

Why, then, when the choice was announced some two months later, did it occasion the surprise that it did? The answer lies in its unusual nature. Basil Hume was, after all, not even a bishop, and selecting him meant that every member of the existing Hierarchy had seen his claims overlooked. It was not true, however, that there was no precedent for such a choice. It *had* happened before, if only once. When Henry Manning was named as Cardinal Wiseman's successor in 1865 he also was not a member of the episcopate but merely the Provost of the Westminster Metropolitan Chapter. So the notion of a priest of the Second Order being first ordained bishop and then put in charge of what was in effect the primatial see was not entirely novel.

What it did represent, at least for the laity, was a refreshing change. Since the appointment of Herbert Vaughan, who succeeded Manning in 1892 and came of old recusant stock, successive Archbishops of Westminster had tended to conform to type. Solid, well-trained priests (normally at the English College in Rome), they had usually come up the hard way, with lots of parish experience behind them but little or no pretension to learning or scholarship. (Hume was, in fact, the first

Westminster Archbishop since Manning to have attended Oxford University.) The seven years of training in Rome – an experience Basil never had – may have left a certain surface veneer, but essentially, if the conventional bishops were representative of anyone, it was of the predominantly Irish flocks to whom they ministered. Now, in the light of what had largely been a Patricians' Revolt, they found themselves confronted with an Archbishop who, as a son of the professional middle class, was recognisably not one of their own. (He even had a place, if a vicarious one, in the power structure. It was carefully noted in the press release which accompanied the announcement of his appointment that his brother-in-law – also a Roman Catholic – was Secretary of the Cabinet.)

It is probably time, though, to consider the mood of the Archbishop-Elect himself, and how the news of his appointment was broken to him. In an effort to lead as normal a life as possible, the Abbot of Ampleforth had gone during the first week of February 1976 to St George's House, Windsor, to take part in what was somewhat portentously known as 'A Study Course for Senior Church Leaders'. (The timing of his participation could hardly be put down to the workings of the Holy Spirit. The invitation had been accepted the previous summer and anyway, though he had never been to St George's House before, it was the third such seminar that Basil had attended.)

At first all went very much as before – Anglicans, Roman Catholics and Free Church representatives mingling with each other in what was predominantly an academic atmosphere. By the Thursday night Basil felt liberated enough to invite himself out to dinner with an old school friend, Lieutenant-Colonel Johnnie Johnston (the same man who as a schoolboy in 1941 had mocked and derided Basil's decision to enrol in the monastery rather than join the Army). Colonel Johnston was in the 1970s the Assistant Comptroller of the Lord Chamberlain's office and, as such, lived in a grace-and-favour residence in Windsor Home Park. He, his wife and his guest had just sat down to a kitchen supper when the phone rang and a male voice inquired whether he might speak to the Abbot. Despite its trace of a foreign accent, the voice meant nothing to Colonel Johnston and he duly summoned Hume into the adjoining sitting-room, where the phone was kept.

The conversation gave singularly little away. The 52-year-old Abbot's first words were 'No, no' (this in response to a question as to whether he was alone). Next he could be heard giving a seemingly reluctant assent (this to a proposal that it was important that he came to see the Apostolic Delegate in just two days' time before he returned to Ampleforth). He did not have to be Sherlock Holmes to guess what such an interview was likely to be about – which explains no doubt, why he reappeared at the supper table looking rather pale and murmuring something about 'a family problem'. He left surprisingly early, perhaps because he still had one matter to wonder about. What he was not told on the phone was whether the offer on the coming Saturday would be of Westminster or of Liverpool.

Here he was behind even his own family, for the other thing he did not know was that earlier that very same evening Bruno Heim had gone round the corner from his home in Wimbledon to knock on the door of his near neighbour, Sir John Hunt, at the time Secretary of the Cabinet under Harold Wilson. The Apostolic Delegate had one simple purpose: to discover from Sir John's wife, Madeleine, how he might get in touch with her brother. (Having already established via a phone call that the Abbot was away from the monastery, he did not want to have to put the same 'fishing' request to Ampleforth lest it gave too much away.) As good luck would have it, Madeleine knew precisely where her brother might be found as he had been staying with his sister and brother-in-law before leaving for

Windsor and had laid out his plans for the coming week. The price, though, of that knowledge was that the Apostolic Delegate felt bound to reveal the reason for his request. Under the strictest vow of secrecy the Cabinet Secretary and his wife thus became the first people outside the diplomatic chain of command from Rome to learn the identity of the next Archbishop of Westminster.

The candidate himself did not take long to catch up. On the Saturday morning, when he visited what was to become the Nunciature in Wimbledon, the first thing he noticed was a rather grand visitors' book resting on a table in the hall. Unable to resist taking a crafty look at who else had been there, he immediately spotted that the last visitor to be received had been Derek Worlock. That told him all he needed to know – he guessed in one that it must mean (since there was a proper order of doing these things) that Worlock would have been asked to go to Liverpool and that he would now be invited to become the next Archbishop of Westminster. After the formal offer had been made and accepted, Heim tried to make small talk by asking Basil whom he thought would turn out to be the next Archbishop of Liverpool. 'Oh, there's no doubt about that,' he was told, 'it's going to be Derek Worlock' – an answer that caused some consternation to the Pope's diplomatic representative. In his earnest, German-Swiss way, he professed himself mortified and bewildered that the news of such an important appointment should already have leaked out. It was a tale that Basil used rather to enjoy telling, though whether he ever let the slightly humourless Bruno Heim into the secret that it was the evidence of his own visitors' book that had enabled him to answer the question with so much confidence has never satisfactorily been established. There are those who maintain, however, that the visitors' book was never on show in quite such a prominent way again.

The name of the new Archbishop of Liverpool was, as things worked out, released a full week ahead of the news of Basil's own appointment to Westminster. This was to prevent the people of Britain's second most important Catholic archdiocese – the Archbishop of Liverpool is always Metropolitan of the Northern Province – from feeling that they were being required to play second fiddle to Westminster. Whether his week of solo glory did anything to salve the hurt feelings of Derek Worlock – twenty-one years of whose life as a priest had been spent in the Westminster archdiocese – is an entirely separate issue. He deserves great credit, however, for the chivalrous nature of the letter he wrote to Basil Hume two days after the latter's appointment was announced on 16 February. It cannot have been an easy letter to write, but the sometimes inhibited Worlock for once threw caution to the winds:

I offered Mass for your intention this morning and later was glad to see that Baden Hickman in the *Guardian* had suggested that we would work together. That is my earnest hope – and I will never tell you anything about the South of England unless you tell me about the North. In spite of the press, you will have a good diocesan machine at Westminster and priests who will rally to you as you bring them a message of hope.

Enough! The picture always seems overwhelming once we analyse. I am thankful that Ladbroke's [the bookmakers who had run a book on the Westminster Succession Stakes, with Worlock at 9–4 and Hume at 10–1] is behind us and that we now can, under the Holy Spirit, get on with the work of the Gospel. Please God, we can together fire some of the hopes that are not far below the surface.

I look forward to seeing you soon and in the meantime promise you continuing prayer. Do please remember me. It will be as hard for me to leave Portsmouth as it will for you to leave Ampleforth. Liverpool has gone ahead with my installation for 19 March, St Joseph. When your plans are fixed, you must let me know what under the unusual circumstances you would wish to do. Come if you can, but I shall understand.

Yours affectionately,

+Derek

In the end Basil did not go to Worlock's installation, but that was merely because the five weeks' interval between the announcement of his appointment on 17 February and the date of his own installation on 25 March proved altogether frantic. The Archbishop-Designate was later to reflect that the worst period was the ten days in which he was required to keep all knowledge of what was about to happen entirely to himself and thus became caught up in a web of dissimulation and deceit. (He was allowed to tell only one other person and that was his private secretary, Father Geoffrey Lynch, to whom he broke the news on the platform of York station on his return from London.) Miraculously, though, the secret was kept, and it was only when it became known on the morning of Monday 16 February that the Abbot was once again leaving for London – and that he had asked to have his best pair of trousers pressed – that rumours, originating with the novices, started running wild within the monastery.

The actual formal announcement was made at 11 a.m. on Tuesday 17 February, when the Archbishop-Elect appeared before a news conference held just off Fleet Street in the London Press

Club. Schooled through most of the previous afternoon and evening by the Catholic Information Office (the bishops and certain Catholic officials had been forewarned that morning as to what to expect), the Abbot-Archbishop conducted himself with some aplomb, particularly pleasing the popular papers with his frequent references to his interest in both soccer and rugby and his expressed determination to go on playing 'geriatric squash'. The results may have gone a bit further than he intended – 'Sporting Monk is new RC leader' proclaimed the *Daily Mirror* the next day – but at least the new Archbishop had got himself off to a flying start. Even the wintry joke with which he ended his final answer on fee-paying education – 'I'm in favour of all freedoms, even freedom of the press' – failed to raise any hackles.

On his return to Ampleforth Basil already bore the burden of having become a public figure. There were over 1,000 letters and 400 telegrams to answer, to say nothing of a host of requests for interviews whether on television, radio or in the newspapers. (Ruefully Basil would remark that he had already done his fair share of these in London on what he now began to refer to as 'my ghastly ego trip'.) The appetite of the media, however, proved insatiable and members of the Community had to grow accustomed to finding television cameras hidden behind every bush. For the Abbot himself there was respite in a trip to Newcastle to see his mother* who had already greeted the news of his appointment with the distinctly maternal comment, 'I feel deeply sorry for him because of all the work it will mean, but I am confident he will carry it out very well.'

The most daunting experience for the outgoing Abbot was

---

* Lady Hume was to make the trip to London in order to attend, in a wheelchair, her son's episcopal ordination. She died in a London nursing home on 18 December 1978, aged eighty-one. Basil presided over her Requiem Mass held in Newcastle upon Tyne ten days later.

probably the High Mass held in the Abbey on 22 February at which he had both to preside and preach.

It was the kind of occasion to which Basil nearly always rose, and this particular Sunday was to prove no exception. As a preacher he was never shy of wearing his heart on his sleeve and that morning he certainly did so:

What am I to say to you on an occasion like this? It would be all too easy to become sentimental about Ampleforth and all that it has meant to me since my first arrival here in 1933; that would be embarrassing. Or I could take refuge in clichés and pious phrases to mask the deep sadness that I feel on leaving; that, too would be embarrassing.

No, we are in the presence of God, and that is a serious matter. Since I am talking to the Community – monks, happily many parents and boys – it is right for me, I think, to take you into my confidence . . .

The generosity of the Press and the expectations of so many people have been to me personally a profound shock. That, my dearly beloved, is why I need your prayers and your friendship.

The gap between what is thought and expected of me and what I know myself to be is considerable and frightening. There are moments in life when a man feels very small and in my life this is one such moment. It is good to feel small because I know that whatever I achieve will be God's achievement and not mine . . .

A High Court Judge, Sir Michael Davies, who happened to be in the congregation – he was not himself a Catholic, though his wife was, and they had a son in the school – claims to have felt there and then that either he was listening to the greatest actor he had ever encountered or that he really was in the presence of a man of God. Certainly upon those in the Abbey Basil's words made a deep impression – not least because of the tribute he went on to pay to all that Ampleforth had meant for him ('What I am is what you have given').

All in all, it was probably as well that within the week the Archbishop-Elect was on his way to Rome, for as a farewell that High Mass would have been hard to surpass. The Rome visit, though, in a sense was an accident: Basil had been scheduled to go there on official business in his capacity as chairman of the Benedictine Commission on Monastic Renewal, and the public happenings of the past few days simply lent the visit an additional significance. Having disposed of his Benedictine work on the Saturday and the Sunday, Basil was able to devote the rest of his time to the preparations for his future.

His first visit on the morning of Monday 1 March was to Gammarelli's, Rome's best known clerical outfitters, to be measured for his purple soutane. There are, no doubt, some priests for whom such an experience would represent the high-point of their lives; but always a shade ungainly, and never at all clothes-conscious, Basil found the whole ordeal somewhat unnerving. He made his way (with some relief) from Gammarelli's to keep an appointment at 11 a.m with Cardinal Casaroli, the Secretary to the Council for the Public Affairs of the Church and, therefore, in effect, the Vatican's Foreign Secretary. His next, and even more important engagement – one added since his selection as Archbishop of Westminster – was a half-hour audience with the Holy Father in the papal apartments within the Vatican.

Basil, except perhaps in his preaching, was never an emotionally demonstrative man, but this particular encounter left a lasting impression upon him. Although he was to meet Pope Paul VI again, when he came back to Rome three months later to be made a Cardinal, this meeting represented the longest time he and the Pope ever spent together. Only the two of them can have known what exactly transpired, but Basil was later to confide in more than one friend that, without the strength with which the Pope supplied him, he could never possibly have managed to cope with the responsibilities of the job for which he had been chosen.

What appears to have happened is that Basil started off by explaining just how unqualified he felt for the task that had been thrust upon him. He made, as it were, a full confession of his various limitations and weaknesses – only to be silenced eventually by Paul VI insisting that it was God's command that he was being summoned to obey. The grace that he himself had been vouchsafed in order to meet his worldwide responsibilities would now, the Pope promised, equally be made available to the Church's newest archbishop. Whether it was the age-gap between them – Pope Paul VI was, after all, twenty-five years older than Basil – or merely the awe that the Englishman felt for the papal office, must remain a moot point: what matters is that the meeting between the two of them was crucial, with the Pope's final advice to him – 'Always remain a monk' – proving particularly decisive. Ever afterwards Basil would never hesitate to talk of the debt he owed to Paul VI, who, he seems to have come to feel, had exerted much the same influence on his life as Abbot Byrne had done all those years ago when he was a young novice. Although in later years his contacts with John Paul II would be perfectly cordial, Basil's relationship with him never came close to matching that between Paul VI and his hand-picked English archbishop.

After his meeting with the Holy Father, Basil did not linger in Rome, but flew back to London and thence on to Ampleforth for the few weeks of monastic life that were left to him. At Ampleforth he faced a flurry of farewell parties – with the real work going on in the Abbot's office, where Father Geoffrey Lynch had set up camp in company with three members of the Catholic Information Office who had been drafted in to serve as his media advisers. Here, with the additional help of a dynamic young Ampleforth monk, Father Felix Stephens, the plans were laid for the transition period, which would start at Westminster with the new Archbishop taking possession of the *jurisdictio* (or what Anglicans would call 'the temporalities') of his see on Friday 12 March.

That date saw the strangest contrast of all – a day starting with the reading of the Papal Bull of appointment to an impressive collection of Westminster Cathedral officials gathered in the Throne Room of Archbishop's House and ending with Basil's departure for a modest convent in Wimbledon, where he was due to spend his pre-ordination retreat. Relative strangers to London, he and Geoffrey Lynch, who was acting as his chauffeur, had difficulty in finding the way, and Basil, possessing the short fuse that he did, gave vent to a certain degree of bad temper before the Marie Reparatrice Convent was safely located. The new archbishop spent a week there, taking time off only to give an interview to Clifford Longley, the religious affairs correspondent of *The Times* (always Basil's favourite newspaper). This duly appeared in the shape of a profile on 22 March, three days before his ordination and installation in the cathedral on the Feast of the Annunciation.

Headed 'A Man of God, and of Doubt', the profile proved to be a remarkably candid assessment in which the subject made it clear that he had been through periods of 'doubt and despair'. This ability to empathise with those struggling to maintain their faith was to prove an enduring part of the new archbishop's appeal – though whether the *Times* writer was correct in equating this with 'belonging to the tradition of Newman' is more open to question. (It was Newman, after all, who once famously pronounced: 'Ten thousand difficulties do not make a doubt.')

By and large, however, the new archbishop – as he himself had acknowledged in his farewell service at Ampleforth – had no reason to complain against the 'generosity' of the media treatment he had received. To journalists, who had grown slightly weary of the grandeur of Cardinal Heenan, this fresh player on the ecclesiastical stage had one great advantage: he was 'the new kid on the block' with no past to live down and with all the added attraction of novelty. For instance, as in his original ordination as a priest twenty-six years earlier, Basil would be required to prostrate himself before the High Altar at his installation. Predictably, this proved too much of a temptation for the secular press – the *Daily Express* explaining what was supposed to be the most sacred moment of the service with the caption: 'Hume Makes it Flat on his Face.'

Even before his installation Basil managed to participate in ceremonies that emphasised his human side. On his last Saturday at Ampleforth he had, for example, kept a promise by baptising the grandchild of the family who ran the local post office just a few steps up the road from the monastery; and within days of arriving in London he was to be found officiating at the weddings of two of his nieces, the second service taking place in Westminster Cathedral just four days before his own formal installation.

There can be no question that Basil took his episcopal ordination extremely seriously. In his first pastoral letter to his archdiocese he asked that all its 220 parishes and 195 religious houses join him in the hour-long vigil he would be keeping on the eve of the service. (Most of them – including such far-flung non-diocesan outposts as Ampleforth – duly did so.) By now Basil was living in Archbishop's House, so his own vigil was kept in the private chapel.

When the Feast of the Annunciation dawned on 25 March, it did so under a slight shadow. The previous day had witnessed the death at the age of eighty-eight of the country's best known soldier, Viscount Montgomery of Alamein. The papers, therefore, were full of patriotic and martial sentiments. That did not, though, end up by mattering much, since, at least in the popular eye (and the whole service was televised), the Roman Catholic Church was also that day engaged in panoply and pageantry. No fewer than 2,500 people packed the cathedral, led by four cardinals, eight archbishops, thirty-six bishops and 130 Ampleforth monks. It was predominantly the clerical contingent who provided the blaze of colour – the bishops in their mitres and purple skull caps, some monsignori in choir dress, the monks in their various monastic habits of black, white and brown. It was not, though, a ceremony for the faint-hearted, lasting two-and-a-half hours and involving a Mass in which 600 priests concelebrated. The service reached its climax in the installation of the new Archbishop upon his throne. It was only at this point that the former Abbot of Ampleforth became the central figure of the occasion. Once invested with his ring, mitre and pastoral staff, he went out of his way to give a special welcome to the Archbishop of York (the Archbishop of Canterbury was away in the West Indies) and a dozen other Anglican bishops who also attended. This was a notable ecumenical gesture on both sides, but an even more important one was to come.

After only a brief break – during which a tea reception took place in Archbishop's House – the 130 monks, who had come specially down from Ampleforth, together with their former Abbot were on the move again. This time their destination was Westminster Abbey at the other end of Victoria Street, where for the first time in 400 years – and by special invitation of the Dean – a service of Latin Vespers was to be sung according to the Benedictine rite.

In retrospect, this moment of unprecedented fellowship between the Church of England and the Church of Rome may look more like a romantic gesture than an exercise in practical ecumenism, but, coming on the day it did, it certainly made its mark – so much so that in some press reports it entirely overshadowed the earlier events of the day in Westminster Cathedral. One reason for that may well have been the address that the new Archbishop chose to deliver from the Abbey pulpit. Whereas his homily in his own cathedral had been essentially conventional, the words he spoke in Westminster Abbey seemed deliberately designed to strike a chord and evoke a response. Perhaps the most memorable passage came when Basil referred to one of the many tombs in the Abbey – the one shared by Queen Mary I and Queen Elizabeth I – which, the preacher suggested, still spoke to the world 'with a poignant, indeed tragic relevance'. The two characters, he went on, had been 'two sisters, estranged, not on speaking terms, misunderstanding each other'. Yet should they not all learn from the inscription that their joint tomb bears: 'Consorts both in throne and grave, here we rest, two sisters, Elizabeth and Mary in the hope of one resurrection'? It was, admittedly, a piece of imagery that had been suggested to Basil by a former Dean of Westminster, but he brought to its deployment great grace and tact, and there must have been many in that vast evening congregation (the Abbey, like Westminster Cathedral earlier in the day, was packed) who felt that they were about to see an entirely new departure in inter-church relations.

If anything, they would probably have found such hopes strengthened had they been present at the subsequent reception given by the Dean and Chapter for all their Benedictine visitors in the great hall of Westminster School. Here was a moment of real reconciliation, with the successors to the Benedictine monks who had been driven out of Westminster by Henry VIII being entertained in the very building that had once served as their forebears' monastic dormitory. For a moment it was as if 400 years of religious bitterness had been washed away.

It had certainly been a red letter day for the new Archbishop, but then so also had it been for the monastic community which, he never tired of insisting, had made him what he was. The most affecting moment probably came the next morning when more than a hundred monks from Ampleforth gathered in a coach park near Vauxhall Bridge, waiting for the coaches to take them back home. As the sun came up on this particularly brisk March morning, an old black Wolseley hove into view and drove slowly to a halt. Out of it clambered a familiar tall figure – the fourth Abbot of Ampleforth who was now the ninth Archbishop of Westminster had come to make his farewells of all those with whom for forty years he had lived, worked and prayed. As one of them was later to say, it was only then that 'we had our strongest sense that, leaving us with all the entrails of parting, he had been quite simply taken from our midst'.*

---

* The quotation is taken from Father Alberic Stacpoole. I am indebted to him and to his two articles 'Abbot to Archbishop' (*Ampleforth Journal*, Summer 1976) and 'The Making of an Archbishop' (*The Month*, March 2000) for much of the detail contained in the latter part of this chapter.

VII

SETTLING IN

ARCHBISHOP'S HOUSE IN AMBROSDEN AVENUE, WEST-minster, has never enjoyed a good press. That distinguished twentieth-century Catholic journalist Patrick O'Donovan once remarked that its interior reminded him of 'a nursing home for upper-class alcoholics', while the contemporary Catholic writer Peter Stanford has described its ambience as being 'about as welcoming as a North Country station hotel during a period of national mourning'. It was this vast, forbidding pile that now served as home for a man who had spent the previous forty-three years living either in an isolated Yorkshire monastery or at the public school next door.

The new Archbishop immediately did his best to reproduce the conditions to which he was accustomed. Rejecting the capacious, second-floor bedroom that had been Cardinal Heenan's, he instead chose for himself a much smaller room on the top floor that he always afterwards referred to (with some justice) as 'my cell'. True, there was little or nothing he could do about the State Rooms, though he did ensure that at least one of them (the grandest) was put to an unorthodox use. He had hardly been in office a year before he was excitedly reporting to a former young novice at Ampleforth how 'uncommonly well a frisbee bounces off the Throne Room floor'.

In truth, though, his new life did offer the freshly elevated Prince of the Church some compensations. He did not hesitate to tell his friends how nice it was to have his own private bathroom and he also took pleasure in possessing a cheque book, something again that he had never enjoyed before. However, he was also at pains not to alter the pattern of his life too dramatically. Although no longer summoned by a bell, he regularly rose at 6 a.m (only an hour later than had been his practice in the monastery, where he would have gone to bed much earlier) and his day continued to start with prayer. He would make his way to his private chapel by 6.30 a.m. where he and his private secretary would spend the next three-quarters of an hour in silent devotion. At 7.15 a.m. they would be joined by the three elderly nuns who cooked and cleaned in Archbishop's House and together all five of them would say Lauds, the first Office of the Day. The Archbishop would then go on to celebrate Mass if he was not due to do so later in the day on some parish engagement. At 8 a.m. – or earlier if there had been no Mass – he would leave the chapel and go for the first session of the day at his desk. This often proved a convenient time for priests in the archdiocese (all of whom were supplied with the number of a private line reserved for their use only) to ring him up if they needed help or wanted advice.

After breakfast – a glass of fruit juice, coffee and a slice of bread or toast – it would be back to his desk to deal with that morning's correspondence (he always insisted on opening his own mail). Incoming letters averaged some thirty a day, although that number could go up dramatically if the Archbishop found himself embroiled in some controversy. Astonishingly, Basil continued to write a good number of his letters by hand. He was never much of a typist and, though he did not mind 'face-to-face' dictation, he loathed using a tape recorder. He was always punctilious about sending out prompt replies. This applied particularly to those correspondents who had written in to complain about him or to criticise his actions (what he characteristically called his 'Boo' letters), and over these he always took special trouble. In the absence of any more active commitments, the rest of the morning would normally be taken up with sermon preparations, interviews or administrative matters of one sort or another.

If the working day had a high-point, it normally arrived with lunch. At Ampleforth – except for the two or three weeks in the year that counted as holiday – this meal would always be taken in silence, broken only by a reading aloud from a lectern first of a passage from Scripture and then of some improving book. This custom, however, was not followed at Archbishop's House. Frequently clergy from the archdiocese would be invited to lunch (in all there were some 500 parochial clergy so they came in batches of five or six) and on those days when there were no outside guests the occasion would have an even more relaxed atmosphere. Although the Archbishop did not like discussing business at meal-times, he would normally be joined by both his private secretary and the vicar-general, with each of whom he enjoyed a light-hearted, almost bantering, relationship. One aspect of his life that Basil maintained at Archbishop's House was his dependence on regular exercise, so most afternoons he would either play squash (at the RAC Club in Pall Mall), go jogging or simply take a walk in St James's Park. All such expeditions, though, had to be organised with some care. The one thing the new Archbishop found that he had sacrificed on leaving Ampleforth was his right to privacy and from the start he never ceased to mourn what he called 'my loss of anonymity'. In those early years – most of the more intense physical activity came to an end with his first hip replacement operation in 1983 – the popular papers would have given their eye-teeth for a photograph of a sweaty Archbishop jogging on Wimbledon Common, in Battersea Park or wherever, so the venues were constantly changed and considerable trouble taken to keep such expeditions secret. Squash was less of a problem since the Archbishop's opponent was normally his private secretary, John Crowley,* one of whose qualifications for the job, to which he was appointed within six months of Basil moving south, had allegedly been his ability to dash about a squash court.

The most taxing part of the Archbishop's day began in the early evening, and by 5.30 he would normally be out on the road. In his predecessor's day there had been a chauffeur but Basil preferred to be driven by his private secretary, so it would generally be just the two of them who would be involved in making parish visits.

Such engagements nearly always took place in the evenings, since it was only then that the faithful could count on getting back from work in order to attend a service in church or a bun-fight in the parish hall. Having to perform at such functions night after night would necessarily put a strain on anyone's stock of amiability, but for a monk used to the Rule of Silence it must have been especially hard. Even when the circumstances were a good deal grander – say at a dinner given by some City Livery Company – the demands on sociability were exactly the same. It was probably fortunate that even at Ampleforth, both in his years as Abbot and before them, Basil should have had the reputation of being one of the more outgoing members of the Community. Yet, from the start at Westminster, there was perhaps a hint of strain in Basil's custom – once he got in at around 10 p.m., and if he had managed to avoid, as he liked to do, a sit-down supper – of having two boiled eggs and a choc ice before going straight up to his 'cell' as soon after 10.30 as could be managed. (There was only one exception to this rule:

---

* Bishop of Middlesbrough since 1993.

in the winter when *Match of the Day* was on BBC1 on Saturday nights, Basil postponed his bedtime and insisted on watching right through to the end.)

This was not his only preoccupation on Saturday evenings, at least in the early days. Very soon after he arrived at Archbishop's House Basil invented something called 'the eleven minus club'. Designed as talks for teenagers not bright enough to have passed the eleven plus, it regularly attracted some sixty or seventy young people who would sit around the Throne Room listening to Basil give what in his Ampleforth days would have been called 'a jaw'. In the grander setting of Archbishop's House it was officially described as 'theology for the eleven minus' and for a time – not least because it represented an entirely novel notion – it enjoyed a great success.* It certainly represented a new way of involving young people in the life of the cathedral.

So far as his own responsibilities to the cathedral went, the new Archbishop could certainly claim to have had a baptism of fire. Before he even appeared on the scene, the decision had been taken to launch an appeal for £1 million to protect its future. One of the Archbishop-Elect's first public appearances had, in fact, been to attend a fund-raising concert held in the cathedral in the presence of HRH the Duke of Edinburgh on 4 March 1976. It was merely the most glamorous of many such occasions.

Opened only in 1903, the work of the Victorian architect J. F. Bentley, the Byzantine-style cathedral had for some years been betraying signs of wear and tear. Its dominating campanile, rising high above the then rather modest tower blocks of Pimlico,

---

* These talks also provided the original source for Basil's one venture into children's fiction, his 1997 book *Basil in Blunderland*. In his thoughtful Prologue to this not wholly successful work he returns to some of the themes he first addressed in talking to the eleven minus club.

had already pushed down the porch by six inches, and the roof (heavily eroded by smog and soot) also badly needed attention. However, the appeal was not just aimed at providing money for running repairs: it was also – at least once Basil took charge – intended to ensure the continuing existence of the choir school by providing it with a badly needed endowment.

This particular objective was particularly close to the new Archbishop's heart (his predecessor had been on the point of closing down the school altogether), and he was to play an active part in reviving the school's fortunes – not least by the decision to open it up to non-singing 'day boys' who were not even required to be Catholics. This move transformed the Cathedral Choir School's economy as well as its atmosphere – a change also reflected in Basil's decision to invite John Rae, the Head Master of Westminster School, to join the governing body and, although a non-Catholic, to become in effect his understudy as chairman of the board of governors. (In an equally interesting if more conventional initiative, Basil also persuaded Patrick Barry, still Headmaster of Ampleforth after eleven years, to make his wisdom and experience available to the choir school by becoming a governor.*)

To the surprise of the pessimists, who had seen similar efforts to raise money for the cathedral fail in the past, the appeal flourished – not least thanks to a very public gift of £100,000 made on behalf of the capital's ratepayers by the pre-Ken Livingstone Greater London Council. Such an unprecedented gesture on behalf of a local authority ensured maximum publicity and, with the help of so munificent a civic gift, the appeal managed to reach its target of £1 million within eighteen months.

---

* Basil always acknowledged how much Patrick Barry had done in broadening the character of Ampleforth and emphasising the more sensitive side of what had previously been a fairly rugged institution.

In this achievement the spotlight that increasingly played on Basil personally was certainly no hindrance. Within five weeks of his installation at Westminster, it was announced that the Pope proposed to make him a Cardinal, a mark of recognition for which his predecessor John Heenan had had to wait for two years (thereby missing the 1963 conclave which elected Pope Paul VI). Basil's was, of course, merely one of nineteen names that featured in the Vatican announcement, but by the faithful in England and Wales (Scotland recently has had its own separate Cardinal) it was seen very much as an honour to their own church. The new Cardinal himself was suitably modest about the appointment: 'It comes with the job, if I may put it that way. The important thing is that the Church in England should have a representative in the College of Cardinals.' (What he could not have been expected to know was that within little more than two years he would have taken part in two papal elections.)

The actual visit to Rome, during which the freshly appointed Cardinal was invested with possession of his titular church of San Silvestro in Capite proved, predictably, of more interest to the religious than the secular press. It involved a week-long stay at the Venerable English College, whose Rector at the time was Cormac Murphy-O'Connor (ultimately to be Basil's own successor at Westminster). It also included a second personal audience with the Pope, which again appears to have made a deep impression on him. On this occasion he was accompanied to the papal apartments by both Father Cormac Murphy-O'Connor and Father Dominic Milroy, a fellow-Benedictine from Ampleforth who happened at the time to be Prior of St Anselmo, the Benedictine monastery in Rome. Many years later Father Dominic, who went on to be Headmaster of Ampleforth, set down his memories of that occasion:

First, Paul VI spoke to the three of us together and then he said 'I would like to see each of you privately'. So Cormac and I retired and Basil went in and about ten minutes later he came out in tears. Then Cormac went in and Basil told me what Paul VI had said to him, which was talking about Westminster and London and England and all that, and not talking about piety.

Then at the end he fixed him with those beady eyes and said, 'Above all, Father dear, be yourself' – which is just what Basil needed to be told. He didn't have to climb on to a sort of pedestal and look like Heenan or whatever. 'Above all, Father dear, be yourself' – and Basil was in tears.

It was certainly sound advice, though the temptation for Basil to play the part of some pretentious prelate was never particularly strong. He proved this when at the first meeting of the Conference of Catholic Bishops of England and Wales following his elevation to Westminster (and consequent introduction into its counsels) he adamantly refused to become its president. Insisting that he was very much 'the new boy', he asked the senior bishop in terms of service, George Patrick Dwyer, the Archbishop of Birmingham, to take on the job in his place. Although occupying what was by common consent the premier Catholic see, he was content in all bishops' meetings over the next three years to take second place to his colleague from Birmingham.

One of the challenges facing any Archbishop of Westminster lies in striking the correct balance between his national responsibilities and those of his own archdiocese. However modest or diffident by nature, no Archbishop of Westminster can hope to function simply as a Father in God to his own diocesan flock. Although lacking the special position of the Church of England's Archbishop of Canterbury – he has, for example, no specific role in the worldwide Catholic Church – the holder of what is in effect the primatial see for Catholics in England and Wales has to make strategic decisions as how to apportion his time.

Basil seems to have accepted this from the beginning. As early as April 1976 – the same month that the Pope nominated him to be a Cardinal – he was already spelling out a plan in his first pastoral letter to divide the archdiocese into five separate 'episcopal areas', each with its own bishop exercising full executive powers. In truth, the new scheme merely represented an extension of something that was already happening in practice, since the three existing auxiliary bishops each had his own special part of the archdiocese to administer. However, the new Archbishop's proposal represented something much more fundamental than that: it envisaged, for example, each separate 'area' of the Westminster archdiocese having its own vicar-general, its own senate of priests together with a wholly autonomous pastoral council.

Even as an 'experiment' – not due to come fully into effect until the year 1980 – it did not prove to be universally popular. As the Anglicans were subsequently to discover with similar schemes – notably one launched in the diocese of London in 1979 – both priests and laity rather like the idea of a single commanding figure being the focus of loyalty and the symbol of unity. An 'area bishop' can never usurp the authority of the diocesan and, although Basil's reorganisation plan was undoubtedly undertaken with the best of motives, it did not long survive his own time at Westminster (his successor, Cormac Murphy-O'Connor, losing no time in restoring the previous much less formal position).

It is not difficult, though, to understand what prompted Basil to embark on his own experiment in devolution. If he needed any reminder of the dual role expected of an Archbishop of Westminster, it came with the arrival, after barely two years in office, of a communication bearing ominously on its envelope the legend 'Private & Confidential' and the address of 10 Downing Street. In the letter inside the Prime Minister of the day, James Callaghan, who had come to office at almost exactly the same time as Basil and had exchanged friendly greetings with him then, explained that he 'had it in mind on the occasion of the forthcoming Birthday Honours to submit your name to the Queen with a recommendation that Her Majesty may be graciously pleased to approve the dignity of a Barony for Life of the United Kingdom be conferred upon you'.

In making the offer Jim Callaghan was breaking entirely new ground. Although the Methodist Donald Soper and the Presbyterian George MacLeod had both been put in the House of Lords by Harold Wilson, neither could claim to be the leader, or anything like it, of their respective churches. (The Chief Rabbi, Immanuel Jakobovits, did not get created a life peer by Margaret Thatcher until 1988, three years before his retirement.) The Callaghan invitation, however, immediately posed the Cardinal with a problem which, in writing to the Prime Minister the next day, he did his best to explain:

Archbishop's House,
Westminster SW1   19 May 1978

My dear Prime Minister,
    I thank you for your letter dated 17 May, 1978, in which you tell me that you propose to submit my name to HM the Queen for the conferring of a Barony for Life upon myself.
    I am grateful – and rather touched – that this should be proposed. You will, I am sure, recognise that this has many implications so far as a Roman Catholic bishop is concerned. The confidential nature of your letter prevents my being in

a position to discuss the matter, and I would need to consider and ponder the implications to which I have referred.

I would, therefore, ask you not to put my name forward, at least at this stage. I have no personal ambition to be a peer – grand and honourable though this is. I would also be unlikely to be in a position where my other duties (in terms of time) would permit my playing a part in the House of Lords, which would rightly be expected of me.

I hope you will forgive my reaction and understand that I am most grateful for the gesture of confidence which it implies.

Yours very sincerely,
Basil Hume

As a letter, it was in many ways a model of tact – even if it did not tell the whole truth. To do that, it would have had to include the awkward fact that the Canon Law of the Church expressly forbids priests to take part in the making of laws, something that had already caused the Vatican problems with the 'liberation priests' of Latin America. At least, however, the Cardinal's reply was diplomatically enough phrased to cause no offence and it certainly did not do so to Jim Callaghan or, indeed, to his successor (Basil was to receive an almost identical letter from Margaret Thatcher in 1987).

As if that invitation was not a sufficient warning of the competing claims upon the Cardinal Archbishop's energies, there was within a couple of months a second one – if of a rather different kind. Paul VI had been elected Pope in succession to John XXIII in 1963, the same year that Basil became Abbot of Ampleforth. When he came to office – he had previously, as Cardinal Giovanni Montini, been Archbishop of Milan – he enjoyed the reputation of being a liberal; but that perception of him had long since vanished in the light of the unexpectedly hard line he took in the debate over birth control as symbolised by his 1968 encyclical *Humanae Vitae*. Yet he had, as we have seen, made a profound impression upon Basil and, if the speed with which the new Archbishop got his red hat was anything to go by, that regard was reciprocated. It must, therefore, have been a particular shock when word reached Archbishop's House on the evening of 6 August, 1978, that the Holy Father had died at his summer retreat of Castel Gandolfo.

It was not just a shock, however. It also – since Basil had been a member of the College of Cardinals for the previous two years – involved an immediate and urgent call upon his time. The telegram from the *camerlengo*, or interim administrator of the Church, that arrived at Archbishop's House said simply: 'The Pope is dead. Come at once.' Basil, therefore, immediately set out for Rome. The rules of procedure, as laid down by John XXIII, required that the conclave charged with the duty of electing a new Pope must open no fewer than fifteen and no more than twenty days after the death of his predecessor. Before that, however, a date had to be found for the papal funeral, which in this case, and for the first time, took place amid all the space and grandeur of St Peter's Square (previously papal funerals were held inside the Basilica). The formal opening of the conclave did not take place for another thirteen days, but the rationale behind that delay was quite deliberate. Cardinals, coming from all corners of the globe, tend not to know each other at all well, and the purpose of their all being together in Rome – and attending daily what is known as the General Congregation – has always been that they should get to know each other better.

This was perhaps especially valuable in the case of the first papal election of 1978. As these things go, it was a remarkably open conclave. Pius XII in 1939, John XXIII in 1958 and certainly Paul VI in 1963 may all have been reasonably obvious choices; but there was no one in quite that position in 1978. The newspapers may have insisted on playing their normal game of promoting their particular favourites but none of the press forecasts got near to spotting the eventual winner. He, after a mere four ballots, turned out to be Albino Luciani, the Patriarch of Venice, who promptly announced (combining the names of his two most recent predecessors) that he wished to be known as John Paul.

Predictably, rather on the Henman-Wimbledon principle, there had been a certain amount of conjecture in the British press that the lot might fall on the 55-year-old Archbishop of Westminster. Although the London bookmakers originally placed the odds against him at 10–1, they soon shot out to 20–1 and failed to shorten even when an American prelate – not a Cardinal – took it upon himself to declare that, in his view, the Cardinal Archbishop of Westminster 'possessed all the qualities to be the next Pope'. With typical diffidence – and, as it turned out, total accuracy – Basil himself immediately dismissed this forecast as 'ludicrous' and 'totally unrealistic'.

He was less happy, though, in the choice of words with which he greeted the election of Albino Luciani to be Pope John Paul. He had been, he rashly opined, 'quite certainly God's candidate' – a phrase that was to return to haunt him when, after just thirty-three bewildering, unhappy days, the man who had initially been hailed as 'the smiling Pope' was found dead in his bed in the papal apartments in the Vatican.

For Basil and his 110 voting colleagues within the College of Cardinals this inevitably meant another expedition to Rome barely a month after the first one had ended. This time, however, the conclave started its deliberations on a rather different basis. At least the electors now knew one another pretty well and were thus much less likely to vote in regional or even national blocs (though, to be fair, Luciani was said to have ended up with 101 out of a possible 111 votes). There had been some speculation even before the August conclave that it might result in the choice of the first non-Italian Pope in 450 years, but, given that the Italians still controlled a quarter of the electorate – Cardinals over eighty were no longer allowed to take part in the conclave – that never seemed a very likely prospect. On this second occasion, however, it looked from the beginning as if things might go the other way. After a papal reign of only just over a month, it might have appeared rather odd to replace the former Patriarch of Venice with, say, the Archbishop of Palermo or, worse, with some member of the Curia which – it was already being muttered – had not given the late Pope sufficient support.

In how apprehensive a mood Basil set off for Rome for the second time in seven weeks it is impossible to know, but it may have been indicative that he should have gone out of his way to emphasise to his private secretary the importance of making sure that he picked him up at the right place in the Vatican Gardens the moment the conclave was over. (He plainly did not want to linger around in case he found himself in a position of potential embarrassment.) In October, as in August, Basil's name had usually been included in any list of the *papabile* appearing in the British press. In addition, this time round, he even rated as one of the top half-dozen candidates in *Time* magazine, to say nothing of being selected by a computer in Chicago as the fifth most likely successor to John Paul I. (As a salutary warning to any contemporary Vatican soothsayers, the candidate who was eventually elected, Cardinal Karol Wojtyla of Cracow, failed to get a mention either from the computer or from *Time* magazine, though we now know that he had collected at least four votes in the previous conclave.)

But if one non-Italian was considered, why not another? Over and above the fact that Poland is far more of a Catholic country than is Britain, a further part of the explanation probably lies in the undoubted seniority enjoyed by the Archbishop of Cracow. The two men may have been roughly the same age but Wojtyla had been an Archbishop since 1964 and a member of the College of Cardinals since 1967. Put alongside that, Basil's own record – only two-and-a-half years as either an Archbishop or a Cardinal – necessarily looked like that of a Johnnie-come-lately. The timing of what became known as 'the year of the three Popes' could hardly, in fact, have been less helpful to any hopes of there being a second Englishman (after Nicholas Breakspear in 1154) to make it to the papacy. A few years later, when he was already president of the Council of European Bishops' Conferences, Basil might well have looked a formidable candidate; but in 1978 he was not even president of his own national Bishops' Conference and was altogether too much the ecclesiastical *ingénu*. Add to that his lack of familiarity with Rome (he didn't even speak Italian) and his general distaste for Curial politics – and the wonder perhaps is that his name was in the frame at all.

Only once – years afterwards – did he give anything away about the whole experience. 'You know,' he remarked to a friend, 'it's a very odd thing when you're a member of a conclave. No one says anything to you – but then you suddenly realise that your name must be under consideration because no one comes up to talk to you any more.' It may just conceivably be that there was a hint of wistfulness about the way Basil kept among his most private papers a note that was passed by Jim Callaghan as Prime Minister to the Archbishop's brother-in-law, the Cabinet Secretary, on the day – 16 October 1978 – that Karol Wojtyla was elected Pope. A hand-written scribble, it read: 'I imagine Basil Hume won't be disappointed – probably relieved! But on the spiritual plane he would have been good.'

It is not necessary to question the conditional prediction involved in the second sentence to wonder about the total accuracy of the assessment contained in the first.

VIII

HOPE DEFERRED

T HE NEW POPE WAS ONLY THREE YEARS OLDER THAN Basil Hume. This meant that in the normal course of events – since Popes, unlike Archbishops, do not retire – Karol Wojtyla's active life would outlast that of the man who had come to be spoken of simply as 'the English Cardinal'. But if the ninth Archbishop of Westminster imagined that this would leave him free to concentrate exclusively on the affairs of his own country and diocese, he was soon to learn his mistake. One of John Paul II's first actions was to nominate Basil to take his place on the fifteen-man general secretariat council of the International Synod of Bishops.

Although essentially an advisory body to the Pontiff, the council exerted considerable influence – not least because it was expected to liaise with the various regional or national bishops' conferences. It also carried the burden of drawing up the agenda for the regular meetings of the international synod itself. The next one of these was due to take place in 1980, so Basil found himself immediately plunged into making frequent visits to Rome in order to plan and prepare for the first such meeting to take place in the new papal reign.

Perhaps in an effort to reassure his own flock, he also in 1979 took over the presidency of the Bishops' Conference of England

and Wales. This was the post he had declined in 1976, urging that it be filled instead by the senior Catholic prelate among the Hierarchy, but, after three years of deferring to the septuagenarian Archbishop Dwyer of Birmingham, Basil clearly felt that the time had come for him to assume the titular leadership of the English and Welsh bishops. It was a position that necessarily reinforced the practical (though not constitutional) primatial role that any Archbishop of Westminster is bound to exercise.

More significant, if also perhaps more surprising for such a fresh recruit to Catholic Hierarchy, was Basil's election in 1978 to the presidency of the Council of European Bishops' Conferences, the body that – in those years still heavily influenced by the Iron Curtain – brought together the Catholic bishops of both Western and Eastern Europe. Basil was to hold this influential post for the next eight years and, had there been a further papal election during that period, he would almost certainly have been able to count on a hard core of support from the other European Cardinals. This was not, however, the kind of speculation – despite the attempted assassination of the Pope in 1982 – that Basil himself ever encouraged. It was events, more than any inclinations of his own, that ensured that his name was kept in the public spotlight. The year 1980, for example, had seen the 1,500th anniversary of the birth of St Benedict – and what could have been more natural than that the most prominent Benedictine (and the only one to be a member of the College of Cardinals) should have been called upon to play the most prominent part in it? Basil spent a sizeable proportion of 1980 preaching abroad, delivering addresses in honour of St Benedict in America, France and Italy.

He was by no means inactive at home either. One of his earliest initiatives as Archbishop had been to give a public speech before the General Synod of the Church of England (the first holder of his office ever to do such a thing). There may have been some disappointment with the message he delivered – Roman Catholics, he insisted, could not in conscience join in the work of the British Council of Churches – but there was widespread appreciation of the ecumenical spirit he had shown in appearing at all. Sometimes this spirit could reveal itself in small, if eloquent, gestures. On 25 January 1980, for example, Dr Donald Coggan was due to retire after five years at Lambeth. That morning *The Times* carried a 'lead' letter from the Archbishop of Westminster paying fulsome tribute to the outgoing Archbishop of Canterbury. Officially 'absolutely null and utterly void' though Anglican Orders may have remained in the eyes of the Roman Catholic Church, Basil still praised Coggan as 'a Christian whose sincerity and integrity I very much respect' and went on to describe him as a man 'who knows the things of the spirit which really matter'.*

Almost certainly this spontaneous gesture paved the way for the next decisive step in relations between the two Churches. Just two months later, when Coggan's successor, Robert Runcie, was enthroned in Canterbury Cathedral, Basil was not only present but took a formal part in the service (he read the Epistle). No one could have envisaged Cardinal Heenan playing an equivalent role at the time of Coggan's own enthronement a mere five years earlier.

Nor was the world of politics left entirely alone. The opening of the new decade witnessed what was one of the most trenchant statements ever made by a Catholic leader on the arms race. In a New Year article he contributed, again to *The Times*, Basil contrasted the plight of the ten million children of the world suffering from malnutrition with the huge sums being

---

* The warmth of this encomium appears to have caused some bewilderment at *The Times*. Its Editor was reduced to publishing the letter under the slightly bemused heading 'Prelate's tribute to a Prelate'.

spent by the superpowers on the manufacture of weapons of mass destruction. To make matters worse, he proceeded to question the whole underlying ethos of the then fashionable doctrine of mutual deterrence: 'If it is wrong to unleash such weapons against civilian targets, can it be morally defensible to threaten to do so, even against an unjust aggressor? Can we, in fact, base a defence policy on such threats?'

Such questions may not have done much to add to his stature within Margaret Thatcher's Downing Street, though even there he was accepted as a figure of consequence. That much had been made clear a year earlier when the new Prime Minister had written directly to the Cardinal at the time of the formation of her Government. She had just appointed a Roman Catholic to be a Minister of State at the Northern Ireland Office and wanted the Cardinal to reassure the Tory MP concerned – Hugh Rossi, the Member for Hornsey – that he had done the right thing in accepting the post.

The respect in which Basil had come to be held extended across party boundaries. Few things pleased him more than the invitation he got from the Labour-controlled council of Newcastle upon Tyne to accept the freedom of the city in which he was born. The ceremony took place in the summer of 1980 when the Cardinal received the freedom in the company of Jackie Milburn, the local Newcastle United sporting hero. He certainly did his 'street cred' no harm by humbly asking his fellow-honorand for his autograph – and he added to his populist stature a year later by taking part in a *This is Your Life* ITV programme devoted to Milburn's career.

By the beginning of the 1980s Basil had to accept that, like it or not, he had become a public figure of considerable interest to the media. This meant, for instance, that if he spoke out (as he did) against the new Conservative Government supplying arms to General Pinochet's Chile, he had to expect to make headlines – just as he was bound to if he inveighed against 'the great scandal of the homeless'.

In part, the Cardinal owed the growth in his popular standing to an hour-long television documentary that had been made about him in the second half of 1980 (but which, thanks to an ITV strike, did not go out until February 1981). Entitled simply *Basil Hume OSB* and the work of an experienced Thames TV producer, Robert Fleming, it did everything for his public reputation that an earlier, ill-judged encounter with Ludovic Kennedy on the BBC *Tonight* programme had failed to do.* Very much a portrait in the round, taking in all its subject's years at Ampleforth, it was a model piece of documentary television, which went on to win the Sandford St Martin prize for the best religious programme of the year. Curiously, however, its first impact on Hume himself was one of irritation. Taken aback by all the newspaper pre-publicity about it, and in particular by the press unanimously zeroing in on some (perhaps unguarded) remarks he had made about marriage, he went for a pre-emptive strike by issuing a slightly pompous press statement. In it, while not criticising the TV profile itself, he regretted the fact that 'newspapers single out from an hour-long programme a reference to the human and emotional sacrifices involved in the faithful observance of celibacy'. The product of what was becoming known at Archbishop's House as 'Basil's short fuse', it was a foolish thing to do. In mitigation, though, it deserves to be said that there had been a good deal of provocation on the part of the press – the *Sun*, for example, headlining its story 'Cardinal: I Yearn For A Wife' and the *Mirror* using 'Why I'd Wed By Cardinal'.

---

* Basil had not properly prepared for this interview – undertaken in September 1976, within six months of becoming Archbishop – and it showed, particularly in the way he allowed himself to be roughed up by his interviewer. There was subsequently some correspondence in *The Times*, protesting at TV 'aggression'.

Probably, though, Basil's sensitivity is best explained by what he knew to be the changing mood of the faithful on such a delicate issue as a married priesthood. Indeed, the previous year, 1980, the views of the Catholic clergy and laity were exposed to the public gaze in a way that they never had been before. The occasion was the Liverpool National Pastoral Congress – the brainchild of Archbishop Derek Worlock – at which some 2,000 men and women came together to discuss a whole variety of contentious issues. Eventually seven 'final reports' (prepared by separate committees and then approved in plenary session) came out of the Congress, on matters ranging from artificial contraception, through social justice, to the possible ordination of women and, indeed, of married men.

Probably to the secret relief of the Cardinal, the face the Catholic Church presented to the world turned out to be much more tolerant and less repressive than had been foreseen. From the admission of divorced or remarried Catholics to the Sacraments, through the reception of non-Catholics at Mass, to the whole vexed question of birth control, this predominantly lay assembly came out decisively for liberal positions. However, whatever his private views, such an outcome was bound to cause the Cardinal some anxiety, not least so far as the reactions of the rest of the English and Welsh Hierarchy were concerned.

The method chosen for dealing with what was seen by the more conservative bishops as little better than a popular insurrection followed a time-honoured course. The responsibility for incorporating the seven reports into a single document was passed to a drafting committee. It was not in itself illiberal, since heading it was Archbishop Worlock, and another member of it was Basil's own assistant for public affairs, Monsignor George Leonard (the other three individuals involved were all drawn from the laity). The drafting committee finished its work in six weeks and the result was a comprehensive summary known as

The Easter People. Visibly toned down from the seven raw 'final reports', the strategy behind it was still plain enough: as a document, which also took into account the responses of the Bishops' Conference to the proposals made, *The Easter People* had been deliberately presented in such a way as not to court automatic rejection in Rome.

The task of taking it there fell to Basil Hume and Derek Worlock. When they set out in August for the Pope's summer residence at Castel Gandolfo in the Alban Hills, they can hardly have been in any doubt as to the delicacy of the mission on which they were engaged. According to the account that he gave afterwards, Basil at the audience handed over a copy of *The Easter People* to Pope John Paul II, expressly drawing his attention to the section on artificial contraception – only to see the Holy Father impatiently wave it away. It is probably only fair to add that Derek Worlock, always inclined to put a brave face on things, never endorsed this version of what had occurred.

What, however, is common ground between them is that at some stage in the same audience an invitation was issued to the Pope to come on a papal visit to the Catholic Church in Britain – and that, even if without too much grace ('It is inevitable'), John Paul II accepted it. Although Hume and Worlock had arrived armed by their colleagues on the Bishops' Conference with the authority to issue such an invitation, the outcome appears to have taken them by surprise. In particular, they had not foreseen that the Pope would indicate a readiness to come at as early a date as he did. The timing was fixed then and there for the early summer of 1982, a matter of only just over eighteen months away.

As soon as he got home, the first thing the Cardinal had to do was to alert the Queen at Balmoral, the Archbishop of Canterbury on holiday in Greece and (since the Pope was planning to visit Scotland as well as England and Wales) Cardinal

Gray at his home in Edinburgh as to what was afoot. He did not have to act with the same urgency towards the Prime Minister since it had already been agreed that the Pope's visit would be in no sense a State, or even official, one but rather be strictly pastoral in nature.

Gratified and excited though they were by the Pope's positive response, both Hume and Worlock must have realised what its effect would be. In terms of the English Church, it immediately shifted the focus of attention away from the reforming proposals so carefully put forward in *The Easter People*, and instead firmly onto the preparations for what would inevitably be viewed as an historic event. No Pope had ever visited Britain before. Whether by accident or design, John Paul II had thus succeeded in deflecting any immediate threat posed by the proposals contained in *The Easter People* – notably its plea for a reinterpretation of the teaching on birth control contained in *Humanae Vitae*. Not surprisingly, by the time the International Bishops' Synod opened at the end of September, both Hume and Worlock found that they had their work cut out to get their fellow prelates even to discuss it.

Of the two it was probably Hume who was the more depressed. Entirely lacking the Pollyanna streak that was always an integral part of Worlock's make-up, he did not deceive himself as to the reality of the defeat that the reformers within the English Church had suffered. That autumn he made a couple of interventions at the Bishops' Synod held in Rome but, though each was well received, both, in effect, involved a recognition that – faced with so conservative a Pope – it was futile to fight on.

That was certainly the message that Basil ultimately delivered to his more radical clergy back at home, but it was not a view that they were at all inclined to endorse at first. When the Archbishop of Westminster and the Archbishop of Liverpool met the standing committee of the National Conference of

Priests, they found that out for themselves. The leaders of this body expressed their disappointment that the English Hierarchy appeared to have moved away from the proposals so recently passed by the National Pastoral Congress and reproached the bishops for being too ready 'to give up their rights as a local Church and . . . too willing to give way to the Roman Curia'. For their pains and anxieties all they got was a brisk telling-off from the Cardinal. From the sole original minute of the meeting to survive, it is perfectly plain that he found it necessary to strike a warning note:

> The Cardinal considered that conservatism was succeeding in many parts of the world and was now rising in Rome. We had to remember that Western Europe was now a minority in the Church and that places like Africa and South America were very conservative. Our local Church has to find its way in present circumstances and it is not always clear how it should proceed.
>
> The Cardinal was sure it would not help to have public calls on our bishops to act by themselves. There were some conservatives in this country who were already attacking what had been done by himself and by Archbishop Worlock.*

In the end this minute was considered too dangerous to circulate and the flexible, tactful pen of Archbishop Worlock was brought in to compose a far more anodyne version of it. However, there can be little doubt that it represented an accurate picture of the situation. The meeting of the National Pastoral Congress in May and (if in a more subdued form) the publication of *The Easter*

---

* The minute appears in full in *The Worlock Archive* by Clifford Longley (Geoffrey Chapman, 2000).

People in August had symbolised a high-water mark for the spirit of liberalism within the Church. For one reason or another it then receded and we shall probably never know how much of that decline was due to a loss of nerve on the part of the English Hierarchy.

Basil's own spirit, however, was by no means entirely broken. He demonstrated that when at the end of 1981 he took the bold step of coming out openly in criticism of Opus Dei, the Catholic evangelising movement of priests and laity founded in Spain in 1928 which had always enjoyed the full support of the papacy. Basil had been unhappy about its more repressive tendencies for some years, and in December 1981, just five months before the Pope himself was due to arrive in Britain, he pointedly issued what he called 'guidelines' for the behaviour of Opus Dei within his own diocese. These were largely concerned with Opus Dei's involvement with young people, since this was the area in which most criticism had arisen. The guidelines, which were published and made available to the newspapers, made four substantial recommendations:

1) No person under eighteen years of age should be allowed to take any vow or long-term commitment in association with Opus Dei.

2) It is essential that young people who wish to join Opus Dei should first discuss the matter with their parents or legal guardians.

3) While it is accepted that those who join Opus Dei take on the proper duties and responsibilities of membership, care must be taken to respect the freedom of the individual – particularly the freedom to leave the organisation without undue pressure being applied.

4) Initiatives and activities of Opus Dei within the diocese of Westminster should carry a clear indication of their sponsorship and management.

Short of slapping the phrase 'health warning' on the document, Basil could hardly have made his meaning more explicit. Despite their powerful friends – and the personal prelature about to be granted to the 80,000-strong organisation by the Pope – Basil had, in effect, relegated Opus Dei to being essentially a touch-line organisation – and that was something he did, as we shall see again on page 296, with total deliberation.

For the moment, however, that was about the sole crumb of comfort that aggrieved Catholic liberals got. Most of their policy concerns, thanks at least in part to the impending arrival of the Holy Father, had been placed firmly on the backburner. In fact, from the time of the announcement of the Pope's visit, the Roman Catholic Church in Britain looked as if it was riding something of a triumphalist wave. There were some rumblings from what a caustic Anglican bishop once called 'the Protestant underworld' – Dr Ian Paisley lost no time in making a formal protest to the Prime Minister against the papal visit – but it soon became clear that, at least on the mainland, the old cry of 'No Popery' had lost most of its evocative power. As a mature, multi-faith nation, most people seem to have felt, Britain should be able to take a papal visit in its stride.

Yet that is not to imply that there were no apprehensions on the part of the Catholic community, though most of these tended to concentrate on financial and administrative issues. The aim – necessarily an expensive one (not least in terms of security) – was that the Pope should be seen by as many people as possible, and that meant arranging for him to appear in a whole range of population centres. On this occasion, since it recognised that it was dealing with *terra incognita*, the Vatican was content to leave the planning of the visit in the hands of the English Church. Once the decision had been transmitted that the Holy Father would want to take the Seven Sacraments as the theme and framework of his tour, all the detailed preparations were undertaken in London, the majority of them at Archbishop's House.

Here Basil himself very much took the lead. That can be seen from a long and detailed letter that he wrote to the Pope on 27 January 1982, just a week before he was due in Rome to discuss the whole project with the Holy Father. In his letter Basil made four specific requests – that the Pope should agree to take lunch with the Queen *en famille* at Buckingham Palace on the day of his arrival in Britain; that the next day he should do the same with Anglican and Free Church leaders on the occasion of his visit to Canterbury; that the following week in Liverpool he should visit not merely the Catholic cathedral but the Anglican one as well; and, finally, that when in London he should reside not at the Nunciature in Wimbledon but rather – if only on grounds of security and geographical convenience – under his own roof at Archbishop's House, Westminster.

The fact that, despite closely arguing each point, Basil returned from Rome successful on only one of them – in Liverpool it was agreed that the Holy Father would look in on the Protestant cathedral on his way to the Catholic one of Christ the King – tells its own tale of the uphill struggle faced by anyone who tries to challenge the custom and practice of the Vatican. Basil took particularly hard his failure to persuade the Pope of the importance of accepting the Queen's invitation to lunch, and he also appears to have harboured some resentment over the role of the Papal pro-Nuncio in blocking the scheme for the Holy Father to make Westminster rather than Wimbledon his base.*
He could just about claim to have fought the Canterbury proposal

---

* The man, however, that Basil mainly blamed for this – and for his other disappointments over the papal visit – was Archbishop Paul Marcinkus, the Pope's American bodyguard and close aide who also ran the troubled Vatican bank. He was a highly influential figure whom Basil consistently regarded with the deepest suspicion.

to a draw, since the meeting with non-Catholic Church leaders survived, although without the symbolic benefit of the two sides being seen to break bread together.

This was not the only area in which difficult issues surfaced, sometimes defying the best efforts at diplomacy. The Scottish Catholic Church was co-host to the visit and was very conscious of its own independent entity although, fortunately for Basil, Cardinal Gray was an easier figure to negotiate with than his successor, Cardinal Winning, would probably have proved to be.

There was also the even more prickly question of how to involve the Church of England. Here the Cardinal was to display a remarkable capacity for self-effacement. Very early on, the commitment was made that the Pope would come to Canterbury, where the co-star of the occasion could only be the Anglican Archbishop, Dr Robert Runcie. For historical and emotional reasons, the Pope's presence at the shrine of English Christianity – where St Augustine had first arrived in 597 – was bound to provide the high-point of the visit. This was something that Basil appears to have accepted with complete equanimity. Even when the Pope's factotum, Archbishop Paul Marcinkus, tried at the last moment to scale down the time the Pope was due to spend at Canterbury, the Cardinal dug in his heels and insisted that not merely the service in the Cathedral but the meeting afterwards with the non-Catholic Church leaders should go ahead as planned (even if now as a more frugal occasion than Basil had intended).

As things worked out, however, these were by no means the most serious hiccups to threaten the Pope's visit. At the eleventh hour the Argentine invasion of the Falklands almost wrecked the entire project. With fewer than eight weeks remaining before the Pope's planned arrival, it began to look as if all the advance preparations – to say nothing of what was already a considerable financial outlay – might have gone for nothing. Once the

British task force sailed for the South Atlantic it seemed to many that the Pope would feel compelled to pull out, if only because it would be singularly inappropriate for him to visit any country that was at war with another.

From the start no one seems to have confronted this threat with more realism than the Cardinal himself. In fact, it was he who first drew public attention to it by remarking at a press conference that if Britain, by the time the visit was scheduled to begin, was already engaged in armed conflict in the South Atlantic, then the Pope would 'find himself in an impossible position'. Yet any suspicion that this represented a none-too-subtle effort to put pressure on the British Government to seek a negotiated settlement could hardly have been wider of the mark. Only eight days later Basil was to be found declaring, via a special article published simultaneously in the *Universe* and the *Catholic Herald*, that the use of force by Britain in order to recover the Falkland Islands would meet all the conditions for a just war and could certainly be morally justified.

The background to that statement was not as clearcut as it may have appeared. Although the Archbishop of Canterbury had already taken a position virtually identical with the Cardinal's, not all Anglican – or, indeed, Catholic – bishops shared their view. The Free Churches, too, were much exercised over any resort to force and strongly favoured a peaceful settlement through the United Nations. However, largely because of the proximity of the papal visit, it was within the Catholic Church that the real argument took place, and it proved to be a disagreement that found Basil seriously at odds with some of his leading colleagues.

Just before the final crisis over the visit broke, the Cardinal himself had been in Rome, though his purpose in being there was merely to discuss security questions pertaining to the proposed visit. (He had, in fact, got back to Heathrow before any

Argentine troops landed at Port Stanley.) But as matters developed – and the threat to the £6 million that the English Church had already invested in the Pope's visit began to look ever more serious – at least one member of the Hierarchy became increasingly agitated. Towards the end of April Derek Worlock resolved that he had no alternative but to try to save the day himself.

His initiative was to lead to the most serious breach ever to take place between him and the Archbishop of Westminster. Broadly, Worlock's view was that it was worth paying almost any price to make sure the visit went ahead; the Cardinal, on the other hand, felt that basic principles were involved – and one of his more personal concerns was to ensure that the robust line he had already taken on the war was in no way compromised. Inevitably, the lines of battle were drawn up between the two men.

It was to prove a tough struggle, with Basil at one stage failing to get his way even in an emergency session of the Bishops' Conference. The final *casus belli* became Worlock's demand that the Cardinal should fly to Rome and agree to take part, along with Cardinal Gray, in a 'Mass of Reconciliation' in which the two other participants would be Cardinals from Argentina. Having failed to get his colleagues on the Bishops' Conference to back him up in his initial instinct that such a gesture would inevitably be misunderstood, Basil finally, if reluctantly, fell in with Worlock's plan. He duly flew to Rome, took part in the Mass with the Pope presiding, and at least was able to announce on his return to Britain that the papal visit was 'now secure'. Apart from the Pope's diplomatic intimation that he would be visiting Argentina just a week after he got back from Britain, only one political price had to be paid. Somewhat to his chagrin, Basil had to ask Downing Street whether the Prime Minister would mind forgoing her scheduled meeting with the Pope – and this sacrifice Margaret Thatcher (far more mindful of the damage that would be caused to Britain internationally by the Pope's refusal to come at all) willingly accepted. It had been a close run thing – not least because the Battle of Goose Green actually took place on the day the Pope arrived – but at least the British Catholic Church had been spared the humiliation that any decision on the Pope's part to withdraw would certainly have represented.

The new danger, of course, was that – taking place against the background of the war now being waged in the Falklands – the papal visit would turn out to be something of an anticlimax. If it did not do so,* it was largely because of the meticulous planning that had gone into making the forward arrangements covering the entire six days (five spent in England and Wales and one in Scotland). Deliberately designed to embrace what was still generally known at the time as the Whitsun weekend – thus incorporating a Bank Holiday – the whole project had been organised with an almost military precision. This was not perhaps surprising since one of the key planners behind it was the Duke of Norfolk who, in his time, had been a distinguished professional soldier. It was, in fact, he – the former Major-General Miles Fitzalan-Howard – who, along with an ex-ambassador, Sir Paul Wright, and the local Bishop of Arundel and Brighton, Cormac Murphy-O'Connor, first greeted the Pope when his plane touched down at Gatwick on Friday 28 May. On emerging from the aircraft at 8 a.m., John Paul II followed what was then his normal custom of immediately kneeling down and kissing the ground. There were 2,500 Catholics present at the airport to see him, but his visit started in earnest once he reached London by train.

---

* In one sense, though, it did. Sales of souvenirs and mementoes of the Pope's visit proved disappointing, perhaps because of the long period of uncertainty that had surrounded it. The Church was left with a number of aggrieved dealers on its hands, one of whom threatened to complain direct to the Pope in Rome.

It was only the shortest of journeys from Victoria Station to Westminster Cathedral, and there at 11 a.m. the Pope celebrated Mass before a packed congregation. From the Cathedral John Paul II went to Buckingham Palace where he had his brief meeting with the Queen, and then it was on to St George's Cathedral, Southwark, for a service of the anointing of the sick (one of the Seven Sacraments). The Pope's first day in England ended with his taking supper with – and giving a formal address to – the whole array of the English and Welsh Bishops who were assembled at Archbishop's House. John Paul II did not, however, spend the night there, going to sleep instead at the home of the former Apostolic Delegate, Archbishop Bruno Heim, whose diplomatic status had been raised to that of a pro-Nuncio to coincide with the papal visit.

The following day, Saturday 29 May, remains probably the one that is most firmly embedded in the public memory. After an early morning meeting at Roehampton with some 4,000 men and women drawn from the Religious Orders, the Pope set off by helicopter for Canterbury, where the plan had long been that he should attend a service – formally described as 'A Celebration of Faith' – in the cathedral. In terms of dramatic impact nothing could match the sight of the Pope being greeted by the Archbishop of Canterbury, or of the two of them praying side by side at the tomb of St Thomas à Becket or again of their jointly signing what was called 'The Common Declaration', which set out what were hoped at the time to be the future avenues of co-operation between the two Churches.

The crowds at Canterbury were fairly sparse but that did not matter as the entire morning's events were covered live on television, providing most viewers with the first chance they had of seeing the Holy Father being driven through the streets in his glass-walled Popemobile. That vehicle was to feature again later in the day, when the Pope celebrated Mass in front of 80,000 people at Wembley Stadium and before the service drove around the pitch that only a few weeks earlier had been used for the FA Cup Final. When the service was over it was also to provide the one unintended moment of comedy of the day. As the Popemobile moved off, bearing John Paul II out of the stadium, a figure was to be observed running rather desperately behind it. Dressed in crimson, that figure turned out to be none other than the Cardinal Archbishop of Westminster who, having been left behind, had to be hauled aboard.

That could, indeed, be said to have been not only a moment of comedy but also one of truth. A striking aspect of the Pope's visit was the way in which Basil, as the man who had first issued the invitation, kept himself firmly in the background throughout. It may have been a stance that came naturally to a self-effacing Benedictine, but that did not make the Cardinal Archbishop's reluctance to share the limelight with the Pope – or, for that matter, with the Archbishop of Canterbury – any less remarkable.

Oddly, it was outside London and the South-East that John Paul II best demonstrated his credentials as a crowd-puller. In Liverpool an estimated half-a-million people turned out to cheer him as he made his way from the Anglican Cathedral to the Catholic one. Another massive crowd had assembled earlier in the day to take part in an open-air Mass held at Coventry Airport. In Scotland he enjoyed an equal success: on the penultimate day of his visit he drew a congregation of 250,000 to an open air Mass held in Bellahouston Park in Glasgow. If there was a disappointment, it occurred on the final day which he spent in Wales. A mere 35,000 young people, drawn from both England and Wales, failed to fill Ninian Park for what was described as a National Youth Event.

Broadly, though, Basil and the rest of the Catholic Hierarchy had every reason to feel pleased with the way the papal visit had

Basil Hume's parents 'Mimi' and William in the 1920s.

The five Hume children on the beach at Wimereux in 1929. Basil is on the far left.

Opposite: The young fisherman: while still a schoolboy Basil was taught to fish by his father.

Father Paul Nevill, Headmaster of Ampleforth 1924–54. The boys knew him as 'Posh'.

Ampleforth First XV. Basil is third from the left.

Basil as a young priest with his father
Sir William Hume in Ampleforth village.

Abbot Herbert Byrne, Basil's predecessor,
who presided over Ampleforth for twenty-
four years.

The British contingent in the annual Fribourg Summer Procession. Basil is in the second row on the far right.

Ampleforth Monastery and College at the time of Basil's departure for Westminster.

Basil Hume on the day of his installation as the ninth Archbishop of Westminster.

Basil Hume with Pope Paul VI on the day he became a Cardinal in May 1976.

Next page: Pope John Paul II leaving Archbishop's House, Westminster, on the first day of his papal visit to Britain in May 1982.

gone. Despite a few efforts at disruption, notably a demonstration in Edinburgh by Ian Paisley and his friends, no serious Protestant backlash had developed; in defiance of the fighting in the Falklands media interest had held up remarkably well throughout; and from a notoriously unsentimental press the Pope's personal notices had been uniformly favourable.

Indeed, if there was any damage done, it came in the shape of expectations raised and hopes unfulfilled. When Pope John Paul II and Archbishop Robert Runcie met to pray together at Canterbury that Saturday morning at the end of May 1982, it seemed certain that some kind of breakthrough in relations between Rome and Canterbury must be round the corner, but, despite 'The Common Declaration' they both signed, there was no follow-through: in fact, if anything, over the next ten years (in 1992 the Anglican vote in favour of women priests of course changed everything) there was, at best, a standstill rather than a coming together.

In that sense, while 1982 may justifiably be seen as a year of hope, it can also be regarded as one that witnessed no more than a mirage. For a moment the sight of it was thrilling, but the promise it held out proved neither lasting nor permanent. That was something with which even Basil Hume – at that stage only a quarter of the way through his reign at Westminster – had eventually to come to terms.

IX

FALLOUT FROM
THE BOMB

WHEN BASIL HUME BECAME ARCHBISHOP OF WEST-
minster in 1976, he can hardly have foreseen that the
first, and in some ways the fiercest, controversy to
confront him would involve the nuclear bomb. The Campaign
for Nuclear Disarmament may once have been a great force in
the land – its annual Easter Aldermaston Marches (from the
late 1950s to the mid-1960s) providing a formative experience
for a whole generation of duffle-coated young people – but, as
with the queen bee, CND's strength began to drain away at the
very moment it delivered its sting. No sooner had it captured
the Labour Party – as it did when its policy in favour of unilateral disarmament prevailed at the 1960 Scarborough conference – than its influence started to wane. The Labour leader,
Hugh Gaitskell, fought back to save, as he put it, 'the party we
love', and at Blackpool in 1961 he managed to reverse the
previous year's unilateralist decision.

Meanwhile the ban-the-bomb movement itself fell victim to
internal divisions, with its titular leader, Canon L. John Collins
of St Paul's Cathedral, quarrelling in spectacular fashion with
the aged philosopher Bertrand Russell and all the other celebrity

advocates of direct action enrolled by the Committee of 100. This internal split caused great bitterness and, by the time Harold Wilson's Labour Government came to office in 1964, CND had shown itself so ineffectual that it proved quite unable to prevent the new Prime Minister from going back on his public promise to 'renegotiate' the Nassau Agreement.*

When Wilson returned to office in 1974, CND had become so quiescent that he experienced not the slightest difficulty in continuing the Heath Government's policy of smuggling through the modernisation of the Polaris fleet via the new Chevaline anti-ABM system. To all intents and purposes CND looked as if it was over – a history of sad decline from a movement of mass influence to one of evident impotence in less than two decades.

Of course, concerns continued to be expressed over nuclear policy. Indeed, as was noticed in the previous chapter, Basil raised some of them himself in an article he contributed to *The Times* at the beginning of 1980, but it was another measure of how quiet things had gone by then that even his moral questioning of the whole principle of deterrence should have provoked little or no public debate. CND was certainly in no position to start one up. Although in 1978 it had had some success in mobilising public opinion against the use by Nato of the American neutron bomb, by 1980 it was an organisation with a paid-up membership of barely 3,000, an annual income of no more than £30,000 and a headquarters staff (on a time-share basis) of three-and-a-half individuals. Miraculously, though, by the end of that same year it still

---

* This was the deal struck in December 1962 between John F. Kennedy and Harold Macmillan whereby, in recompense for the collapse of the Skybolt air delivered missile programme, the United States agreed to sell to the United Kingdom its recently adopted Polaris missile system, thus renewing the life of the so-called 'independent British deterrent'.

managed to get 80,000 people to turn out for a demonstration in Trafalgar Square.

By then, however, there had just been a significant development, even if, understandably, no one spotted it at the time. Towards the end of 1979 the still relatively new Archbishop of Westminster received – by appointment – one of his own clergy at his residence next door to the Cathedral. This particular priest was certainly no stranger to those slightly intimidating premises; he had worked there himself some fifteen years earlier as private secretary to Cardinal Heenan. He had then gone on to be chairman of the Diocesan Schools Commission, afterwards serving as Catholic chaplain to London University. Given the title of Monsignor by Heenan, he had for the previous three years been parish priest of the economically depressed but vibrantly Catholic area of Somers Town, that part of north-west London lying behind the three railway termini of Euston, St Pancras and King's Cross. In addition, he had become increasingly active in such bodies as the Catholic peace organisation Pax Christi, the secular charity War on Want, to say nothing of CND itself (of which he had been chairman since 1977).

It was this double tug on his time and energy – the one represented by the demands of his parish, the other by his involvement in the world outside – that the priest concerned, the then fifty-year-old Bruce Kent, wished to lay before the Cardinal. The immediate occasion, though, for their meeting was rather more urgent than that. As chairman, Kent knew that the CND's existing general secretary was about to retire and he wished to succeed him in what was a full-time, if modestly paid, post. The rest of the story, and in particular the Cardinal's reaction to his plea, is probably best told in Kent's own words:

I can't say that he thought this a wonderful idea but in a tolerant way he said that if that was what I felt I ought to do, then at least I ought to try it. I'm sure he felt that this was an enthusiasm that I would get out of my system in a relatively short time. It was a generous decision but one which he clearly later came to regret.

If Basil Hume did come to regret granting one of his priests temporary leave of absence from serving in his diocese, it was far more the consequence of the unforeseen political repercussions that followed than of any sense on his part that his original decision had been mistaken – and in feeling as he did he was probably justified: for a period at least all went smoothly and no conflicts appeared to arise.

The new CND general secretary was at pains to preserve his priestly ministry, at least part-time. He celebrated the early morning Mass on both weekdays and Sundays at St John's, Duncan Terrace, Islington, where the parish priest had offered him accommodation within the presbytery. Nor initially was there much sign of a right-wing backlash. All remained relatively quiet on the nuclear front until the public debates began over the acceptance of Cruise missiles on British soil and the decision to modernise the UK's submarine force by replacing Polaris with Trident missiles.

That there should have been so much popular agitation over this was, admittedly, largely CND's own achievement. The movement, under its new energetic general secretary, was determined that what he called this 'ratcheting up of the arms race' should not be allowed to take place without some attempt to rouse public opinion – hence the CND encampments at Greenham Common and, later, Molesworth. This, in turn, led to overt political retaliation, with the newly appointed Secretary of State for Defence, Michael Heseltine, leading the charge against CND.

Since everyone knew that a general election was in the offing – it was called by Margaret Thatcher on 9 May and took place on 9 June 1983 – the stage was set for a shoot-out between the peace movement and the Government, with the Church as ricochet victim.

As so often happens, though, it took a bizarre and wholly unpredictable turn of events to set the whole thing off. As the election drew closer, the number of letters arriving at Archbishop's House querying the propriety of Monsignor Kent's position began dramatically (and possibly suspiciously) to increase. In the absence of the Archbishop, who was in Westminster Hospital undergoing a hip replacement operation,* a decision appears to have been taken that a *pro forma* document should be prepared that could be sent out to all correspondents who had written in seeking reassurance. Copies of the document first went out above the Cardinal's signature on April 15 and, inevitably, surfaced in the press within a fortnight, causing in Basil's own characteristic phrase (he received in the end more than 1,000 letters) 'a row that was deafening'.

The trouble probably was that in a single document the Archbishop, or his staff, tried to say too many things. The statement could hardly have opened more robustly – it started, indeed, with what sounded uncommonly like a put-down for the more indignant right-wing complainants:

The issues of war and peace and the questions of nuclear warfare and deterrence are supremely important in our

---

* Hume entered hospital in early March but did not resume his duties until 10 April, just in time for Easter Day and the Bishops' Low Week Conference. The operation was not an immediate success: four months later the Cardinal, always impatient, was still complaining of a limp and of having to use a stick.

time. They are not simply political and secular matters. They are moral issues which confront the Christian conscience and require serious and urgent consideration.

So far nothing for even the most ardent champions of the right of a Catholic priest to work for CND to complain about. Yet when the document moves away from the proclamation of general principles and starts considering instead the particular case at issue, its whole tone seems to change. Defensiveness takes the place of defiance and, while absolutely no apology is offered, appeasement seems very much the order of the day:

About three years ago, Monsignor Bruce Kent sought my approval to leave temporarily the full-time service of the diocese of Westminster to devote himself to the work of the Campaign for Nuclear Disarmament. I agreed

a) because war, peace and deterrence are moral issues and not just matters of political and military strategy;

b) because at that time the role of CND in stimulating public debate and educating public opinion was of great significance and the political aspect of its work was not as highly developed as it is today;

c) because Mgr Kent saw campaigning for the cause of peace and disarmament as a dimension of his priestly ministry, and I did not feel justified in standing in the way of his commitment to a work which in conscience he felt bound to undertake;

d) because Mgr Kent has never claimed to be an official spokesman for the Church in this matter; my own views on these issues are publicly known and the expression of his view is unlikely to be confused with mine.

There is, it has to be said, a definite smack of committee prose about this four-pronged justification, and the suspicion has to remain that it was more the work of the Archbishop's staff (and especially of the assistant for public affairs, Monsignor George Leonard) than it was of the Archbishop himself. The real damage, however, was done in the final paragraph where – a very far cry from the rousing opening – an almost minatory note appeared to be struck:

Should the political aspects of CND develop further and become predominant in its work, it would be difficult for a priest to hold responsible office in the direction of the movement. Such a task might more fittingly be undertaken by a lay person whose witness could more suitably be given in contentious issues of a secular character. Although recent developments have caused me serious misgivings, I do not feel that at the present time the grounds for my decision of three years ago have been invalidated. I have made known these views to Mgr Kent and I shall continue to keep the situation under careful review.

It did not require any close understanding of the ways of Fleet Street to realise which part of the statement the newspapers would immediately pounce upon. The 'splash' story in *The Times* of 27 April 1983, which revealed the existence of the Cardinal's letter, wholly predictably carried the headline: 'Hume's Concern over CND's Catholic leader'. That story, in turn, produced an enormous postbag at Archbishop's House, nearly all of it vociferously in Bruce Kent's favour. One typical letter read simply: 'I have always thought of you as a man of Christ. Now I know you for what you are – a creature of the Establishment.' Certainly, the least happy legacy of the whole affair, from Hume's own point of view, was the widespread assumption that he had been forced to fire a shot across CND's bows by 'considerable pressure from leading lay Roman Catholics, particularly Conservative politicians' (a phrase actually used by *The Times* in its news story). In Archbishop's House that was not considered at all helpful, and perhaps the only consolation it brought in its wake was this cheerfully irreverent letter addressed to 'Dear Basil' from a former head boy of Ampleforth. By now Hugo Young was joint deputy editor of the *Sunday Times* and this is how he opened his letter:

> I see from this morning's paper that you have been regularly receiving letters about Bruce Kent's position at CND from 'senior lay Roman Catholics'. I am never sure to whom this phrase, regularly used, is supposed to apply. But could I add a small cheep from further down the pew?

Young went on to make a sober and reasoned case in defence of Kent's continuing right to remain at the helm of CND – with every word of which the Cardinal himself (though not necessarily all his advisers) probably agreed.

Fortunately, events conspired within the next few days to afford him the opportunity of making clear what his position was. First came an allegation, originally made by the *Daily Express*, that he had been forced to act by a direct instruction from Pope John Paul II (who had just compelled an American Jesuit priest, Father Robert Drinan from Massachusetts, to give up his seat in the US Congress). Despite the American precedent, there was no truth at all in the charge that the Pope had had anything to do with the decision to send out the Archbishop's letter – something that the *Daily Express*, at the insistence of Monsignor Leonard, was eventually forced to acknowledge. The Vatican, too, officially denied the story. That was probably just as well. Nothing, as his staff well knew, was more calculated to make the Cardinal furious than the suggestion that he was merely a puppet controlled on a string by Rome.

Yet, as ill-luck would have it, within a week or so that again was to be the impression created. In a wholly improper excursion into British politics the Papal pro-Nuncio, Archbishop Bruno Heim, injudiciously wrote a private letter to a prospective Conservative candidate in which he called Bruce Kent (in Lenin's phrase) 'a useful idiot' and accused him of doing the Kremlin's work for it. Inevitably, the letter was leaked, and the fat once more was in the fire. Here, after all, were the Pope's personal representative in the United Kingdom and the titular head of the Church in England and Wales apparently on opposite sides of a political argument.

Basil, understandably, was outraged and, because a day or two before it surfaced in the newspapers he had foreknowledge of Heim having sent the letter, he pointedly arranged a public display of solidarity between himself and the general secretary of CND. At short notice they both attended a reception held at Archbishop's House in London for a visiting American prelate, the US chairman of Pax Christi, Bishop Thomas Gumbleton. This took place on 12 May (just three days after the election had been called). Although the assembled company can hardly have known what was going on, each proceeded to make a speech in fulsome praise of the other.

It was a measure, though, of Hume's anger – and of his feeling of resentment that Kent had been quite improperly traduced – that he still did not feel that he had done enough to restore justice to the situation. With that objective in mind he agreed to appear on ITN's Saturday night news bulletin on 14 May, the day on which the existence of the pro-Nuncio's incendiary letter had broken in the press. His intention was to express his full confidence in the unruly priest who on this occasion was in his view blameless for all the trouble that had been caused.

With that in mind, he sketched out in advance on the day of the broadcast the points that he wished to make. The hand-written document survives to this day and this is what it says:

> I have renewed my permission (on 15 April) for Mgr Kent to continue his work for CND.
>
> The giving of that permission is my responsibility, and mine alone. I have a great respect for Mgr Kent personally, for his integrity and for his commitment to peace.
>
> We must not underestimate the importance of the debate in which it is vital for us all to listen carefully to each other's arguments.
>
> There can be no difference of opinion among Christians concerning our ultimate aim which is to prevent nuclear war from ever taking place. The debate concerns only the means to be adopted to achieve this aim.

The last paragraph in particular cannot help seeming a slightly woolly conclusion, but, in fact, it concealed a real confusion in the Archbishop's own mind. The truth is that Basil Hume never succeeded in reaching a settled view on the whole nuclear issue (or 'thing' as he slightly irritatedly sometimes called it). He knew he was not a unilateralist – indeed, he frequently explained as much to his many correspondents on the subject. However, he equally knew that the full rigour of the doctrine of deterrence was not for him. For all his agonising, this – to most experts – contradictory position necessarily made him risk sounding neither consistent nor convincing,

A case in point was a lecture he delivered to an international disarmament conference held at the Methodist Central Hall in Westminster in April 1980, just three months after he had written his original article for *The Times* questioning the moral legitimacy of the doctrine of deterrence. Giving the lecture was a challenge he took very seriously and he certainly did his best to spell out his position in strategic as well as ethical terms. The dilemma, though, which faced him was that, while he was prepared to condemn the use (or even the threat to use) nuclear weapons, he was not willing to rule out on ethical grounds the possession of a nuclear arsenal. That left him searching for an escape clause. The one he found would not probably have passed muster with more sophisticated military minds. Placing his emphasis on the immorality of nuclear strikes (whether pre-emptive or retaliatory) against centres of civilian population, he simply went on to assert that it was possible to conceive of circumstances in which a nuclear attack could be launched against a purely military target. He proceeded, however, rather to undermine his own case by adding that even then two condi-tions would need to be met if such limited resort to nuclear weapons were to be justified. The first such condition was that it must be possible 'to draw a clear distinction between military installations and personnel who will be destroyed and the civilian population that may be affected'. The second condition was, if anything, even more improbable. It was that there must be an assurance that 'the use of weapons of this type will not lead to escalation'. At least in his Westminster Central Hall address – though he was less forthright about this in a subsequent similar lecture he gave in Cologne some two years later – Hume had the grace to admit that the chances of both (or even either) of these conditions being fulfilled was pretty slight. But then so also was the cogency of the case he tried to make.

It may be because he realised the vulnerability of the posi-tion he attempted to defend that Basil eventually ended up estab-lishing a 'nuclear issues committee', specifically charged with the task of producing a discussion paper that the Bishops' Conference could then consider. The document it produced was never published – partly, it is said, because the distinguished (mainly academic) participants, who included a formidable anti-Bomb Dominican Father Roger Ruston, could not bring themselves to attach their names to propositions which they fundamentally opposed. It did, however, if rather late in the day, succeed in clarifying the underlying moral issues – though not, as events turned out, in a way particularly helpful to the Cardinal.

The technique the committee adopted was to list four separate policy positions which, as it was tactfully put, 'commanded the attention of Catholics'. These were:

a) All uses of nuclear weapons are morally excluded but their possession to deter aggression is justifiable.
b) There are possible (extremely limited) moral uses of nuclear weapons and their possession to deter aggression is justifiable.
c) All categories of nuclear weapons involve immoral threats and there is a moral obligation to renounce them.
d) Nuclear deterrence involves unacceptable risks of nuclear war (involving immoral actions) and the only responsible public policy is to dismantle it.

In the light of those four options, though they were not laid out until 1986, the difficulty of Basil's position becomes immediately apparent. He did not so much take elements from each as try to straddle them all – and this in face of the discussion paper's warning that, in terms of a coherent defence policy, they were mutually incompatible.

In fairness it has to be conceded that prelates are seldom at their best when grappling with issues of higher military strategy.*

---

* Geoffrey Fisher, as Archbishop of Canterbury, once announced that the 'worst an H-Bomb can do is to sweep a vast number of persons at one moment into the other, and more vital, world into which, anyhow, they must all pass at some time'.

St Thomas Aquinas's definition of the requirements needed to meet the criteria of 'a just war' may remain sound principles; the problem lies in applying them to a far more technologically terrifying world than he can ever have envisaged. It did not help either that even when Basil started out feeling his way in the great nuclear debate – there is no sign of it having preoccupied him at Ampleforth – the new Archbishop did not find himself an entirely free agent.

The Second Vatican Council had already ruled that 'any act of war aimed indiscriminately at the destruction of entire cities or extensive areas along with their populations is a crime against God and man himself'. But that robust position had subsequently been modified by Pope John Paul II when he told the United Nations Special Session on Disarmament in June 1982 that the doctrine of deterrence could be regarded as 'morally acceptable' provided it was seen not as an end in itself but rather as a stage towards general disarmament. (This increasingly became the text on which Basil Hume relied and may explain why his unilateralist critics detected a hardening in his attitude as the years went by.)

He faced pressures at home, too. The Church of England had just commissioned a working party under one of its leading theologians, John Baker, the Bishop of Salisbury, to produce a report on the whole nuclear question. When it came out in 1982 under the title of *The Church and the Bomb*, it was widely interpreted as having a distinct unilateralist flavour and, though in the end the C of E's General Synod refused to endorse it, the general feeling, even among the Anglican Establishment, was that the anti-Bomb forces had had rather the better of the argument.

Even more embarrassingly, in March 1982 the Scottish Roman Catholic Church, at the instigation of the unilateralist Archbishop of Glasgow, Thomas Winning, had come out strongly against any country possessing nuclear weapons – thus repudiating the Pope's own view that nuclear stockpiles could at least temporarily be tolerated, if only as a bargaining counter in a wider process of world disarmament. As if that did not represent troubles enough, Basil Hume also seems to have been in no doubt that the vast majority of his own diocesan clergy – he once during an informal conversation put the figure as high as 75 per cent – wanted him to take a more radical anti-Bomb position than he eventually did.

Not that the pressures all came one way. There were a number of efforts to influence the Archbishop's judgment on the nuclear issue, and a particularly crude one came early on via the American Embassy in London. On a visit to the United States in 1981 Basil had been given to understand that a very prominent American military figure (whom he took to be General Bernard W. Rogers, the Supreme Allied Commander, Europe, who happened to be a Catholic) wanted to have a general discussion with him. Through an intermediary he conveyed a message that in principle he would be very willing for the two of them to meet.

Back home in Archbishop's House he was almost immediately the recipient of a letter (and full *curriculum vitae*) from one Colonel Ervin J. Rokke, the air attaché at the American Embassy in Grosvenor Square, offering to give him a briefing on current Nato policy. Basil was not normally a man to stand upon his dignity, but on this occasion a certain feeling of resentment against *lèse majesté* appears to have prevailed. The American Air Force colonel was sent away with a flea in his ear – or, more precisely, a suggestion that, if he wished it, there might be a possibility of his having a discussion with a couple of clergy in the diocese. (The unfortunate air attaché does not appear to have been heard from again.)

All the available evidence suggests that Basil reacted with

similar hauteur to any efforts made by domestic politicians to lobby him. He had little or no sympathy with the concerted propaganda attacks that the Ministry of Defence under Michael Heseltine continued to launch against CND. Indeed, it was as much thanks to them as it was to the clumsy interference of the pro-Nuncio, Bruno Heim, that his attitude towards Bruce Kent so visibly softened. He always bridled at any suggestion that he had allowed himself to be manipulated by Conservative ministers and there is no record of his having met even once with the Defence Secretary, Michael Heseltine.

What, perhaps surprisingly, did take place, however, were regular contacts with the Civil Service. In part, these were probably due to the Cardinal's brother-in-law, Sir John Hunt, who, although he retired as Cabinet Secretary in 1979, continued to maintain close contacts with members of the Civil Service in a private capacity. In fact, it seems to have been at Sir John's instigation that a rising young mandarin – who was to end up as Permanent Under-Secretary at the Ministry of Defence – first got in touch with the Cardinal. Michael Quinlan's letter addressed to Archbishop's House was such a model of modesty and discretion that it deserves to be preserved. It certainly catches the well-mannered atmosphere in which the academic side of the debate was conducted at the time, as well as reflecting the whole ethos of the British Civil Service:

8 August 1982   75 Grange Road,
                                                              Sutton, Surrey

Dear Cardinal,

I venture to send you herewith, at Sir John Hunt's request, a copy of a talk that I gave earlier this year at a Catholic Institute for Justice and Peace meeting in the Portsmouth diocese on the ethical problems of the nuclear deterrent.

Father Roger Ruston was in the opposite corner on that occasion.

I have much respect for Father Ruston's arguments. His latest pamphlet for CIJP is a very powerful statement of the case against my views. I am unfortunately, as a current civil servant now moving out of the defence field, debarred from undertaking an equally extended public statement of the case for my views; but the main line of my disagreement with Father Ruston can perhaps be deduced from my Portsmouth piece. If it would be of value to you or your helpers to have a more direct critique, I should be very willing to attempt one on a private basis.

Yours sincerely
Michael Quinlan

It is almost possible to feel the sense of relief with which Basil (still trying to come to terms with the Pope's coda to the original Second Vatican Council statement) leaps on the offer when he replies to the letter:

24 August 1982   Archbishop's House,
                                              London, SW1

Dear Michael,

I must thank you very much indeed for your letter dated 8 August and for the enclosure. I am pathologically incapable of writing letters when I am on holiday but I have read your document over and over again. In fact, I spent a lot of time reading about this ghastly problem and I have to confess that I am still not clear whether the possession of the nuclear thing as a deterrent is morally in order or not. You suggest that you might be able to supply me with a further critique of Father Ruston's paper. I would be very grateful to have that if it were not too much trouble for you.

Yours sincerely,
Basil Hume

As an assessment of what really was going on in his mind, this personal letter is more revealing than any of the Cardinal's public statements at the time. It at least demonstrates that whatever convictions he eventually proclaimed were not reached at all easily, but it does look as if Michael Quinlan's efforts – apparently backed up by those of another prominent lay Catholic, the former Permanent Under-Secretary at the Foreign Office, Sir Michael Palliser – had some impact. Certainly by October 1982 there were signs of Basil's thoughts crystallising. It was then in his lecture in Cologne that he steeled himself to announce: 'Intellectually I can accept that the policy of deterrence is morally acceptable, but only on the understanding that it must be no more than a stage towards multilateral and total disarmament.' That still did not solve the practical problem of how a deterrent can be a deterrent if you serve notice in advance that it will never be used except against strictly and exclusively military targets. This, however, was probably more a worry for those likely to attend meetings of such bodies as the Institute for Strategic Studies than it was for the ordinary Catholic struggling to reconcile the modern nuclear era with the traditional concept of the just war – and at least Basil never claimed that he had succeeded in bringing that off. Even in the most hard-line article he ever wrote – one entitled 'Towards a nuclear morality' and published in *The Times* on 17 November 1983 – honesty was still compelling him to admit: 'To condemn all use and yet to accept deterrence places us in a seemingly contradictory position.' Some of his more clear-headed multilateral supporters would have found that proposition just as difficult to dispute as did, from their own viewpoint, his generally more scathing CND critics.

Yet if Basil never exactly covered himself in glory during the intellectual debate over the bomb, he could not be faulted for the loyalty of the stand he took in defence of Bruce Kent. There had been a clamour for Kent's activities to be repudiated almost from the start and this inevitably increased in strength once it became clear that the Catholic Church in England and Wales (with Scotland going the other way) was not going to endorse the unilateralist case. To his credit, however, Basil never wavered, sending out reasoned replies even to those who wrote to him in far from temperate terms. This is how he addressed one such correspondent at the very moment that he was changing his own mind on the question of deterrence:

There are many people who are troubled in conscience on this matter. And I think that it is fair to say that, even if there are others involved in questioning the nuclear thing who are more concerned with politics than morality, this does not invalidate the position of those anxious about the moral criteria. The involvement of Bruce Kent is certainly due to his deep concern about the moral questions. I suppose that right down through history there have always been those who have said and done unpopular things in order to shake our various assumptions. For my part, I find the issue an extremely complex one and I can't say that I personally am a unilateralist . . .

As we have seen, whatever movement there was in Basil's own position finally went the other way, but that was never permitted to affect the consistency with which – after one bad wobble in his statement of April 1983 – he sought to uphold Bruce Kent's right as a priest to follow his own conscience. This was all the more impressive an achievement as Monsignor Kent by no means always made things easy for Basil. There was sometimes a tendency on his part to kick over the traces.

There was a particularly glaring example of this in the autumn of 1983, just after Margaret Thatcher had won her greatest electoral victory (achieving a majority of 144 in the House of Commons). It was then, for reasons best known to himself, that Bruce Kent accepted an invitation to address the annual congress of the then still extant British Communist Party. He successfully avoided making any too obviously compromising policy statements, but when he referred at the beginning of his remarks to the Communist Party and CND being together 'partners in the cause of world peace' he had, in effect, offered his enemies a pretty hefty hostage to fortune. In no time the old repertory company of indignant Catholic Conservative MPs was in full cry, demanding that, at the very least, this recalcitrant priest be disowned or that, better still, he should be required to renounce either his Orders or his allegiance to CND, but at Archbishop's House there was no sign of panic. A simple statement was put out saying that the Cardinal had asked to see Monsignor Kent, and later, after they had met, a further explanation was issued saying that the secondment of this particular parish priest to the work of CND continued to be sanctioned.

Although there were those on his staff who would have preferred more draconian measures, Basil's low-key, undramatic response to this latest episode in what was to prove a long-running controversy was almost certainly the right one. It deprived the press of its prey and ensured, at least for a time, that a period of relative calm prevailed so far as CND was concerned. Of course, on lean news days, articles with titles such as 'The Case of the Misguided Monsignor' continued to appear, but, for the most part, the press preferred topics of greater novelty. Always promiscuous in their interests, both the broadcasting and print media began to be much more taken up with such matters as Mrs Victoria Gillick's pertinacious campaign to make parental consent essential for any prescription of the contraceptive pill for teenage girls.

Nor did the Cardinal himself fail to make his own contribution. His visit to Ethiopia towards the end of 1984 attracted a great deal of television attention, and his insistence on his return that it was essential that British aid should not be cut guaranteed that this was followed up by domestic political controversy. It was the only visit that Basil ever made to Africa – an Archbishop of Westminster is not like the Archbishop of Canterbury in being the leader of a worldwide communion – and there is no doubt that what he saw of the famine there had a profound effect upon him. Thereafter he always liked to refer to himself as 'the ambassador for the hungry', and his strong support for the Catholic Fund for Overseas Development (CAFOD) became a new and important element in his life.

It could, indeed, be thought to be more than a coincidence that a revival of interest in the controversy over the appropriateness or otherwise of Bruce Kent's position in CND – this had anyway changed in 1985 from being general secretary to being unpaid vice-chairman – should have again come about only when another general election came into view. Especially in light of the direction from which the attack came, both the Archbishop and Monsignor Kent were probably entitled to feel that they were the targets of a planned, concerted assault. The first hint that Basil had that the whole business was about to start up again came in the shape of a letter received out of the blue at Archbishop's House. Its purpose, according to his correspondent, was to congratulate him on an article he had recently contributed to the *Observer*, but, as the author of the letter went on to describe himself as one of those 'engaged in political research and campaigns in countering, to some significant effect, the activities of the Campaign for Nuclear Disarmament', it should have been reasonably clear that this was something more than a letter from a casual admirer.

If that was not sufficient by itself to cause alarm bells to ring, then the pointed questions the author – Dr Julian Lewis* (writing from the Athenaeum) – proceeded to put, should certainly have done so. These questions were:

1) Has Father Bruce [sic] asked for, and been granted, permission for a further placing in abeyance of his priestly duties now that the original CND role for which he was effectively given leave-of-absence has terminated?
2) If not, why has he not been directed to resume his duties as a priest of the Church if he wishes to retain his status as such?
3) On the other hand, if he has been given permission for full-time political campaigning, is there ever going to be a time-limit set to this gentleman's political campaign activities?

Resisting what must have been the strong temptation to tell his non-Catholic correspondent to mind his own business, Basil dispatched within a fortnight a reasoned and rational reply. Since Dr Lewis in his letter had intimated that he would want to circulate it to both 'the Papal Nuncio and the Chairman of my party, Mr Norman Tebbit', Basil did, however, take the precaution of marking it 'Private'.

In his answer he explained that, 'while Mgr Kent and I do not always agree on the issue of nuclear disarmament', it remained his judgment that 'the contribution he makes to this

---

* In 1997 to become Conservative MP for New Forest East.

debate is an important one'. Furthermore, he argued, the nuclear issue posed 'one of the most difficult and important moral issues of our time and that this aspect of the matter tends to get neglected'. If there was one passage in the Cardinal's letter that went halfway to meeting his correspondent's concerns, it lay perhaps in its opening sentence in which he declared: 'The prominent part that Mgr Kent plays in CND causes tension for any bishop, not least his own.' But even that was balanced by his parting shot, which was a somewhat *de haut en bas* final paragraph making it clear that the whole enterprise had been recognised for what it was – a fishing expedition:

> This letter is private and is not to be circulated or published without permission. If Mr Tebbit wishes to discuss this or any other matter with me, he knows well enough how to contact me; and as far as the Papal Nuncio is concerned I am, of course, in constant touch with him.

On any test it was an impeccable response, but it was not the one the Cardinal's correspondent had been looking for. Predictably, therefore, within ten days a further interrogatory missive arrived – though this one, unlike its predecessor, at least gave away its provenance. It was written under the letterhead of a body called Policy Research Associates which, as well as having Julian Lewis as its director, turned out to possess such redoubtable figures as Lord Chalfont and Norris McWhirter among its patrons.

Whether this by itself would have been enough to discourage the Cardinal from further correspondence we may never know, but certainly Lewis got no immediate answer. There could, however, have been another explanation for that. Included in the files on CND in the Westminster Diocesan Archives is an internal memo – arising out of Lewis's first letter – addressed to the Cardinal by his assistant for public affairs. This is what Monsignor George Leonard – never a man shy of speaking his mind – had to say:

> The letter from Dr Julian Lewis is deadly. It will be difficult to get off this particular hook.
>
> Your reply will be published (he has warned of this).
>
> I'm afraid I feel your present standard letters leave many questions unanswered and do not meet the central issue of the discharge of pastoral responsibility towards a priest of your diocese.
>
> I feel that to say 'he appeals to his conscience, so what can I do?' may be the hard truth but it would be disastrous to admit this publicly. Everyone believes that priests are obedient and bishops are omnipotent!

That cannot have been an easy memo to write or a comfortable one to receive, and it may be that it was responsible for the first false step that Basil took in the whole imbroglio. Instead of sending a brisk (and brush-off) reply to Lewis, he resolved to forward both of Lewis's letters and his own slightly lofty answer to the first one – together with a covering note – to the subject of the controversy, Bruce Kent himself.

This proved a terrible psychological error, producing an immediate anguished response from an overwrought, beleaguered priest who plainly felt he was being offered up as a sacrifice by his own Father-in-God. Monsignor Kent's sense of distress can still be felt after two decades:

> It was a terrible shock to me to learn when I opened your letter tonight that you have been in correspondence with Julian Lewis. It cannot be right for a bishop to discuss his priests in this way with strangers. Julian Lewis is one of

the most brutal critics of both myself and CND. I will write to you again over the weekend when I have thought this thing through. At the moment I am too upset to think clearly.

Basil, not perhaps realising how lonely and exposed a controversial priest can feel, appears to have been genuinely taken aback by the anguished nature of the reaction he had provoked. He immediately wrote an emollient letter by way of response and was rewarded with a second and far more balanced reply from the vice-chairman of CND. At least one piece of advice it offered was obviously taken: Bruce Kent seems to have believed that getting into an argument with Julian Lewis would be a pointless endeavour – and this counsel appears to have been accepted. No substantive answer to Dr Lewis's second letter was ever sent.

Meanwhile, however, a somewhat surprising development had taken place. Lord Chalfont – once Minister for Disarmament in the Wilson Government of 1964–70, but long since a Labour defector – made a direct approach to the Cardinal and requested that they might meet. He had, he explained, seen copies of the letters sent to Archbishop's House by Dr Julian Lewis, 'who is one of my Research Associates', and had 'profound worries' about Bruce Kent's position with CND.

Basil seems to have greeted this intervention with relief. It would, he seems to have felt, at least spare him having to endure any further correspondence with Lewis. In this, though, he was wrong. No sooner had he agreed to meet Chalfont on a mutually convenient date than Lewis was back at it again, asking when he might expect 'a considered response' to the second of his two letters. Here at least Chalfont did come to Basil's rescue. Showing just a flash of steel, the Archbishop replied to Lewis with a brief note saying that, since he had assumed they were acting together, a face-to-face meeting with Chalfont had seemed to him the logical next step. He had, therefore, not thought any reply to Lewis's second letter was necessary.

In fact, the Chalfont visit to Archbishop's House, while originally scheduled for July, did not in the end take place until October – and by then Julian Lewis had ingeniously opened up a second front. On 2 October 1986, another letter arrived at Archbishop's House, this time bearing the letterhead of a right-wing quarterly publication called the *Salisbury Review*. It contained as an enclosure a tear-sheet from the next issue of the magazine, a page headed 'An Open Letter to Cardinal Hume' and intimating via a strap-line that he was being invited to reply.

Sure enough, the 'open letter' bore the signature of Julian Lewis and its text was, in fact, synonymous with the second (unanswered) letter that its author had sent to Archbishop's House the previous May. By now, however, Monsignor George Leonard – the man who had described the original Lewis letter as 'deadly' – had been joined by a volunteer colleague who would eventually take over the role of public affairs assistant to the Cardinal. He was a former Regular Army officer named Patrick Victory and he soon proved his mettle. With a couple of flicks of the wrist – first the announcement that 'the Cardinal has no wish to conduct correspondence with Dr Lewis through the pages of any publication' and then the direct rebuke that 'it is surprising and, I would suggest, rather unprofessional' to trail a reply from him without first obtaining his permission – the managing editor of the *Salisbury Review* (and, for that matter, Lewis himself) were both effortlessly sent on their way. Nothing further seems to have been heard from either of them again.

In a sense, the odd saga of the Lewis/Chalfont intervention

may be regarded as a mere postscript to the whole Bruce Kent/CND story that had started six years earlier when the parish priest of Somers Town arrived on the doorstep of Archbishop's House, asking for what became in effect a dispensation to lead a political life. However, it can also be argued that it had more significance than that. Unconsciously, if understandably, it seems to have led to a parting of the ways between prelate and priest. There was perhaps just a hint of what was about to happen in the last official letter sent from Archbishop's House to Bruce Kent at the presbytery in Islington. In it the Cardinal expressed his apprehension that, in the light of his dismissal of the *Salisbury Review* proposal, there might now follow 'an active campaign to get at you through me'. He then, perhaps unwisely, added the comment: 'I would like to think, if it gets difficult for me, that I could count on your assistance.'

It is hard to imagine how Bruce Kent was intended to interpret this – if not as a warning that, if things got too tough, he would be expected to comply with a direction to return to his normal priestly duties. Certainly, it is difficult to believe that it was a coincidence that, within two months of getting that faintly ominous letter, Bruce Kent should have been found once again on the steps of Archbishop's House, this time to seek permission to retire from the active priesthood.

It was a decision that badly wounded Basil, not least because he was not even consulted about it. (Kent had initially presented himself before Monsignor David Norris, the Vicar-General of the diocese and – despite all they had been through together – not in front of the Archbishop.) However, the decencies were still observed. On the day the news broke – 25 February 1987 – press statements were issued on either side with each expressing regret, though in the Cardinal's case of a slightly formal kind. In one sense the way had been made easy for him. Kent, by now back as chairman of CND, had already gone public with his intention of speaking in as many constituencies as possible in the run-up to the next general election (now widely expected in the summer of 1987). It was, therefore, predictable that the Cardinal should have concluded his own press statement with the comment that such a course 'is clearly incompatible with the traditional pastoral role of a priest which obviously I would have preferred him to have chosen'.

How disappointed did Basil really feel that things had ended in this way? There was certainly an element of testiness in the private letters he wrote at this time to those (including priests) who contacted him deploring Kent's departure from the ministry. He always went out of his way to point out: 'I can assure you it was entirely his decision and nobody else's . . . he did not really discuss it with me, just presented me with his decision.'

It may be, of course, that Basil sensed that Kent had already set his mind on an entirely different future. That would certainly explain why he did not even try to intervene in the two months that elapsed between Kent's visit to the Vicar-General in December 1986 and the announcement of his 'retirement' from the active priesthood in February 1987. (The two of them had only one brief meeting, and that was a purely formal one in which the Cardinal accepted that Kent's decision was final.)

If that could be seen as a rather surprising failure of pastoral care on his part (soon to be redeemed, as we shall see), the Cardinal was entitled to feel that his non-interventionist attitude had at least been prudent. For within just over a year Kent announced his marriage to a fellow peace campaigner, a former general secretary of Pax Christi, Valerie Flessati. He thus – by failing to keep to his vow of celibacy – necessarily abandoned his Orders.

Basil would not have been unduly shocked by this development. He had had quite enough experience in this area with other priests (including his close friend, the prominent theologian, Adrian Hastings) to accept that such things took place.

Inevitably, though, Bruce Kent's marriage and his refusal to submit himself to the Vatican's somewhat arbitrary process of laicisation altered his relationship with his former diocesan. While he and Basil met again from time to time, their main means of contact was via correspondence. Two examples of this survive. One of the more personal letters preserved in the Westminster diocesan archives is a short, badly typed note. Dated 17 May 1987 (just three months after the man who wrote it announced his 'retirement' from the active ministry), it reads:

Dear Cardinal Hume,

Many thanks for that unexpected, but very welcome, cheque for £2,000. It will certainly help with the task of finding somewhere to live. The price of even the smallest flat is quite incredible anywhere in London.

Yours sincerely,
Bruce

The second letter is, if anything, even more touching. Written in response to a note Bruce Kent had delivered by hand in June 1999 to the St John and St Elizabeth Hospital in St John's Wood, it proves that, whatever the tensions and irritations between the two men of all those years ago, there remained a bond of friendship. Addressing his former priest by his Christian name and above a distinctly shaky signature – the letter was dictated just two days before he died – the Cardinal Archbishop wrote in the following terms:

Dear Bruce,

I have received a great many letters but none gave me more pleasure than yours. It was kind of you to write as you did.

I have always remembered your great gifts and I know that they will be made use of for the Gospel. Once again thank you so much.

With kindest regards and best wishes.

Yours devotedly,
Basil Hume

If the six-year battle over the rival claims of politics and religion had left its scars, at least the two chief protagonists did not part as anything but friends.

X

THE CARDINAL
V.
THE HOME OFFICE

IT WAS JUST BEFORE CHRISTMAS 1978 THAT BASIL HUME paid his first visit – he was to make several more down the years – to the largest men's prison in his archdiocese. His visit had not come about by chance. Among the letters received at Archbishop's House earlier in December had been one from Prisoner 462817 at Wormwood Scrubs. His name was Patrick Joseph Conlon – although always better known as Giuseppe (a nickname acquired from his Italian ice-cream-selling godfather in Belfast) – and he wrote to the Cardinal to protest his innocence of the charge of possessing explosives of which he had been convicted at the Old Bailey almost three years earlier:

> Well, Father, first of all I want to tell you right away that I am completely innocent of the charge that they framed me with. I have never been in trouble in my life, and the Chief Constable got in touch with the police back home in Belfast and he could not find anything to connect me with the IRA . . .

It was the kind of letter that turned up frequently enough at Archbishop's House, but on this occasion its arrival appears to have been anticipated. The Roman Catholic chaplain at Wormwood Scrubs was Father George Ennis, a priest who was held in particularly high regard by the Cardinal. It was Father Ennis who had first suggested to Giuseppe Conlon that he should write direct to Archbishop's House and it was he again who saw to it that, when the Cardinal arrived on his pre-Christmas visit, he spent time alone with Giuseppe talking to him as he sat on the bed in his cell.

Since this encounter was eventually to have such crucial and far-reaching repercussions for the reputation of British justice, it is natural enough that it has come to be surrounded by more than its fair share of legend. It is not the case, for example, that the Cardinal heard Giuseppe Conlon's confession – on this occasion or any other. Given the circumstances, in which his help was, in effect, being enlisted for an effort to overturn a conviction, Basil would have regarded any such action on his part as wholly inappropriate. Nor, as some versions have had it, was it the attitude of Giuseppe Conlon's fellow-prisoners that proved decisive. Certainly, the Archbishop was struck by the way in which they all insisted that not only Giuseppe but all the other male members of what came to be known as the 'Maguire Seven' should not be in jail at all; but one of Basil's small vanities was the pride he took in his intuitive judgment of people. He always made up his mind for himself, and it was when he sat listening to the 54-year-old Giuseppe's story that he first became convinced not only of the truth of what he was being told, but also of the innate honesty of the already seriously ill man who was telling it to him.

Nevertheless, even Cardinals have to take care to do their homework, and it was not a coincidence that three months were to pass before any follow-up action was pursued at Archbishop's

House. During this period Monsignor George Leonard made it his business to soak himself in the background of the case of the Maguires – Maguire being the name of the Irish family who lived in north London, at 43 Third Avenue, Harlesden, and who three years earlier, along with Giuseppe, their visiting brother-in-law from Belfast, had been charged with running a bomb-making factory there. The accusation against them was that their activities had lain behind the two successive pub bomb outrages at Guildford and Woolwich which, in the autumn of 1974, had claimed a total of seven lives, as well as badly injuring no fewer than sixty-eight people. Three months later, and in the wake of further even more severe bomb atrocities in Birmingham, a measure optimistically entitled the Prevention of Terrorism Act whistled through Parliament in eighteen hours.

There could hardly have been a less promising climate for anyone – and especially perhaps for a Roman Catholic prelate – to take up the cudgels on behalf of a middle-aged Irishman serving a twelve-year sentence who had been publicly branded as a bomb-maker. It was probably, therefore, no more than prudent for Basil to resolve initially to fight on as narrow a front as possible. Accordingly, when he first wrote to Merlyn Rees, the Home Secretary in James Callaghan's 1976–79 Government, it was not with a plea for him to reopen the case but rather to show compassion towards a prisoner who had probably not got long to live anyway:

Archbishop's House,
Westminster, SW1   26 March, 1979

Dear Mr Rees,
   I have been troubled for some time about the case of Mr Giuseppe Conlon, who is a prisoner in Wormwood Scrubs. My anxiety arises from the fact that there are strong indi-

cations that this man is not guilty of the crime for which he was convicted. I have met Mr Conlon in person myself and would have little doubt in my own mind that he is innocent.

I realise, of course, that it would not be at this stage a question of putting into motion a judicial process to reconsider the verdict which was passed on him. The reason I am writing to you about Mr Conlon at this stage is the fact that he is a very sick man and I am gravely concerned about the state of his health. This anxiety is shared by many other persons who are concerned with his case. So I am asking you, quite frankly, for an act of clemency towards him and that he should be released on compassionate grounds. I know that this act of clemency would be very favourably received by many people in the Catholic community in Northern Ireland.

I appreciate how much I am asking of you but it would be a humane and merciful response to what is, in my opinion, a very delicate situation.

With kindest regards,
Yours sincerely,
Basil Hume

This was the first of ten letters that over the course of the next decade the Cardinal was to write to four successive Home Secretaries. If early on he may have hoped that the best way of making progress would be to make his case modestly (if also slightly politically), he was soon to be disabused. Merlyn Rees, like his predecessor Roy Jenkins (who had piloted the anti-terrorism measure through the Commons), was later to become a close ally, but there was no sign of that at this stage. Replying to the Cardinal's letter almost a month later – and to an intervening one the Cardinal had also sent to Brynmor John, the

Minister of State at the Home Office in charge of prisons – the Home Secretary did not yield an inch. Any action on his part, he explained, would require invoking the Royal Prerogative of Mercy – and that, in line with the consistent attitude taken by his predecessors to similar cases in the past, was not something that he was prepared to do. He was good enough, however, to say – or maybe it was a formula always suggested by the Civil Service for use on such occasions – that he had arranged for Mr Conlon's case 'to be kept under continuous review so that, if there should be any significant deterioration in his condition, consideration can be given immediately to the question of his early release'.

Since the Labour Government, of which Merlyn Rees was a leading member, was to be defeated barely a month later at the polls, that particular promise soon proved to be made of piecrust. Also, in any event, the Cardinal's whole initiative (through no fault of his own) had not been especially well-timed. Barely was the ink dry on the signature to his original letter to Merlyn Rees than Airey Neave, the Conservatives' Northern Ireland spokesman, was blown up in the underground car park of the House of Commons, thereby making it virtually impossible for any Home Secretary – and particularly perhaps a Labour one – to display any form of clemency towards an alleged IRA activist. (In the public mood of the time it hardly seemed to matter that the perpetrators of this particular atrocity were not the IRA at all but rather the much smaller splinter group, the Irish National Liberation Army.)

Basil was never, however, a man to give up easily and, after the change of government had taken place, he took advantage of his first courtesy visit to Margaret Thatcher in Downing Street to put to the new Prime Minister the argument for the early release of Giuseppe Conlon on compassionate grounds. (His health had got markedly worse as he was by now suffering not just from tuberculosis and emphysema but from bronchitis as well.) Mrs Thatcher, who owed Basil a favour for the help he had given her in overcoming Hugh Rossi's doubts about joining the Northern Ireland Office when she formed her Government,* at least gave the impression of listening sympathetically, and it was at her suggestion that he went, on 4 July 1979, to call on the new Home Secretary Willie Whitelaw, at the Department's headquarters in Queen Anne's Gate.

Once he got there, he discovered, to his dismay, that Whitelaw was flanked on either side by a whole array of civil servants. The new Home Secretary took exactly the same line as his Labour predecessor had done in the letter he had written to the Cardinal three months earlier (not perhaps surprising since precisely the same civil servants would have advised both Ministers on the issue). Once more, despite Giuseppe Conlon's evident deteriorating condition – Basil had since been back to prison to see him – he could extract no commitment to his early release.

In fact, he fared worse than that, getting a lesson in the way governments tend to treat not just their critics but also those who seek to force unpopular courses of action upon them, Within three months of his supposedly private talk with Whitelaw, a story surfaced in the loyal Thatcherite *News of the World* with the provocative, if revealing, headline: 'Fury at plea by Cardinal to free IRA man'. The source of the report – 'Cardinal Hume has personally asked Willie Whitelaw, the Home Secretary, to release Giuseppe Conlon because he is seriously ill' – could only have been someone with knowledge of the meeting held the previous summer.

It may even have been a sense of shame that led Whitelaw to make a small act of official contrition, if by then a fairly meaningless one. Giuseppe Conlon died in Hammersmith Hospital

* See page 122.

on 23 January 1980 having first been allowed out of jail on 31 December 1979 and then, in the face of some security scare, returned to prison some ten days later before going back to hospital just before he died. Writing to the Cardinal at Archbishop's House on the day after his death Whitelaw felt moved to say: 'I thought I should let you know in confidence that I had already in fact come to the conclusion that, should Mr Conlon recover sufficiently to be discharged from hospital, it would not be right to return him to prison.'

Such a 'confidential' disclosure of an intention – especially as it simultaneously was leaked to at least two national newspapers – may not have been much to carry away from what had been a two-year struggle on behalf of an individual prisoner; but as the cause he was subsequently to press on the Government widened in its scope, it was all the progress that Basil was able to claim over the next nine years.

From the moment of his first rebuff at the hands of Merlyn Rees, he had, in fact, adopted a two-track strategy. His first aim had been to get the oldest (and easily the most frail) of the seven Maguire defendants released from jail. That objective had now been frustrated, Willie Whitelaw's 'deathbed conversion' coming too late to do anyone any good, but all the time there was a much longer-term second quest: to assemble enough new evidence – or at least 'a consideration of substance' (to borrow the phrase that Roy Jenkins, as Home Secretary, used in referring the Confait* case to the Court of Appeal in 1976) – in order to overturn convictions that by the time of Giuseppe's death were already four years old.

---

* This was the case in which three young men who had been convicted of murdering Maxwell Confait had their convictions quashed because of doubts as to the time at which the crime had taken place. The local Labour MP, Christopher Price, who led the campaign for their release, was also to play a valuable part in having the police's scientific evidence analysed in the Maguire case.

Here, admittedly, things started slowly. As Basil was later to concede – after the final victory had been won in the Court of Appeal by the Maguires in 1991 – all he originally had to go on was a strong personal hunch that a very sick and innocent man had been convicted of a crime he did not commit. He was gradually forced to realise – despite the manifest absurdity of Giuseppe being suspected of bomb-manufacture when he had only arrived in Britain (as it happened for the first time in seventeen years) on the day he was arrested – that it would take more than this to persuade a Home Secretary to intervene in a case that had already been decided by a judge and jury. Hence the sustained effort to test and examine the evidence that lay behind not just the convictions of the Maguire Seven but also the life sentences handed out to the three young men and a girl found guilty of doing the actual bombing. In an echo of a fashionable American usage of the time, these latter inevitably became known as 'the Guildford Four'.

It was a daunting task that the Archbishop and his public affairs staff had taken on. A close examination of the two trials soon showed that, although they had taken place separately, they were, in fact, inextricably linked. The Guildford Four case had been the first to be heard and, in a sense, was the more awkward to challenge. Here verdicts of guilty had been obtained purely on the basis of pre-trial confessions made by the accused, who ranged in age from seventeen to twenty-four. Two of the defendants – Giuseppe's son Gerard (21), whom he had come over from Belfast to try to assist, and his friend Paul Hill (24) – had in the course of their admissions to the police implicated the Maguire family in bomb-making activities, to the extent that the prosecuting counsel felt able to refer in open court to 'Aunt Annie's bomb factory' (meaning the modest terraced house in Harlesden where Anne Maguire and her family lived). It is hard to think of a more prejudicial remark, and what made it worse was that it was delivered to the jury by a former Solicitor-General and future Attorney-General, Sir Michael Havers. Significantly, he was also to lead for the prosecution in the Maguire trial that followed three months later. Even more suspiciously, the judge, too, proved to be identical in both cases – the Heath Government's former President of the Industrial Relations Court, Sir John Donaldson. In truth, so intertwined were the two cases (Anne Maguire was even originally charged with murder alongside the Guildford Four) that the argument for trying them together was overwhelming. There can be only one plausible reason why this did not happen: someone seems to have thought that it would be easier to secure convictions if the two cases were treated as quite separate entities – as both Donaldson and Havers kept insisting that they were.

They were not, of course, as subsequent events were to show. It remains odd, though, given the Crown's chosen method of proceeding, that no one – apart perhaps from Basil as he gradually mastered the detail of both trials – seems to have smelt a rat until many years later. At first it was the convictions of, and life sentences, imposed upon the Guildford Four that commanded the more press attention. This was largely because as early as 1977 those convicted in the Balcombe Street Siege case had volunteered that they had planted the bombs in the two Guildford pubs and also had claimed that three of them had been responsible for the Woolwich bombing as well. Proudly parading their credentials as members of an IRA Active Service Unit, they had refused to plead to any of the charges brought against them because they did not include what they regarded as their successful operations at both Guildford and Woolwich. They denied all knowledge of the Guildford Four who had actually been convicted of carrying out the murders, evidently wanting it to be known that the Provisional IRA set higher standards for membership of its Active Service Units than would be reflected in recruiting young people who lived in squats, took drugs or relied on alcohol. However, this claim, plausible as it later was recognised as being, cut no ice with the three-man Court of Appeal, presided over by Lord Roskill.

The three judges threw out the Guildford Four's appeal in October 1977 (the Maguires' own appeal had been rejected three months earlier). By the time Cardinal Hume began to take an interest (which is probably best dated as coinciding with his visit to see Giuseppe Conlon in Wormwood Scrubs in December 1978) both cases thus looked as if they had run their judicial course. The popular mood of the late 1970s – and, indeed, of the early 1980s after the Harrods and Regent's Park bandstand bombings – was hardly conducive to any public criticism of the legal system. The voices prepared to speak up, even over so tragic a case as that of Giuseppe Conlon, were few and far between. There was, though, a certain agitation in the Commons, where two MPs as different and distinct as the SDLP's Gerry Fitt and the Conservative Party's Sir John Biggs-Davison, went to see Giuseppe Conlon in his dying days in prison. As a result, they each tried to raise the matter of his treatment by the authorities on the floor of the House, but the Government, anxious not to revive an issue that it hoped had been put to sleep, remained strangely unmoved. It even maintained its policy of passive inaction when, much later on (in January 1986), 200 MPs signed an Early Day Motion calling for a review of the entire Maguire case.

However, the factors that gave the Government pause were precisely the same ones that drove Basil on. If Giuseppe could be shown to have been innocent – and there was at least an intimation of that in Whitelaw's reluctant and belated intention to free him – would not the same have to go for the other five members of the Maguire household, together with a family friend, Patrick O'Neil, all of whom had been convicted on the sole finding of having nitroglycerine traces on their hands (or, in Anne Maguire's case, on her plastic gloves)? And, if the scientific evidence could be proved to be unsound, where would that leave the three young men serving life sentences and the one female juvenile being detained at Her Majesty's Pleasure for planting the bombs at Guildford and Woolwich? If these bombs were not supplied, as the police and the prosecution had alleged, by 'Aunt Annie's bomb factory', then the whole cumulative case against them must collapse. The more Basil brooded, the stronger became his feeling that this was not a case that could be left where it was. Justice must prevail, even if the heavens fell.

How much Basil was influenced in reaching such a conclusion by other people – as, for example, by the valiant solicitor for both the Guildford Four and the Maguire Seven, Alastair Logan – can never now be fully known, but what is certain is that he tended very much to keep his own counsel. The entire 'miscarriage of justice' question does not seem to have been discussed once by the Catholic Bishops' Conference and, initially at least, all the Cardinal's activities took place behind the scenes. He made a deliberate resolve not to go public, believing (until he was forced to accept otherwise) that he was likely to have more influence that way, and he stuck to this resolution even in the face of grave provocation. One particular judicial outburst as early as January 1980 (within days of Giuseppe Conlon's death) must, however, have put even his sense of patience under strain. Lord Denning, having heard a civil action in which the alleged half-dozen perpetrators of the Birmingham bombings of November 1974 sought to obtain legal aid in order to sue the police, then saw fit, in delivering his judgment, to include this extraordinary statement:

If the six men win, it would mean that the police were guilty of perjury, that they were guilty of violence and threats, that the confessions were involuntary and were improperly admitted in evidence, and that the convictions were erroneous. That would mean the Home Secretary would either have to recommend they be pardoned or would have to remit the case to the Court of Appeal. This is such an appalling vista that every sensible person in the land would say: it cannot be right that these actions should go any further.

That sort of outburst was not merely revealing of what was threatening to become a judicial mindset in all cases involving alleged terrorists. For the Cardinal it must also have awoken disturbing echoes of Caiaphas, the High Priest in St John's Gospel, declaring just before the Crucifixion: 'It is expedient for us that one man should die for the people.'

The trouble, however, was that, as the forces on each side got more and more dug in – and the public argument was fought even more fiercely in Northern Ireland than it was on the mainland – it was this type of attitude that increasingly came to characterise the advocates of law and order. On the other side, those who despaired of the legal system ever offering any form of redress gradually succeeded in getting their case made in the media, particularly on television. As early as February 1980, BBC Northern Ireland had run a programme in a series called *Spotlight* which was harshly critical of the quality and reliability of the scientific evidence on which Giuseppe Conlon (and the other Maguire defendants) had been convicted back in 1976. This particular programme was not shown on the national network, but it provoked enough of a stir within Northern Ireland for the Cardinal to become aware of it. He was in touch at this time, if still very much in the background, with the altogether more vocal Cardinal Tomàs O'Fiaich, the Roman Catholic Archbishop of Armagh.

He was still not prepared, however, to associate himself with any popular campaign to reopen the cases. It required a further television programme – 'Aunt Annie's Bomb Factory' made by Yorkshire TV for its *First Tuesday* slot – even to get him to renew his correspondence with the Government.

This time, more than four years since he had last heard from Willie Whitelaw, he chose to write direct to the Prime Minister. His letter to her is so indicative of his growing sense of frustration that it is worth quoting in full:

Archbishop's House,
Westminster, SW1   12 July, 1984

Dear Prime Minister,

For a number of years now I have experienced grave disquiet over the case of Giuseppe Conlon who died, you will recall, on 23 January, 1980, in Hammersmith Hospital, while still serving a sentence of 12 years for his alleged involvement in the alleged manufacture of explosives in the house of the Maguire family in 1974.

I discussed my misgivings with you soon after you first arrived in Downing Street. I must confess that I have not been at all satisfied with the official answers that have so far been offered. I know that my anxiety over Giuseppe Conlon's innocence, and how he and those accused with him were convicted, is shared by some public figures including Lord Fitt and Sir John Biggs-Davison, surely no friends of the IRA. His protestations of innocence until his death – and his funeral in Belfast with no hint of a paramilitary presence – must surely give rise to the most grave anxiety about the likelihood of a major miscarriage of justice. Whatever the forensic evidence may seem to prove, every other indication would argue for the intrinsic improbability of the charges levelled against the Maguire family in general and against Giuseppe Conlon in particular.

I am disturbed by the evidence produced by Yorkshire Television's programme on this case screened on 6 March 1984. I would hope that the relevant authorities have called for a transcript of that programme and have weighed the serious doubts and questions it raised.

I am well aware that it is normal practice to produce fresh evidence to justify the re-examination of a judicial sentence. As events subsequent to the trial have cast doubt on the justice of its conclusion, I would suggest that an examination of the evidence actually presented in court needs to be considered.

I am understandably reluctant, as you will well appreciate, to cause fresh controversy in the present state of Anglo-Irish relations. That, however, can never be the only consideration. Justice remains an absolute priority. I am sure I speak for others when I say we would only be reassured if we could be convinced that every aspect of this case has been objectively and fairly reviewed after the death of Mr Conlon, and every reasonable anxiety allayed not only about his case but that of the people convicted with him, one of whom, Mrs Annie Maguire is still in prison.

I would ask you to ensure that the Home Secretary looks carefully at this whole case and its consequences. There are so many indications which cast doubt on the justice of the Court's verdict.

Yours sincerely,
Basil Hume

Predictably, though Mrs Thatcher wrote a perfectly civil letter in reply ('I am sorry to say that there is no action I can properly take in this case'), she offered the Cardinal no comfort, save perhaps in her intimation that the new Home Secretary, Leon Brittan – to be transferred to the Department of Trade and Industry only a month later – would be quite ready to see him. For obvious reasons, especially given the summer holidays, that does not seem to have been an invitation that was ever taken up, and Basil's subsequent contacts with the Home Office were nearly all with Brittan's successor, Douglas Hurd, who was to serve there for the next four years.[*]

By February 1985, Anne Maguire – the last of the family to remain in prison (she had been allowed bail to look after her children in the run-up to the Old Bailey trial of 1975) – had been released after serving ten years of her fourteen-year sentence. She was probably the most articulate member of the family[†] and her finally being at liberty had the reverse effect from that for which the authorities must have hoped: far from making the episode part of history, it brought the whole thing back into much sharper focus. This was partly because Anne and her husband Paddy found themselves pressed to take their case to the court of public opinion, appearing in two TV interview programmes in the course of a single week.

The viewers of both programmes – Robert Kee's *Seven Days* on Channel Four and David Frost's *Good Morning, Britain*, on TV am – simply found it impossible to recognise in this highly respectable north London housewife 'the evil Auntie Annie' or 'the armourer to the IRA' that she had been depicted as being during her trial more than ten years earlier. Instead, she and her husband (who had always been a regular drinker

---

[*] These started with a letter from the Cardinal dated 19 November 1985 in which, for the first time, he referred to the Birmingham Six, arguing that their case should be reviewed along with that of the Maguires and the Guildford Four.
[†] She subsequently published a moving account of her ordeal, *Why Me?* (HarperCollins, 1994). Cardinal Hume contributed the Foreword.

at his local Conservative club) came across as a perfectly normal couple, far too well-known to their neighbours to have been able successfully to keep any sinister activities from them.

However, the emergence of Anne Maguire from jail did far more damage to the Home Office's position than that. She had so impressed her interviewer Robert Kee, when they first encountered each other at a press conference held in the London Irish Club on the day of her release (22 February 1985), that – having already started to research the case with help from Christopher Price and documentation from Alastair Logan – he determined to go ahead with a book about it. When the book – with the excellent title of *Trial and Error** – was published, it immediately altered the whole tenor of the debate.

One of the first people to realise that this would be its effect was Basil Hume, whose own name – in a tacit tribute to the discretion he had up till then displayed – did not even appear in Kee's index; but he was still a person greatly admired by the author and twenty years later Kee can still recall the day he spotted the tall, gangling figure of the Cardinal loping his way across Westminster Bridge and thought to himself, 'Now, if only we could get him involved, we might actually get somewhere.' Given the extent of the commitment Basil had already privately shown, first towards the cause of Giuseppe Conlon and later to that of the Maguires in general, Kee's aspiration did not prove all that difficult to achieve. It was also helped by one stroke of good luck. It was at this time that Patrick Victory had just come aboard in the Archbishop's public affairs office and, from the moment he arrived in June 1986 (first as deputy to Monsignor George Leonard and then as his successor), he had shown a passionate dedication to the cause of justice and

* Hamish Hamilton, 1986

truth.* Mainly thanks to Paddy Victory, arrangements were made for Kee to come to Archbishop's House and formally present a copy of his book to the Cardinal. It was part of an elaborately planned launch for a work that set out with the deliberate intention of trying to change the nature not so much of public as of official opinion.

Basil recognised that that should be its purpose from the start, making the point to Kee that what was needed now was not so much protest as persuasion. Somehow the book's publication must be made the cue for the introduction of a sophisticated debate which would be separate from, if complementary to, the various grassroots campaigns that were already noisily underway. Partly by good fortune, events came together to make this possible. On 2 October 1986 *The Times* had happened to run a leading article suggesting that, while things had recently improved, all was not necessarily quite as it should be in the pre-trial procedures in the courts of England and Wales. This slightly tepid criticism offered the opportunity for others to pile in: the leading liberal Law Lord, Leslie Scarman, with a plea for French-style inquisitorial justice but also referring specially to the Guildford and Maguire cases on 7 October; the Cardinal himself even more directly and trenchantly on 10 October; and the Olympian jurist, Lord Devlin, fully backing Hume's own plea, but dressing it up in rather more scholarship, on 15 October. All at once it looked – though it was not, of course, an accident but rather the result of careful co-ordination – as if the desired debate was up and running. Insofar as there can be a declaration of war by one section of the Establishment on another, this was it.

---

* *Justice and Truth* was to be the title of Patrick Victory's own book (Sinclair-Stevenson, 2002). It remains easily the best and most comprehensive account of the whole struggle and its aftermath.

The most powerful barrage certainly came from Basil himself, if only because he flagrantly broke all the Establishment's rules by revealing his private contacts with the Government, going back to his original letter to Merlyn Rees in 1979. (The former Home Secretary, though, plainly took no offence since a few days later he entered the debate on the Cardinal's side.) There had been a clear switch in tactics. What had brought it about? The precipitating event had indisputably been the publication of Robert Kee's formidable case study of both the Maguire and the Guildford Four trials and appeals, but that was the occasion rather than the cause. From a broader perspective, it is hard to resist the conclusion that, after years of battering his head against a brick wall, Basil had simply decided that there was nothing for it but to go public. It can't have been an easy decision for him to take: by taste and temperament he always belonged behind the battlements rather than the barricades. (His brother-in-law, after all, had been the Cabinet Secretary and few, if any, of his colleagues, whether at Ampleforth or Westminster, dreamt for a moment that he had ever voted anything but Conservative.) However, on the principle of 'In for a penny, in for a pound', he appears to have had no second thoughts. Within a few months he had even agreed to appear in a controversial TV programme, Yorkshire TV's sequel to its 'Aunt Annie's Bomb Factory' of 1984. This latest documentary, itself a follow-up to 'The Guildford Time-Bomb' of 1986, was called 'The Case That Won't Go Away' and it went out on the ITV network on 3 March 1987.[*]

By then, of course, Douglas Hurd, as Home Secretary, had already announced that, while he was prepared to refer the case of the Birmingham Six to the Court of Appeal, he was not ready

---

[*] The co-producers of the programmes, Grant McKee and Ros Franey, eventually published a well researched book entitled *Time Bomb* (Bloomsbury, 1988).

to follow the same course with either the Maguire Seven or the Guildford Four. That only caused the Cardinal to redouble his efforts. In response to the Home Secretary's decision, he resolved to invite those public figures who, in *The Times* or elsewhere, had already expressed their doubts about both the cases to join an informal body that came to be known under the rather grand title of 'The Deputation'. As well as the Cardinal as convenor, it comprised two former Home Secretaries (Roy Jenkins and Merlyn Rees) and two retired Lords of Appeal in Ordinary (Patrick Devlin and Leslie Scarman). It held its first meeting at Archbishop's House at the beginning of February 1987 and took the collective decision to assess the situation reached in each case before publicly presenting its 'submission' to the Home Office in July 1987. The submission, when it was completed, proved to be a powerful document and, even though the actual meeting with the Home Secretary (at which the entire Deputation was present) lasted only forty-five minutes, Douglas Hurd undertook to consider afresh at least the case of the Guildford Four.

This, once that process had taken place, inevitably made the decision of the Home Secretary more than a year later not to order a referral of the Guildford Four case to the Court of Appeal all the more disappointing. To his credit, Hurd chose to break the news personally to the Cardinal, calling upon him at Archbishop's House. He can hardly have been in much doubt as to the reception he was likely to get. A month or so earlier, while staying at a backbench Tory MP's villa in Tuscany, he had been warned at a lunch party by a fellow guest, Roy Jenkins, that the Cardinal would 'never give up'. According to Jenkins, Hurd 'visibly blanched' at hearing the news.

On 8 September 1988, the two representatives of Church and State met alone in the Cardinal's first-floor study, with the Home Secretary first presenting and then seeking to justify his decision (which had yet to be formally announced), and the Archbishop instantly responding by refuting each and every reason Hurd had given.

It was the nearest approach to a 'summit' meeting on the issue since the long, troubled story of the Guildford and Woolwich bombings had begun almost thirteen years earlier, and in addition it had something of a medieval flavour to it – but there was absolutely no echo of a Canossa: far from suing for peace and asking for absolution, as the Holy Roman Emperor, Henry IV had done with Pope Gregory VII, Hurd was there to insist that there could be no modification in the position that a modern secular State had felt it right to adopt.

Having given his own personal reaction, the Cardinal went on to mobilise the forces of the Deputation. After discussions within the group, with Lord Scarman declaring, 'Now the struggle really begins', he got the agreement of his four colleagues that he should send an intransigent letter to the Home Office. Dated 22 September 1988, although courteous in tone, it was designed to chill the blood not only of the bureaucrats in C3 (the section dealing with 'wrongful imprisonment' within the Department), but also of the Home Secretary himself. This, they found themselves being sternly warned, was an issue that was by no means over yet:

I am writing to you following our meeting on 8 September, 1988 concerning the Guildford Four/Maguire cases . . . Having looked again at the points you raised, I have to say at the outset I am now even more convinced than ever that the convictions in these cases cannot be regarded as safe or satisfactory. This view is shared by the whole of our Deputation. Unless a reference is made now to the Court of Appeal, or to a Tribunal set up under the 1921 Act, the country will have to face up to the fact that not only will the Deputation continue what it regards as the pursuit of

justice, but your successor, and probably mine, will be left
to continue grappling with the problem.

It was, no doubt, mere coincidence that at around this stage
a proposal was floated that it might be possible to bring about
the release of the youngest member of the Guildford Four –
Carole Richardson who had gone to prison at the age of seventeen, but who was now nearly thirty – provided some assurance
could be given that the agitation on behalf of the other three
would thereafter cease. According to Douglas Hurd's own
account, he raised this possibility with the Cardinal at their
September meeting (he even goes so far as to say that he believes
he made 'some impression' with it),* but, except as evidence of
the first crack in the Home Office's defences, this seems highly
unlikely. The Cardinal had come a long way since the days when
he would have been satisfied by the early release of Giuseppe
Conlon, if only to allow him to die in dignity – and, concerned
as he was by Carole Richardson's mental and physical condition, there was no way in which he (or any other member of
the Deputation) could have accepted her compassionate release
as a *quid pro quo* for closing down their activities on behalf of
the other defendants in both cases.

In fact, the Deputation proceeded to take the opposite course.
Far from scaling down its activities, it began to escalate them.
November 1988 saw the first breach in its own self-imposed
policy of confidentiality. A meeting held at Archbishop's House
on 14 November resolved that matters had now reached such a
point that a long, closely reasoned letter, which went two days
later to the Home Office, should be released to the press. Nor
was that the only sign of a new aggressiveness. Possibly of more
immediate impact, the Deputation's heavy legal guns were for

---

* Douglas Hurd, *Memoirs* (Little, Brown, 2003) p. 354.

the first time brought into play. Lords Devlin and Scarman had jointly produced a paper headed 'Justice and the Guildford Four' and, while this had also been sent to the Home Office, the decision was now taken to try to get a newspaper to publish it as well. There was only one non-negotiable condition; whatever paper took it must agree to print it in full without alteration or emendation. That was a tall order since the piece, forcefully argued though it was, dealt primarily with an arcane point of law: was it within the powers of the Court of Appeal, in effect, to re-hear a case rather than send it back for re-trial by a judge and jury? (It was Devlin's contention, which Scarman endorsed, that by agreeing to hear the evidence of the Balcombe Street Siege witnesses and then going on to refer to what they had said in their judgment on the 1977 Guildford Four appeal, Lord Roskill and his two colleagues had acted quite improperly.) Nevertheless, after a certain amount of toing-and-froing, *The Times* agreed to publish all 4,500 words, clearing the whole page opposite the leading articles for the purpose on 30 November 1988.

Yet, before that, it may be that the most significant breakthrough to date had already taken place. On 24 November 1988, the Home Secretary replied to the Cardinal's tough letter of a week earlier – the one in which notice had been served of the Deputation's intention to make its case in public if it felt that was the right thing to do. In his reply the Home Secretary disclosed something that he had never made explicit before: that he, for his part, was concentrating solely on the case of the Guildford Four, and that he did not regard any of the representations that had been made to him on behalf of the Maguires as constituting 'new evidence' or even (though Hurd was always a bit shaky about this alternative formulation invented by his distant predecessor, Roy Jenkins) as amounting to 'a consideration of substance'.

At first sight that may well have felt like a blow to the Deputation's campaign, in which the two cases had always been treated as inextricably intertwined. But, in fact, it was the reverse – for the mere dismissal of the arguments on behalf of the Maguires as representing no more than repetitions of points that had already been considered and dismissed inevitably implied that the 'new evidence' presented on behalf of the Guildford Four was being taken seriously.

It says much for the sophistication in the ways of Government that the Deputation had acquired during the eighteen months of its existence that it drew back from any automatic denunciation of the Home Secretary for seeking to divide the two cases. To have done so would only have been to court further delay, and the members of C3, the unit that advised Hurd on what the world outside was beginning to call 'miscarriages of justice', were certainly no slouches when it came to dragging their feet. In any event, with its own considerable knowledge of the background to each case, the Deputation was in very little doubt that, if the convictions of the Guildford Four were to be found 'unsafe', then the verdicts in the Maguire case could not long survive either.

Inevitably, however, as the months went by, there was mounting nervousness as to what the Home Secretary's final decision on referral would turn out to be. Hurd indicated in his letter to the Cardinal of 24 November 1988, that he hoped to be able to make an announcement early in the New Year and plans were, therefore, laid for the Deputation to come together once more in the Lower Library of Archbishop's House on 17 January 1989.

This meeting duly took place, but in a rather different spirit from that which the gloomier members had anticipated. For on 16 January 1989, by means of a Written Parliamentary Answer (notice of which was sent in advance to the Cardinal), the Home

Secretary announced his intention of referring the Guildford Four case back to the Court of Appeal. It amounted to a complete reversal of the decision he had communicated at the face-to-face meeting at Archbishop's House only fifteen months earlier. This change of mind on Hurd's part was made all the braver by the fact that the referral of the Birmingham Six case had failed to find any support within the Court of Appeal – with the Lord Chief Justice, Lord Lane, even making some disobliging remarks to the effect that the Home Secretary had 'wasted the Court's time'.

Of course, no one the following day at Archbishop's House was rash enough to believe that the victory was already won – but if not the beginning of the end, it was at least (as someone put it, echoing Churchill on El Alamein) 'the end of the beginning'. In fact, thereafter, things moved reasonably swiftly, if not wholly satisfactorily, with the Appeal Court suddenly advancing the scheduled date for the Guildford Four hearing from January 1990 to October 1989. Two days before the case was due to be heard the Crown Prosecution Service let it be known that it would not be seeking to uphold the convictions and the hearing thus became something of a *pro forma* affair, with counsel for the appellants not being required even to put forward their arguments. There was some suspicion that this had been done to protect the reputation of the police, though Roy Amlott, QC, counsel for the Crown, did outline a fairly horrifying tale of malfeasance, particularly on the part of the Surrey Constabulary. The four defendants were not best pleased. They believed that, after serving nearly sixty years in jail between them, they should at least have been entitled to their day in court. As it was, they didn't even get half a day, as the entire hearing was over in just two hours. From the point of view of the Cardinal and the Deputation, however, the central fact was that justice had at last been done, if only, so far, in one of the two cases that had always formed their primary concern.

That they were not at all disposed to give up on the case of the Maguire Seven was demonstrated by the preparation of a press release within Archbishop's House that ended with a sharp warning to the authorities that the campaign on behalf of the Maguires would continue. In the end this concluding part of the proposed text was never issued since, on the same day as the Appeal Court met, the Home Secretary announced in the Commons a judicial inquiry to be presided over by Sir John May, a Lord Justice of Appeal, to look into not only the way the Guildford Four case had been handled but also into the circumstances attending the decision to bring the Maguires to trial. As some at least of the police officers were common to both cases, it began to look as if at last the Maguires' complaints – mainly concentrating on the authenticity of the scientific evidence offered at their trial – were being taken seriously. (Another sign of this was the decision of the Director of Public Prosecutions to launch a criminal investigation into the conduct of certain members of the Surrey police force.) The Deputation agreed to co-operate with the May Inquiry and a meeting duly took place between Sir John and three of the five Deputation members at Archbishop's House on 22 January 1990.

Meanwhile the hand of the critics of police tactics had been greatly strengthened by the transmission of a BBC *Panorama* programme entitled 'Guildford – The Untold Story' in December 1989. It was a devastating indictment of the methods the police had chosen to follow, made all the more memorable by what in its context sounded almost like a plea in mitigation on their behalf made by the Cardinal himself:

I think one has got to put oneself in their situation. These were terrible crimes and I don't think one ever wants to minimise that. What happened at Guildford, just as what happened at Woolwich, were terrible crimes, totally to be condemned and everyone was outraged – and I was outraged at the time. They had to find somebody; they had to get the people. The fact that they got the wrong people was the tragedy, but they had to get somebody and I can see how a certain logic then begins to take over – especially when they confessed to having done it.

If Basil had not been moderately confident by then that victory, even on the second front of the Maguires, was now in sight, would he have risked striking quite so magnanimous a note? It is, of course, a fact that in the case of the Guildford Four his had been a stand based primarily on principle. (In contrast to his close contacts with individual members of the Maguire family, the only member of the Guildford Four he ever met while they were serving their sentences was Carole Richardson – and that was only in the last year of her imprisonment.) The campaign on behalf of the Maguires had been a much more personal matter and, had the choice been left to him, he would probably have wished to give it priority. (It would also have been a less difficult case to present to the authorities as it only marginally involved allegations of police brutality, resting instead on the possibly innocent misrepresentation of scientific evidence.) One factor, however, above any other militated against the Maguire case taking precedence over that of the Guildford Four: the latter, after all, were still in jail while the Maguires, except for Giuseppe, had all been at liberty since Anne Maguire became the last to be released in February 1985.

Yet that did not mean that their claim to justice was any less strong. The fact that their convictions had been brought within the scope of the May Inquiry was encouraging, but their wait for any form of official acquittal still went on. The first sign that things might be about to change came when the Director of Public Prosecutions revealed to a session of the May Inquiry in June 1990 that their convictions were no longer accepted as being safe and satisfactory by the Attorney-General. That same day the new Home Secretary, David Waddington,* intimated to the Commons that he would be ready to refer the Maguire cases to the Court of Appeal just as soon as the May Inquiry produced its findings. But this, again, purposelessly involved a delaying tactic, if a short one. It was not until Sir John May produced his first, interim report, specifically concerned with the Maguires, in July 1990 that the Home Secretary (six weeks later) made the referral. Even then the unfortunate Maguires had to wait a further year in order to make their second appearance – the first had been over fourteen years earlier – in the Appeal Court.

Alas, it was to prove as messy and frustrating a business as the Guildford Four experience had been in October 1989. True, this time the hearing ran its proper course, lasting a full eighteen days, rather than two hours, but the reserved judgment, when it was eventually delivered, proved equally spare and sparse. The three-man court found for the appellants but on the narrowest possible ground: that the traces of nitroglycerine which the police claimed had been discovered on their hands (and in the case of Anne Maguire on her plastic gloves) conceivably could have been there for an innocent reason. Or, as Lord Justice McCowan put it: 'It is impossible to identify one or more of the appellants as the primary source of contamination . . . each one could be accounted for by seemingly innocent contamination from a common source, most probably a towel.' In that case it must have been a very convenient towel – never heard of in any of the trials before – but one that just happened to be available for use

---

* David Waddington, the former Government Chief Whip, succeeded Douglas Hurd as Home Secretary on 26 October 1989.

by any contaminating stranger. Since all the police scientific tests, both at the original trial and at the first appeal, had been relentlessly attacked by counsel for the various accused, this was a ludicrous explanation, plainly designed to save the faces of the police and their official laboratory experts. Nevertheless, whatever derision it provoked, the judgment at least cleared the names of the Maguires (and of their family friend, Patrick O'Neil) allowing them, like the Guildford Four before them, to claim financial compensation for all the years they had spent in jail.

The nature of the judgment was, however, greeted with something less than elation within Archbishop's House. Had all the years of fighting for justice ended up with a masterpiece of ambivalence such as this? In public, though, it would clearly not have done to register anything but relief that the Maguires' convictions had finally been overturned. This the Cardinal duly did, but the increasing energy, acting entirely for himself, that he promptly brought to promoting the cause of the Birmingham Six hardly suggests that he was in any mood to let judicial events take their course. While the Maguire case was still waiting its resolution, he had, in fact, written to *The Times*, registering his disquiet at the length of time it was taking to get the Birmingham Six case for the second time into the Appeal Court. (Whether by coincidence or official design, he was rewarded by seeing the Birmingham Six appeal heard and upheld three months before the Maguires' one was.)

There was no question but that a certain scepticism was now creeping into the Cardinal's view of the legal system. The May Inquiry may have started out well; but, partly, because of the complications caused by the simultaneous prosecution of three Surrey police officers (all of whom were eventually acquitted), it was not long before it gave the impression of being totally bogged down. Its preliminary report – that on the Maguire case – asked questions rather than providing answers, thus allowing the Appeal Court to pronounce its judgment on the absurdly slender ground that it did. Then its further two reports – a second one on the Maguire case and a final one going back to the Guildford Four – got some pretty rough press treatment. On the day after the latter one was published the surviving four members of the Deputation – Lord Devlin had died in 1992 – even went so far as to have a letter published in *The Times* conveying their sense of disillusionment.* This was a perfectly fair criticism since a whole year earlier the Deputation had sent a list of eight pointed questions to both the Home Secretary and Sir John May, all of which the latter's final report simply succeeded in evading or ignoring.

Predictably, since normally he was a great believer in trying to work within the system, Basil's thirteen-year foray into the pursuit of justice left him slightly depressed. Of course, in the eyes of the world, he had scored a great triumph. But he was much less sanguine himself about whether he had stopped something of a similar nature and character to the Guildford or the Maguire cases ever happening again, especially as the real culprits had never been brought to book.

Naturally, there had been some consolations along the way. Basil always particularly relished one comment made by a right-wing MP on the day that Douglas Hurd announced the setting up of the May Inquiry. That afternoon Ivor Stanbrook, the Member for Orpington, rose in the House of Commons to declare: 'If we are to allow the due process of law to be diverted at the behest of Cardinals and Archbishops, British justice will be no better than that of Ayatollah Khomeini.' He also enjoyed, especially given the former Master of the Rolls's outburst in the Birmingham Six civil case, Lord Denning's comment: 'British justice is in ruins.'

---

* *The Times*, 6 July 1994.

Yet these were occasions for wry amusement rather than contributions to any lasting sense of vindication. Almost certainly by concentrating on what he had failed to do, rather than on what he had actually achieved, Basil (always a bit of a pessimist) judged himself too harshly. The truth is that no other cleric could have taken on a largely hostile public opinion and turned it around in the way that he did – until at the end people were simply prepared to say: 'Well, if the Cardinal thinks they didn't do it, that's good enough for me.' Nor has any other prelate ever taken on the Home Office and gradually worn it down until it was finally forced into full retreat.*

If there was one tribute that Basil himself valued above any other it lay perhaps in a letter that reached him from Belfast some time in 1990. Opening 'Dearest Cardinal', it went on to say: 'I want to thank you for all you have done for me and all the family. Indeed, we would still have been struggling but for your timely help and consideration. Thank you for looking after Gerard for me – for that and more you have my eternal thanks and prayers. Please take care of yourself and write again when you have time. God bless.' It was signed 'Sarah' – and the writer had no need to add that she was Giuseppe Conlon's widow.

---

* It was not, however, until 9 February 2005, or nearly six years after the Cardinal's death, that Tony Blair as Prime Minister (presumably acting on behalf of the Home Office) made a full apology to the Maguire Seven and the Guildford Four in a special statement delivered from No. 10 on television.

XI

THE LEGATEE OF CHRISTENDOM

W HILE BASIL HUME WAS STILL ABBOT OF AMPLEFORTH he went over one evening in July 1974 to York to attend what was officially described as 'the inaugural dinner of the Anglican Conference of Religious' – meaning those monks and nuns within the Church of England who had found their vocations in membership of Religious Orders. One might have expected that, from the vantage point of an established Benedictine Abbot, it would have seemed a rather small-beer occasion, but Basil was impressed. It had proved to be, as he himself put it, 'a gala night' – with Michael Ramsey, the Archbishop of Canterbury (who was to retire that November), as the main speaker and the Archbishop of York, Donald Coggan (who would be his successor) taking the chair. Something like three hundred representatives of Anglican convents and monasteries were present and, if the Abbot of Ampleforth felt in any need of moral support, it would certainly have been forthcoming from his American friend, Rembert Weakland, attending in his capacity as Abbot Primate of the Benedictine Order.

Back at Ampleforth the next day Basil immediately wrote to one of his younger colleagues, Father Felix Stephens (then temporarily away working outside the Community), to give a report on how the evening had gone. It was a revealing letter, if only because it demonstrated just how far Basil had travelled in the fourteen years since his father's funeral provided the occasion for his first-ever participation in an Anglican service. Now he obviously felt at home with the entire *Ecclesia Anglicana* – describing how captivated he had been by Ramsey ('I had never heard him speak before and he does it well, his handling of questions was brilliant and witty') and going on to relate how he had managed to talk to three separate Anglican diocesan bishops: 'These Anglicans do impress – the combination of holiness, culture and brains and the kind of modesty that goes with really great men is attractive. It is this which makes me such an admirer of the Archbishop of York.'

This feeling of admiration for Donald Coggan was fully reciprocated – indeed, there is some evidence that the voice of the new Archbishop of Canterbury was to prove decisive in getting Basil appointed to Westminster just two years later.* Certainly, when the former Abbot arrived at Archbishop's House in March 1976, he did so with far greater ecumenical hopes invested in him than had been the case with any of his predecessors.

In part, admittedly, this was the consequence of the sharp contrast he presented with his immediate predecessor, Cardinal Heenan. The latter had certainly done what was expected of him in promoting relations between the various churches, even on one occasion delivering the sermon – admittedly to Paisleyite shouts of horror – at the annual service held in St Paul's Cathedral to mark the Week of Prayer for Christian Unity. However, no one ever mistook him for anything other than that which he aspired to be: a traditionalist champion of the Catholic Church as 'the

---

* See page 88 for the visit of the Apostolic Delegate, Archbishop Bruno Heim, to Dr Coggan at Lambeth Palace in November 1975.

PHOTOGRAPH BY BRIAN SMITH, CAMERA PRESS LONDON

Basil continued to play squash in his early years at Westminster. He did not normally wear a cassock to do so, but here he was on a visit to an Essex YMCA.

Next page: Cardinal Hume in 1981 in his office at Archbishop's House, overlooking The Cardinal public house.

Photograph by Rory Coonan   *National Portrait Gallery collection*

©1981 Rory Coonan [Leica M2]

CARLOS REYES

The protagonists: the Cardinal with the turbulent priest Bruce Kent.

Graham Leonard, the Bishop of London, and Basil Hume, the Archbishop of Westminster, flanking Billy Graham during his Mission to London in 1989.

The moment of triumph. Gerald Conlon, the son of Giuseppe, on the day the Maguires finally won their appeal in 1991.

Basil receiving the Dalai Lama at Archbishop's House in 1999.

Opposite: Basil presiding over one of his 'eleven minus' Saturday evenings at Archbishop's House.

Basil with Diana Princess of Wales with whom he had a warm relationship. On her death in 1997 he boldly arranged for a Requiem Mass to be held in Westminster Cathedral.

The last outing: Basil receiving the Order of Merit from the Queen on 2 June 1999.

The final farewell: Basil Hume's Requiem Mass was held in a packed Westminster Cathedral on 25 June 1999.

one true faith'. During Heenan's time at Westminster it was other members of the Hierarchy – such as his own auxiliary Bishop, Christopher Butler (himself a former Anglican), or Alan Clark (then Co-adjutor Bishop of Northampton and later Bishop of East Anglia) – who took the lead in inter-church conversations.

This was especially true of the work of what was known as the Anglican-Roman Catholic International Commission, a body of theologians and scholars drawn from around the world but nominated by the two Churches in Britain. By 1982 it had been labouring for fourteen years and was on the point of producing what was slightly misleadingly called its 'Final Report' (it was to publish another one in 1990). Heenan had tolerated its discussions and deliberations; Hume positively encouraged and protected them, even to the point of writing to the Pope to emphasise how important it would be, when its first report eventually came out, for Rome not to adopt a negative or dismissive tone. He was not entirely successful. Cardinal Joseph Ratzinger, the Prefect of the Congregation for the Doctrine of the Faith, still contrived to sound distinctly less than enthusiastic in his official response, communicated to the Roman Catholic co-chairman, Bishop Alan Clark, in March 1982, just two months before the Pope was due to arrive in Britain.

The impact of this disappointment was still, however, slightly cushioned by a letter John Paul II himself had sent to 'my venerable brother, Cardinal George Basil Hume' only a couple of years earlier. Arising from a conversation the two of them had had in the papal apartments within the Vatican in May 1979, it fully acknowledged the importance of the work ARCIC was doing, and correctly identified 'the problem of authority within the Church' as being 'one of the outstanding, obstinate issues'. Here, though, the Pope was glad to report he had heard that at the Commission's most recent session progress had been made – and he was right about that, too. In fact, when the report came out, the feature within it that attracted the most attention was the readiness of the Anglican representatives to concede 'the universal primacy of the Bishop of Rome' (something which, while received not very enthusiastically in the secular press, provoked a near-riot in 'the Protestant underworld').

The Pope's letter also displayed foresight in spotting the main storm cloud in the sky. It did so with its pointed reference to the fact that 'since the present dialogue began several Anglican Churches have voted in favour of the ordination of women to the priesthood and a few have proceeded to such ordinations'. Although the Church of England had not by then even approved the admission of women to the diaconate (a break with tradition that happened only in 1987), the question of women priests was to be the issue which brought the otherwise promising dialogue within ARCIC effectively to an end. Even then, however, Basil was not prepared to give up without a struggle. As late as 1990, he was still to be found writing to the new Apostolic pro-Nuncio, Archbishop Luigi Barabarito (in the clear hope that his words would be passed on to Rome):

There is no doubt that the issue of the ordination of women is a major obstacle to Church unity. It is sad that it should have become so, for the Churches in this country were making good progress in their dialogue. The present situation is a difficult one but we cannot forget the call of the Second Vatican Council to heed the Lord's command to pray and work for Christian unity. That must go on. If the Congregation for the Doctrine of the Faith were to react in an insensitive manner to the work of ARCIC I [a reference to the Commission's impending 1990 report] then our present difficulties would be greatly increased. We accept entirely that the Congregation may well prove critical of the work of ARCIC I but what is vitally important is the way in which the Congregation makes its points. It would be very important indeed that, whatever negative criticisms the Congregation may wish to make, they should be expressed within a context emphasising the points of agreement. A good statement from the Congregation could help us to build for the future; a bad one could destroy what has been slowly built up over the years.

Of course, in the event, matters were taken out of anyone's control by the vote passed by the Church of England's General Synod on 11 November 1992, approving the admission of women to the priesthood (although no women were ordained until March 1994). Having once seemed so close, the prospect of reuniting the two Churches receded into the middle distance. For Basil, in particular, this was a grievous blow. He had come to acquire an especially warm feeling for the Church of England, the product in part of his own very English ecclesiology. The two Churches possessed, after all, a shared history – something that Basil's own study of such northern saints as Paulinus, Aidan and Cuthbert could not help but bring home to him. For him the Roman and Anglican Churches were not so much permanently divided as temporarily estranged and, as his sermon at the famous Vespers in Westminster Abbey in March 1976 had indicated,* he had even dared to hope that he might live to see them reconciled. That he was not, after all, going to witness any such coming together in his own lifetime was probably his greatest single disappointment, and he had to struggle hard to suppress his private suspicion that it was all the fault of liberal Anglican bishops. These had, in his view, failed to point out robustly enough what the price – in terms of Christian unity – of admitting women to the priesthood was bound to be.

* See page 101.

It says much, therefore, for Basil's native sense of courtesy that he never allowed any feelings of having been let down to affect his relationship with individual Anglican leaders. When Robert Runcie, as Archbishop of Canterbury, found himself in the eye of a press storm over the criticisms made of him by the Anglo-Catholic Oxford don Gareth Bennett in the incendiary *Crockford* Preface of 1987, it was none other than the Archbishop of Westminster who immediately rode to his defence. In a letter published by *The Times* on 5 December, 1987, he demonstrated that, however few qualities might have survived from medieval Christendom, a spirit of chivalry certainly had:

> Sir, Whatever motives may have inspired the notorious *Crockford* Preface, it is now firmly in the public domain. Its anonymous author appears to ignore the brave and imaginative leadership Archbishop Runcie has shown not only in facing the pastoral problems of urban decline but also in advancing the vital cause of Christian unity. He makes, for instance, no mention of the historic encounter with the Pope at Canterbury, their meeting at Assisi or the recent beatification of the 85 martyrs, which the Archbishop welcomed so significantly. Archbishop Runcie has, moreover, done much to earn the gratitude of a great number of people, and not least of
>
> Basil Hume

It was a typical, graceful gesture on the Cardinal Archbishop's part (for which he got a hand-written note of thanks from Lambeth Palace). But then it was never personal relationships that were the problem for Basil: where, in the eyes of his critics, he showed a less than ecumenical attitude was in relation to structures. On his first appearance before the General Synod of the Church of England, two years after he became Archbishop, he had gone to some lengths to explain why the Catholic Church in England and Wales would, under his leadership, continue to resist joining the British Council of Churches. Although it was an issue on which he came under considerable pressure, not least from a resolution of the Liverpool National Pastoral Congress in 1980 (and, later, from a decision on which he was saved from defeat only by his own casting vote within the Conference of Bishops itself), Basil for a long time stubbornly refused to change his mind. For many of his colleagues this seemed all the more strange as he had, after all, as Abbot of Ampleforth, taken a leading part in the formation of the Ryedale Christian Council, to say nothing of going out of his way to attend essentially eirenic occasions such as the inaugural dinner of the Anglican Conference of Religious described at the opening of this chapter. What, therefore was the stumbling block with the British Council of Churches and, indeed, with the World Council, too?

Part of the explanation is probably personal. Essentially pastoral in his own outlook, Basil never had much time for ecclesiastical administrators. If the British Council of Churches – or the World one in Geneva – could have been approached in any other way except through its formidable array of departments, boards, committees and sub-committees, it is possible Basil would have looked on it with more favour. As it was, it symbolised the bureaucratic aspect of religious organisation that always filled him with dread: it was bad enough that he should be expected to put up with bodies and commissions for this and that within his own Church – to see them duplicated and enlarged on an international and inter-faith scale was taking things altogether too far for someone steeped in the prayerful, private traditions of monasticism. It was precisely because at grassroots level the individual local Councils of Churches lacked all this administrative apparatus that Basil had no difficulty with them. Indeed, he went out of his way to encourage their work while continuing to draw the line at full co-operation at the national or international level.

There may also have been one other factor at work. While feeling perfectly at home with Anglicanism and with Methodism (which he regarded merely as a departed daughter of the C of E), the Cardinal, in company with many other Catholics, felt more removed from the Protestant, confessional denominations that to his mind lacked any form of authority. Yet if he had difficulties with the Baptists, the Congregationalists and the English Presbyterians (though the latter two, by the time he became Archbishop, had already combined themselves into the United Reformed Church), these were as nothing compared to the reservations he felt when it came to specifically non-doctrinal, non-sacramental bodies such as the Salvation Army or the Society of Friends. (One of the worst shocks when he had eventually permitted the Catholic Church to enrol under the banner of Churches Together in England was the discovery that the interests of the historic Eastern Orthodox Church were represented there by a woman Quaker who made it crystal clear that she had absolutely no interest in doctrine.)

Yet it was to take years to get Basil to move even that far. The Pope's visit to Britain in 1982 – and, in particular, the memory of John Paul II and Robert Runcie praying together at Canterbury – had certainly given the movement towards Christian unity a fillip, and in both communities there were those who expected progress thereafter to be fairly rapidly made. That virtually nothing happened was largely down to Basil. When the Conference of Bishops of England and Wales met that November, a number of its members hoped to see the question of the Catholic Church joining the British Council of Churches re-opened, but they found themselves stopped in their tracks by the strong resistance offered to any such proposal by their

President (supported, it is only fair to say, by the more conservative bishops). While conceding that there was a perception on the part of the public that the failure to join the British Council of Churches represented 'a lack of commitment to unity' by the Catholic Church, the most the conference was prepared to do at that stage was to offer the BCC the fairly trifling sum of £3,000 towards its work.

However, in private a dialogue had opened, reflected in a protracted correspondence between Basil and the long-suffering general secretary of the BCC, Dr Philip Morgan. Its eventual outcome was an agreement to hold two conferences in 1984 – one in January at Chelmsford, when BCC representatives would be invited to join an 'extraordinary meeting of the Bishops' Conference for joint reflection and deliberation', and the other at Canterbury three months later, when the Catholic Bishops would respond by sharing in 'a weekend of prayer and reflection with the Archbishop of Canterbury and others responsible for leadership in their Churches'.

It hardly sounded like an enterprise that had much of a sense of urgency about it, but, in fact, something decisive had changed. Conferences, even the most informal ones, demand organisation and preparation – and put in charge of this task for the Catholic gathering at Chelmsford were three key figures: Derek Worlock, the Archbishop of Liverpool; Alan Clark, Bishop of East Anglia; and Cormac Murphy-O'Connor, Bishop of Arundel and Brighton. The significance of their selection was that each of them was committed to taking the process forward. Whether he realised it or not, from the moment the three of them were chosen, Basil was bound to find himself under constant pressure to re-open the entire question of Catholic membership of the British Council of Churches.

He always, however, tended to be a figure who played his own cards close to his chest. Even after the announcement in

1984 – following the second joint meeting at Canterbury – that the Bishops' Conference would co-operate with the British Council of Churches in planning 'a major conference' for the autumn of 1987, no one – not even the three principal go-betweens – seems to have been quite certain how the story would end. As the date (the first week of September 1987) approached for what became known as 'the Swanwick conference' (named after the place in Derbyshire at which it was held), the Cardinal's intentions remained remarkably opaque.

Archbishop Worlock, therefore, bravely accepted the challenge of seeking to establish precisely what the Cardinal was proposing to say to the assembled delegates drawn from all the Christian Churches in Britain. The only response he got was a cold, abbatial glare – and it was not until the conference met that even the Catholic delegation learnt (and then only by degrees) what line its leader intended to take. When Basil, occupying a humble place on the floor, rose to his feet on the penultimate day of the conference, the atmosphere was inevitably tense. The BCC had, after all, agreed in advance entirely to reconstitute itself under a new (then unchosen) name in order to accommodate Catholic reservations – and it still did not know whether or not the reward it would get for that would be Catholic membership.

In his speech that evening Basil lost no time in allaying all doubts. The moment had come, he said, for the Catholic Church to 'move quite deliberately from a situation of co-operation to one of commitment', and everyone (including the Archbishop of Canterbury, who was there) seems to have accepted that that sort of language was not used lightly. Some things were, necessarily, left vague. The BCC had still to acquire a new title – and, when it came, it was the pretty clumsy one of the Council of Churches for Britain and Ireland, with subordinate bodies such as Churches Together in England (and similarly for Scotland and Wales).

The Council of Churches for Britain and Ireland was an alto-gether looser body than the old BCC had been, and no longer regarded itself as a direct subsidiary of the World Council of Churches (to which the Catholic Church remained unaffiliated). Instead, very much at the Cardinal's insistence, all the emphasis was on local co-operation – with the model remaining, at least in his eyes, the kind of body that all those years ago he had helped to launch in the Ryedale Valley, and which certainly underlined his own belief, declared at Swanwick, that in matters of Christian unity 'there can be no authentic evolution which does not take place at local level'.

Why were all the other denominations – to say nothing of the more impatient spirits within his own Church – so depen-dent on the conversion of Basil to their cause in order to be able to make any progress? There was a paradox here which perhaps was not fully perceived at the time. All previous Archbishops of Westminster had been sectarian figures – reli-gious leaders, however eminent, whose very existence witnessed to the 400-year-old division of Christendom. It was Basil's perhaps most outstanding achievement to convince at least the Christian community that he was in himself a symbol of unity, almost a pre-Reformation figure and a reminder in his own person of what once had been and conceivably could be again. Any form of inter-denominational organisation to which he did not give his assent would, therefore, have lacked all conviction. Those even within his own Church who favoured a more openly inter-communion approach always knew this – and so did the Anglicans and other Protestants with whom the formation of the CCBI was finally negotiated. So great by the mid-1980s was the esteem and regard in which he was held – not least by the public generally – that any umbrella organisation from which he deliberately stood aside would count for nothing. It is here that the contradiction lies: for far from being the gentle figure of popular imagination, Basil proved a very tough customer to handle, at least until the majority of his own doubts and reservations (principally centring on the former BCC's role as a 'Superchurch') had been met.

The strength of his position lay, of course, in the sheer amount of goodwill on the part of other Christian bodies he had already engendered and built up, and, paradoxically, this had come about almost entirely through personal contact. There had certainly never been any previous Archbishop of Westminster who had made himself so familiar a figure at the various historic and religious celebrations of other churches. As he had shown from the start, with his appearance at Robert Runcie's Enthronement at Canterbury Cathedral, he took his representational function extremely seriously – and, once he had started accepting such invitations, they necessarily came thick and fast.

One of the earliest occasions on which he preached at an Anglican service was at Great St Mary's, Cambridge, in February 1978 – and, highly praised though his address to the students at the term-time 8.30 p.m. informal evening service turned out to be, it was also an experience which left its own warning behind it. For no sooner had he fulfilled this engagement than he found himself being pressed to return the following academic year. Just a flicker of irritation can perhaps be detected in his reply that on the whole he thought it better to allow one generation of students to fade away before inflicting his presence upon their successors from the same pulpit again.

That was a rare moment of relative asperity. In general, Basil found it very difficult to refuse outside preaching engagements, especially when they were persuasively and flatteringly proposed, as they nearly always were. For someone with heavy demands on his time, he adopted the rather curious formula of intimating to those correspondents whose requests he was reluctant to meet that he never liked to enter into commitments too far in advance and suggesting that they might care to write again in a year's time. (This was hardly something that his hard-pressed successive private secretaries can have appreciated, since such correspondents almost invariably did just that.) Before long there was hardly an Anglican cathedral in the land that had not at some time or another been graced by the Cardinal's presence and the C of E cleric organising the 800th celebration of Wells Cathedral in 1982 was entitled to count himself unlucky in getting the unusually firm reply: 'I am trying to be strong-minded and refuse attractive invitations away from London. I am already committed to Worcester and, I think, Gloucester. So what I am trying to say is that, much as I would love to see and pray at Wells Cathedral, I really think I must decline.'

For the most part, however, especially where there was some personal association, Basil found these approaches very hard to turn down – and sometimes he could sound positively ecstatic. For example, to Eric Heaton, the Dean of Durham, he once wrote (admittedly when he had been at Westminster for only just over two years): 'Apart from the joy of seeing your good self again, there is the prospect of being able to preach in Durham Cathedral. That would give me a greater thrill than you can realise. My North Country associations and Benedictine background would make it a special occasion for me. Thank you for offering me that possibility.'

If letters of that sort indicate one thing above anything else, it has to be that Basil was entirely free of the hang-ups that affected so many Catholics of his generation. Confronted by the glories of English religious architecture, he felt no resentment that it was something of which his own Church had been dispossessed. Instead – the product again of his belief in a continuing concept of Christendom – he simply rejoiced in what, despite everything, stayed for him a shared heritage.

Also of course, he did his own bit to make sure that in national terms there came to be a form of diarchy. It was inconceivable, for example, in the case of the planning for the Falklands Thanksgiving Service at St Paul's in July 1982 that the Archbishop of Westminster should not have been just as closely involved as the Archbishop of Canterbury. In fact, his may well have been the more decisive voice – certainly an episode that took place subsequently would suggest that. When in April 1984 an official of the Ministry of Defence suggested that he might call upon Alan Webster, the Dean of St Paul's, to discuss a proposal that there should be a war memorial erected there to the 255 British casualties of the war, it was to the Archbishop of Westminster (rather than to the Archbishop of Canterbury) that the Dean immediately turned for advice and support. It was, of course, perfectly true that the two of them had got to know each other well in the weeks spent preparing for the Falklands Service (when Basil had been the most persistent advocate of the need for some recognition to be given to the Argentine dead), but it is hard to think of any predecessor of Alan Webster's in the Deanery of St Paul's seeking – and getting – help from a Catholic Cardinal in quite the same way. It is a measure of how far the presence of Basil at Westminster had altered the traditional contours of both Church and State that such an episode should not merely have occurred but also today have come to seem quite unexceptionable.

XII

'THE CONVERSION OF ENGLAND'

A HIGH-POINT IN ANGLICAN-ROMAN CATHOLIC RELATIONS – yielding pride of place only to the Pope's visit to Britain in 1982 – was reached with the arrival of the Archbishop of Canterbury in Rome in September 1989. Although Basil himself was not present (Cormac Murphy-O'Connor, Bishop of Arundel and Brighton, and Joint Chairman of ARCIC, stood in for him as the representative of the English Hierarchy), the Archbishop of Westminster had done a great deal of the ground-work in preparation for the visit. It marked the fifth occasion on which Robert Runcie had met Pope John Paul II – they had first encountered each other, almost by chance, in Ghana as long ago as 1980 – but never before had they had a meeting actually within the Vatican. On this first (and last) official visit by the 102nd Archbishop of Canterbury to the Holy See, they ended up talking together five times in four days, so it clearly rated above the level of a mere courtesy call or a purely symbolic occasion.

A more sophisticated figure than his immediate predecessor Donald Coggan (who had caused some consternation within the Curia by openly calling for intercommunion between the two

Churches on *his* visit to the Vatican in 1977*), Runcie skilfully avoided any such pitfalls. Indeed, he delighted his hosts, in formal terms the Pontifical Council for Promoting Christian Unity, by proposing in a sermon he delivered in the presence of the Pope that all Christians throughout the world should join together in acknowledging 'the primacy of the Bishop of Rome'. Of course, here he was merely anticipating the recommendation that the second ARCIC report would make in the following year; but by getting in first he certainly saw to it that his visit attracted a fair amount of attention. At home he may not have got a particularly good press – on the 'primacy' issue a highly indignant Ian Paisley, for once, had the majority of newspapers on his side – but among both Catholics and Anglicans his visit was generally counted to have been a success.

This was all the more remarkable since everyone knew it was taking place under the shadow of a looming storm cloud. The Church of England had been considering the ordination of women for something like twenty years, but now the whole argument looked as if it was approaching its point of decision. Runcie himself had managed to hold off a defining vote on the issue throughout the eleven years of his archiepiscopate, but his successor, George Carey, who would arrive at Lambeth in the spring of 1991, was a committed supporter of women priests and their right to a place within the ministry of the Church of England.

Yet there remained a striking reluctance to make contingency plans on the part of both Churches. To some degree this, no doubt, stemmed from a decent reticence: no one wanted to be caught in the act of making assumptions about the result of a

---

* Since 1960, when by visiting Pope John XXIII that December Geoffrey Fisher ended 400 years of non-communication between Canterbury and Rome, every Archbishop of Canterbury had made at least one pilgrimage to the Vatican.

General Synod vote that (given the requirement of a two-thirds majority to sanction any change) was bound to hang in the balance until the moment it was announced. It was not so much that people failed to perceive the threat to Christian unity. That challenge would exist even if the status quo were to be preserved, for in two provinces of the Anglican Communion there were already, after all, women bishops.* Rather was it that on both sides they preferred to avert their gaze from such a prospect – for fear of having to face up to the consequences.

That was particularly true of the Church of England – hence the hastily cobbled together Act of Synod of 1993 providing for Provincial Episcopal Visitors (or 'flying bishops' as they promptly came to be known) to be appointed in order to offer comfort and reassurance to the defeated minority. For the initial inertia on the part of the Roman Catholic Church there was probably more excuse; had it concerted a strategy in advance of the vote being taken – and in the end if only two members of the General Synod's House of Laity had cast their votes the other way the result would have been reversed – it would inevitably have risked the charge of seeking to exploit the difficulties of what the Pope himself had only recently called 'a sister Church'.

In any case, it is not strictly true that no precautions of any sort were taken. Probably the Anglican bishop to whom Basil felt closest at this time was Graham Leonard, the Bishop of London. They had first met at a dinner party given in the bishop's honour by the then Apostolic Delegate, Bruno Heim, shortly after Leonard arrived back in London in 1981. (Although most

---

* The two outposts of the Anglican Communion that already had women bishops by 1992 were the Episcopal Church in the United States and the Anglican Church of New Zealand – and the Canadian Church was to follow their example within two years.

of his working life had been spent in the London diocese, for the previous eight years he had been Bishop of Truro.) As representatives of two different but no longer diametrically opposed Catholic traditions, Basil and he appear to have got on well together, and something of a genuine friendship soon developed. Indeed, one of the better kept secrets of the women's ordination crisis is concealed in the meetings between the two of them that would from time to time take place in an Anglican vicarage in Pimlico, where the incumbent conveniently happened to be a former chaplain to the Bishop of London. Years later, after Leonard himself had been ordained as a priest in the Roman Catholic Church, he was to write to Basil saying he regarded it as 'providential' that they had each held the jobs that they did at the crucial time. That may have been pushing things a bit – Leonard had, after all, retired at the age of seventy as Bishop of London eighteen months before the Synod women's vote went through – but it does serve to suggest that a certain amount of consultation predated the actual crisis.

They would, however, almost certainly have approached the likely shape of the future from rather different perspectives. From the beginning Graham Leonard seems to have been a 'maximalist', foreseeing a general exodus of both clergy and laity from the Church of England if the ordination of women was agreed upon, which, if he were allowed to lead it, could prove to be highly significant. At an early stage he even appears to have toyed with the idea that he should be awarded a 'personal prelature' in order to make it easier for other Anglicans to follow him. Basil, on the other hand, gave every sign from the start of having entertained much more modest expectations – though that did not inhibit him from putting out the welcome mat, aimed especially at Anglican clergy, once the decision had been taken. It so happened that in the week after the General Synod's vote, the half-yearly Catholic Bishops' Conference was scheduled to meet. This provided its President, the Archbishop of Westminster, with the chance to issue a statement evidently designed to put at rest the minds of any Anglican priests alarmed by the notion that crossing over to Rome would mean having to renounce every aspect of their previous pastoral lives. It was Basil at his most mollifying:

> We recognise that in their ministry they have exercised a call from God. This is the basis of our willingness to assume a continuity of ministry, normally leading to ordination to the priesthood in the Catholic Church, depending on a process of mutual discernment.

It may all have sounded a trifle opaque, but at least it displayed a clear difference in tone from Leo XIII's 1896 Papal Bull, *Apostolicae Curae*, in which the validity of Anglican Orders was totally denied. Basil was also fortunate in that the last week of November 1992 saw him in Rome on what originally had been planned to be quite other business. The trip, nonetheless, offered him the opportunity not so much to consult – the last thing he wanted was to have his footsteps guided – as to get authority to handle things in his own way. This he managed to do, the sole injunction he received from the Pope (and that much later) being contained in the phrase: 'Be generous, be generous.'

It was not until 16 December that the Cardinal and Graham Leonard met together for the first time since the General Synod's fateful decision. It was necessarily now a slightly different relationship from what it had been when their conversations began – with the former Bishop of London recognising his position as now being (in his own phrase) that of 'a suppliant' – but he had by no means given up hope that even if a 'personal prelature' was unlikely to prove a practicable proposition, then at least some form of 'pastoral provision' could, and should, be devised for those groups leaving the Church of England in order 'to preserve our Anglican identity while being in communion with the see of St Peter'.

At first Basil did not wholly crush that notion, although he did firmly rule out any form of 'Uniate Church' – or a quasi-independent organisation built rather on the lines of the Eastern Rite Churches' relationship with Rome.* This was probably as good an indication as any that the more extravagant aspirations among those planning to defect from the Church of England, and hoping to establish a kind of independent dominion under the protection of Rome, were bound to be disappointed – though, oddly enough, at this stage the door was not finally slammed shut on the notion of 'a personal prelature' or, indeed, of the norm being one of parish priests coming over accompanied by their congregations.

This December meeting was, however, one primarily designed to deal with the immediate crisis. In discussing it with Leonard, Basil took the opportunity to spell out the administrative steps he proposed to take. He would, he told his visitor, set up a steering committee consisting of himself and four of his epis-copal colleagues which, once it had got itself established, could regularly meet together in joint session with a similar body of representative Anglican traditionalists. This Leonard found encouraging – as he did the Cardinal's ready acceptance that the ordination of women was not necessarily the sole, or even the principal, point at issue. What mattered just as much as the actual decision to some disaffected Anglicans was the manner in which it had been reached. Where did the future lie for a Church in which not just custom and tradition but even dogma

---

* The Eastern Rite Churches derived from the ancient Patriarchate of Constantinople. They included such independent bodies of believers as the Maronite Church in Lebanon, the Uniate Coptic Church in Egypt and the Greek Melchite Church in Syria and Egypt.

or doctrine could apparently be overturned merely by the force of numbers and a wish to identify with the spirit of the age?

Many of the Anglicans who contemplated leaving were motivated by an uncomfortable feeling that within their own Church 'authority' had simply ceased to exist. This was an important point for the prospective Catholic converts to get across, since otherwise (as the shrewder of them realised) they could all too easily be portrayed as simply a group of malcontents and misogynists whose attitude had been determined by a fundamental incapacity to come to terms with any notion of female equality.

To have this immediately understood by the Cardinal was a great relief to Leonard and his followers, although Basil's attitude was probably at that stage unrepresentative of that of the Catholic Church as a whole. Within it the more liberal elements persisted in regarding the prospective Anglican defectors as being governed primarily by sexual hang-ups – an impression that Leonard's own slightly unfortunate earlier statement that his first instinct on seeing a woman at the altar would be to throw his arms around her did little to diminish.

There was one other highly practical matter that had to be grappled with early on. That was the question of the economic responsibility for those Anglican priests who, albeit voluntarily, decided to sacrifice not only their livelihoods but in most cases their homes as well. In terms of its own resources, this was hardly a financial burden that the Catholic Church could easily take on (nor, of course, could it know what proportion of the departing Anglican clergy would end up as ordained Catholic priests).* Fortunately, however, the problem had largely been taken care of by the Church of England. In an effort to ease the passage of the original measure through the General Synod, it

---

* In the end something like 200 of the 400-plus departing Anglican clergy were ordained Catholic priests.

had included fairly elaborate compensation proposals for those feeling driven by conscience to depart from the Anglican ministry. The fact that the initial, self-chosen title for the organisation of those Anglo-Catholic priests contemplating such action had been 'Cost of Conscience' does not seem to have been an irony that anyone felt much disposed to comment upon.*

The first meeting between Graham Leonard's team and that of the Cardinal and his four bishops took place at Archbishop's House on 15 February 1993; that things even then remained very much in a state of flux is demonstrated by the fact that on Leonard's side of the table two of the Anglican representatives ended up as Roman Catholic priests while two did not (one of them even becoming an Anglican suffragan bishop). The individual who made his personal decision earliest was probably Leonard himself and, once he had charted his own spiritual course (a resolution reached in the full knowledge that no 'personal prelature' or anything like it would, in fact, be forthcoming), he withdrew from these joint sessions, which nevertheless continued well into 1994.

By then, however, an equally important, if much more informal, development had grown up alongside them. At the beginning of 1994 the Cardinal let it be known that he would be holding what used to be known as 'At Home Days' – social occasions of a previous generation for which you needed no invitation but at which you could simply turn up. These particular events – held in the Throne Room at Archbishop's House on alternate Wednesday evenings at 6 p.m. – were aimed specifically at Anglican clergy bewildered about their future. Fifteen such occasions were held between January and June 1994 and,

---

* After ten years the Church Commissioners, the body that deals with financial matters on behalf of the Church of England, estimated that it had paid out a total of £27.5 million to clergy who voluntarily left the ministry as a result of women's ordination.

with the promise of the Cardinal's own presence and the additional bonus of modest refreshments, they succeeded in attracting an average attendance of a hundred or so Anglican priests. They were not, of course, always the same ones and by no means all of them ended up by converting. However, these informal evenings – half seminar, half social conversation – certainly eased the atmosphere. Paradoxically, it could even be claimed that they made their own contribution to a spirit of ecumenical harmony.

This spirit only once came under serious threat, and that, rather surprisingly, was Basil's own fault. March 1993 marked his seventieth birthday and, though not in professional terms a particularly meaningful anniversary (it is at seventy-five, and not at seventy, that bishops in the Catholic Church are required to submit their resignations to the Pope), at least one friendly journalist seems to have resolved that it was an event worth celebrating. On 19 February 1993 John Wilkins, the Editor of the *Tablet*, made the short journey from the paper's then offices in Great Peter Street, Westminster, down Victoria Street to Archbishop's House. His purpose, once he arrived there, was to interview the Cardinal and get him to look back on the seventeen years he had already spent running his archdiocese and, in effect, serving as the leader of the Catholic Church in England and Wales. The article – a thoroughly professional piece of work headed 'Basil Hume at 70' – duly appeared in the issue of the *Tablet* dated 27 February, or just three days before the birthday. It did not, however, turn out to be much of a birthday present.

The reason for that, and the cause of all the trouble, was a single paragraph that appeared in the last column towards the end of what was a 2,000-word piece. At issue here was what is known within the Catholic Church as the Magisterium – or teaching authority – which is recognised as largely belonging to the bishops but in the last resort is seen as resting with the

Pope. There came a point in the article when Wilkins reported on Basil's own attitude to the debate that had arisen over it:

> He [the Cardinal] finds a certain irony in that just at the moment when Catholics seem to be irked by the teaching authority, High Church Anglicans are finding a need of it. He has been struck by the humility of those who have been discussing with him the possibility of a path from the Church of England to Rome. 'This could be a big moment of grace, it could be the conversion of England for which we have prayed all these years. I am terrified we are going to turn round and say we do not want these newcomers. We have prayed for Christian unity and now it could be happening: a realignment of English Christianity so as to bring us together in two blocs rather than lots of little blocs.'

The sentence that caused all the fuss was, of course, the one about 'the conversion of England' (or 'reconversion' as it is usually misquoted). Certainly, Basil was quite justified in reminding *Tablet* readers that this was something that Catholics had traditionally prayed for after each Mass – but that was in pre-Vatican II days when certainty and confidence represented the normal religious ethos. By the 1990s, however, the temper of the times had changed and it had become distinctly unfashionable to lay claim to any monopoly of truth or wisdom.

What made things infinitely worse was that the Archbishop seemed to be giving his backing to an old-fashioned concept at a particularly unpropitious moment. Ever since the General Synod vote, not just the religious but the secular press had been full of pieces suggesting that a new mood of Catholic triumphalism was abroad in the land. (So enraged by it was one distinguished man of letters that he even contributed an article to the *Spectator* suggesting that the passing of the Catholic Emancipation Act of 1829 might have been a mistake.*) Accordingly, with both sides spoiling for a fight, it was hardly surprising if the Cardinal's phrase about 'the conversion of England' was perceived as throwing down a gauntlet.

It was not intended to do any such thing. Neither its originator nor the journalist who took it down and published it had the slightest inkling of the provocation that they were unsuspectingly dealing in. The *Tablet* failed entirely to highlight this particular phrase when it published the interview, while Basil himself had to be rung up by Cormac Murphy-O'Connor to be alerted to the storm that he was all too likely to have provoked. He always, however, prided himself on his sensitive fingertips and, once he had been warned of the danger, he certainly did his best to contain the damage, going so far as to issue an explanation (though not exactly a retraction) of what he had said. A copy of it was even sent personally to George Carey, the relatively new Archbishop of Canterbury. It elicited a polite but still slightly pained response:

Lambeth Palace
London SE1   11 March 1993

My dear Basil,
    I must admit that I did get alarmed when I read reports that you saw the present disturbance within the Church of England as 'an opportunity for the conversion of England

---

* 'No Pontification in this Realm of England' by Ferdinand Mount, *Spectator*, 20 January 1994. To be fair, the then Editor of the *TLS* had been considerably provoked by a number of gloating articles that had appeared both in the *Spectator* and elsewhere over the preceding weeks.

for which we have prayed all these years'. Your statement clarified your thinking – or at least the reporting – and I am relieved to know that 'the conversion for which we all pray' will involve a *metanoia* [a reorientation] that involves us all. So an absorption by one group is automatically excluded.

I assure you of my ongoing thoughts and prayers. Solidarity is important at a time like this!

Yours ever,
+George

With that last sentence Basil almost certainly agreed, and cordial, if never exactly close, relations seem to have been restored. Before long a joint working group had even been set up to advise both benches of bishops on the guidelines to be established for the treatment of those leaving the Anglican Church for the Church of Rome.

One figure, though, forestalled all such preparations. Graham Leonard had, as we have already seen, made up his mind early on that he saw his future as a Roman Catholic priest and, having first been received fewer than three weeks earlier as a layman into the Church,* he was on 26 April 1994 ordained priest by Basil in his private chapel in Archbishop's House. He thus became by eighteen months or more the first of the ex-Anglican clerics to be given such a status. There was one other unusual aspect to the new Father Graham's case. His ordination was officially described as 'conditional' – a quaint expression resorted to in order to concede the possibility that it might not have been

---

* The reason Basil gave to Rome for this very short gap between Leonard being received into the Church and being ordained a priest was that 'it will be hard for him to be neither an Anglican bishop nor a Catholic priest after so many years as an Anglican priest and bishop'.

necessary at all, the explanation being that among those taking part in Leonard's original consecration as an Anglican bishop back in 1964 had been some episcopal representatives of the Old Catholic Church of the Union of Utrecht, the validity of whose Orders are recognised by Rome. In such instances, which tend to be rare, the Catholic Church takes refuge in what is technically referred to as 'a prudent doubt', a concept conveniently implying that, where no one can be quite sure of an existing priestly status, it is better to be on the safe side and go through a second ordination, even if it may not actually change anything.

It fell to Basil to have to try to explain this arcane point of ecclesiology to the newspapers, something which he did in the form of what he called 'a background statement on the Ordination of Dr Graham Leonard'. It was necessarily a fairly convoluted document and it must be doubted whether it was entirely successful in removing the predominant suspicion that Dr Leonard had received preferential treatment simply because of who he was and what he had been. As a former Bishop of London, and thus while in office the third figure in the Anglican hierarchy, he was a much grander 'trophy convert' than either John Henry Newman (a former vicar of the University Church in Oxford) or Henry Edward Manning (a Sussex archdeacon) – a factor which may help to explain the distant and frosty attitude that his former Anglican colleagues tended to adopt towards him.

Once Leonard's ordination was out of the way – a process in which the Pope took an active personal interest, ruling at the very last moment that this new recruit to the priesthood need not be first admitted to the diaconate – relations between the two Churches began to look up. This was partly because there were practical problems to be resolved, some of which needed to be shared.

When a similar breakaway movement, also provoked by the ordination of women, had surfaced a decade earlier in the Episcopal Church in the United States the general pattern had been for a priest, his people and the church in which they worshipped to come across as an entity – and at first that was the model on which the new Anglican secessionists set their sights. It did not take long, however, to prove wholly impractical. The Church of England has never been a 'congregational' Church – the focus of loyalty being not so much the incumbent as the church building and even the historical continuity of the parish. Although a few local arrangements were made, almost exclusively in London, whereby individual churches were shared between the newly received Catholic converts and the Anglican remnant that had been left behind, nowhere did they prove to be anything but provisional. The Cardinal himself was distinctly wary, feeling it was much better for any freshly received converts to be assimilated into their nearest Catholic parish, rather than continue as an isolated pocket of resistance under their old parish priest in a building that legally belonged to the Church of England – and in this stand he and the Catholic bishops certainly had the full support of their Anglican opposite numbers. The latter were inclined to frown even on such few temporary 'church-share' arrangements as were made. None, in fact, survived for more than a year or two.

It was only afterwards that those who had been disappointed at the relatively limited numbers of former Anglicans who had come over to Rome began to rewrite history. They chose to fasten on the reluctance to exploit what became known as the 'pastoral provision' – meaning the acceptance of converts not as individuals but in groups complete with their own pastors – as the key to the failure to secure any significant progress towards 'the conversion of England'. Necessarily Basil became the target of their criticism, but that cannot help seeming a little harsh, not least because Westminster had a far better record in terms of receiving converts into the priesthood than any other diocese. The truth probably is that the original forecasts had all been far too melodramtic. Especially after the passing of the Act of Synod in 1993 (allowing individual dissident Anglican parishes to transfer their allegiance to specially appointed travelling 'Fathers in God' whom they truly believed to be part of the Apostolic Succession), there never was a chance of the kind of mass exodus occurring from the C of E that some newspapers had excitedly forecast. Far from there being something like 2,000 priests leaving Canterbury for Rome there turned out to be fewer than 500 and, though the strength of the Anglo-Catholic wing within the Church of England was certainly reduced, it was by no means obliterated.

Could it be that this was the way Basil – despite his one imprudent statement in the *Tablet* interview – had planned it all along? Certainly, after the Low Week meeting of the Bishops' Conference in April 1993, he gave every sign of pursuing a consistent minimalist policy. No new structures, it was made clear, would be established (thus ruling out not only any introduction of a personal prelature but the adaptation of an American-style pastoral provision as well); no permanent concessions would be made in terms of liturgy (though limited temporary permission might be granted to continue with some aspects of Anglican worship in particular circumstances); and, above all, in a phrase that was, no doubt, calculated to capture the headlines, prospective converts must accept that what was on offer in religious terms was not an *à la carte* but a *table d'hôte* menu.

If that sounded brisk enough, then the instructions for those seeking ordination, when a year later such questions got further down the road, had an equally peremptory tone:

Provisional Guidelines for Single Anglican Clergy

Part 1: Before Reception

a) Talk to the local Catholic priest or a priest of your choice in regard to the possibility of entering into Full Communion with the Catholic Church. He, in turn, will refer you to the Area Bishop if you are seeking ordination in the Catholic Church.

b) The Area Bishop will discuss with you your intentions and your personal situation and, if necessary, appoint a 'priest guide'.

c) If you have not already done so, you must contact your Anglican Bishop informing him of your meeting with the Catholic Bishop and your possible future actions.

d) You will need to discuss with the Church of England authorities your position regarding compensation, housing, pension etc.

e) A decision must be made, in consultation with the Anglican and Catholic authorities, as to when you should offer your resignation and announce it to your people.

f) Reception into full Communion with the Catholic Church.

Part 2: After Reception

a) Placement in pastoral setting for a period of 9–12 months.

b) Continuing reflection with a 'priest guide'.

c) Involvement in pastoral work as part of the team.

d) During period of your pastoral placement there will be an ongoing review of your situation with the Area Bishop, the Parish Priest and the 'priest guide'. This will also be an opportunity to discuss your own personal needs and concerns.

Part 3: Discernment

a) At some stage during the parish placement a process of discernment will take place involving the Candidate himself, the Parish Priest of the placement, the Area Bishop (or Cardinal), the Vicar General, the 'priest guide' and a representative from the Allen Hall Seminary to decide whether to proceed to ordination and what further preparation is required.

b) A period of further preparation which may take the form of either remaining in the pastoral placement and using places of study in London or residential study in England or abroad.

c) During your pastoral placement you will not be provided with an income but your board and lodging will be free. The Diocese is unable to meet any outstanding debts. Once accepted for ordination, a diocesan grant *may* be available.

d) The pastoral needs of the Catholic Church nationally, the Diocese of Westminster and your personal circumstances may indicate the possibility of your applying to a diocese other than Westminster.

7 June 1994

What, of course, that document leaves out is any instructions for married men, but that was for a very good reason. This was one area where Basil was bound to have to consult the Vatican, though once permission had been given by the Holy See for the ordination of Graham Leonard, who had not only a wife but two sons, he must have had a pretty shrewd idea that no obstacles would be put in his way. And so, to his relief, things turned out, with the Pope granting him almost complete discretion.

That was only sensible for this was, as it happened, an area in which Basil had a good deal of experience. From the moment he arrived at Westminster in 1976 he had very much taken under his personal wing the cases of ex-Anglican married priests who – long before the women's ordination issue actively arose – had been received into the Catholic Church only to discover that, as matters stood at the time, they had little hope of ever being anything but a Catholic layman. A few he was even able to help actively – arranging in two or three cases for former Anglican priests who were married to go out to the Catholic Church in America, where the rules on celibacy were nothing like so strictly enforced (as early as the beginning of the 1980s there were eleven married Catholic priests in the United States).* It was an issue on which Basil had always taken a particularly broad-minded view. He once, for example, in his earliest days as Archbishop confided in his old friend the theologian Adrian Hastings – who left the Catholic priesthood in order to get married – that he shared his view that 'the vocation to the priesthood is one thing, the vocation to celibacy another'. It was a point on which he never wavered – which lent somehow a special meaning to his statement before ordaining four ex-Anglican married priests at Westminster Cathedral in November 1996: 'What we are doing today, though novel and extraordinary, has the blessing of God.'

---

* By the end of the 1980s, and before the General Synod's decision on women's ordination, some half-dozen married ex-Anglican clergy had been quietly ordained as Catholic priests in England. They included Peter Cornwell, like John Henry Newman, a former vicar of the University Church in Oxford.

Cynics were, of course, entitled to point out that it was also administratively convenient. Such was the shortfall in vocations, even in the 1990s, that the recruitment of some 200 former active Anglican clergy to the Catholic Church's ministry could hardly have been more helpfully timed. At first the policy was to place those who were married in non-parochial posts – as chaplains to prisons, hospitals, schools or similar institutions – but this approach was gradually eroded and several married former Anglican clergy are now Catholic parish priests in all but name, still being (rather absurdly) required to go under the title of 'administrators'.

That is a development which Basil himself would have welcomed, though the speed with which it has come about would probably have surprised him. As late as 1988 he could be found writing to one of the pre-women's-ordination Anglican married converts whom he eventually successfully 'placed' in America: 'As you know, it is my view that there is no problem about married priests but in the present pontificate it is unlikely that this cause will make much headway. It would be foolish to agitate now with the possible danger of prejudicing the position later on.'[*]

Clearly, he did not at that stage foresee how completely the position would be transformed as a direct result of the Anglican Church's decision to ordain women – though Basil himself would almost certainly have wished for the relaxation of the ban on married clergy to extend beyond the case of ex-Anglicans who had crossed over. The new dispensation was, of course, essentially discriminatory, and those Catholic clergy who had abandoned the priesthood[†] – and, indeed, endured the long and

---

[*] This was the advice he had also given to Adrian Hastings back in 1978 – though without success.

[†] Since *Humanae Vitae* in 1968 there were said in England alone to have been about 1,000 of them.

uncertain laicisation process – solely in order to marry were fully entitled to feel bitter about a new ecclesiastical order reflecting nothing so much as double standards.

It was an area in which Basil himself always behaved with great sensitivity. One of the more affecting pieces of personal correspondence he kept was with a gravely ill 78-year-old ex-Catholic priest who wrote to him saying that his heart's desire was to be allowed to celebrate Mass once more before he died. The Cardinal gave permission for him to do so – on condition that the service was a purely private one – and his reward lay in a letter from the ex-priest's wife describing how her husband had died a happy man.

Yet perhaps the most paradoxical aspect of the entire collision course with the Anglican Church over its decision to ordain women was that it happened to be an issue on which Basil himself appears to have held no deep or unshakeable convictions. When a monk at the Anglican Abbey of Nashdom wrote to him as early as 1978, seeking confirmation that the Cardinal's position fully reflected the traditional Catholic opposition to women's ministry he received a slightly nettled reply, which may well have surprised him:

Archbishop's House,
Westminster, SW1   6 April 1978

Dear Father,

I am not quite certain what you want from me. It is not entirely clear from your letter.

On the question of women priests there is a distinction to be made: my own personal opinion is that a) there is no theological argument either in favour or against women priests; b) the Roman Catholic depends, therefore, on the authority of the Church. As you will know, the Roman

Catholic Church is not in favour of women priests at the present time.

Yours devotedly,
Basil Hume

It cannot have been quite the ringing endorsement of the case for a perpetual all-male priesthood which the young Anglican Benedictine monk was obviously hoping to receive.

There is, indeed, additional – and even more public – evidence that Basil's position on the matter of women priests was far from being entirely entrenched. Only shortly after he sent that letter to the monk at Nashdom, he took part in a BBC World Service phone-in. This is the reply he gave to one American woman caller:

I accept the authority of my Church, which does not advocate the ordination of women to the priesthood. The answer given is 'This is not part of our tradition' – and that may be a good argument and that may be a bad argument. I personally, if the authorities of my Church agreed to the ordination of women, would have no problem about it. But I am a man under authority and I would not be in the Catholic Church if I did not accept that.

Again, hardly a full-throated assent to the kind of case that would have been expected by most of the Anglican converts who came over to the Catholic Church at least partly on the women priests' issue. However, even within his own Church, Basil was by no means alone in keeping an open mind on the subject. (His real quarrel with the Anglican authorities was not on the principle involved, but rather on the 'unilateral' way in which they had taken their decision, which, together with its timing, he thought not only unfortunate but inept.) It was, in fact, those within the

Roman Catholic Church sharing his own temperate views on the ordination of women who provided the kernel of opposition to any prospect of importing into their own Church an embattled array of hard-line, traditionalist Anglo-Catholics. When Bishop Crispian Hollis of Portsmouth declared, 'The Catholic Church is not a flag of convenience – it is not something you can change to just because it suits you', he was not, as it may have seemed to outsiders, making a conservative point: instead, he was speaking up on behalf of liberals who were apprehensive of the impact on their Church of the arrival of a large body of what, rightly or wrongly, were regarded as 'single issue converts'. They would, it was feared, turn the English Catholic Church into a far more reactionary body than it had been before.

Of course, in the end nothing like that happened – but that was because the promise of 'the conversion of England' never materialised either. Precise figures nearly always provoke disputes, but the best estimates would suggest that the final tally of priests (and many of these were already retired) who deserted the Church of England for the Church of Rome over the issue of women priests was nearer 400 than 500, while the number of lay converts fell well short of the once trumpeted 15,000. If the entire episode is remembered for anything it ought to be for the skill and tact – with just one lapse – that Basil brought to its handling; and even that lapse – the ill-judged remark in the interview he gave to the *Tablet* – did not take long to recede in people's memories.

In fact, across the chasm of a decade and more, it no longer looks certain that it was the reference to 'the conversion of England' that supplied the most arresting thing the Cardinal had to say in the course of that interview. In the context of his own personal history, just as interesting – and probably more revealing – was the confessional note on which he chose to start: 'I have always felt I was over-estimated. I don't feel a success.

Any bishop would want to pass on a vibrant, healthy happy Church to his successor. I am not doing that.'

Basil was never one of nature's optimists, but that bleak assessment of what he had failed to do in his first seventeen years as Archbishop of Westminster had an element of grim realism about it. It certainly bore a much greater resemblance to reality than did most of the exaggerated claims put forward by his critics as to what could have come to pass if only he had seized the chance presented to him for 'the conversion of England'. There is, it has to be said, no credibility – and very little plausibility either – to what are essentially romantic, right-wing arguments tied to the 'what might have been' school of history. Nor is there a shred of evidence to support the suggestion that Rome itself came to regret leaving matters so much in the Archbishop's hands.

The truth is that even Basil's own vision of 'a realignment of Christianity in England', as a direct consequence of the Anglican Church's change of heart on women priests, was never something at all likely to happen. His impatience with what he called 'lots of blocs' – meaning the various Protestant denominations – may have been of long-standing; but he can only have deceived himself if he momentarily believed that the decision over women's ordination would by itself prove sufficient of an inducement to persuade them all to shelter together under a single umbrella. Nor was there much immediate prospect of 'two blocs' as he put it – presumably meaning one Protestant and the other Catholic – emerging in their place. Moreover, his prophecy that such an outcome would 'bring us closer together' was hardly self-evident.

Yet all that, of course, was said very much in the heat of the crisis. When Basil came to look back on his role in it – and the way in which the ordination of women (with all its ramifications) was never allowed to develop into a direct confrontation between the two Churches – he was entitled to feel that in the most challenging circumstances possible he had kept the ecumenical flame alive. That in itself was no mean achievement – and one that would certainly not have lain within the reach of any of his eight predecessors in Archbishop's House.

XIII

THE VULNERABLE
FLANK

I F THERE WAS ONE AREA IN WHICH BASIL HAD EVERY REASON
to feel confident, it lay in the close supervision that any
bishop is expected to exercise over the church schools in his
diocese. The first monk ever to become Archbishop of
Westminster had, after all, been a schoolmaster for the first
dozen years of his clerical life and, although he had not been
(as was often later incorrectly stated) Headmaster of Ampleforth,
he had, as its Abbot for thirteen years, served as the Headmaster's
boss – together with his Council the effective equivalent of an
independent school's board of governors and its chairman rolled
into one.

It was, therefore, a wholly unpredictable twist of fate that the
most damaging reverse of Basil's archiepiscopal career should
have occurred in precisely the sphere in which he could claim
to possess the greatest weight of experience and expertise. To
be fair, this was not the result of any incompetent initiative on
his own part. The Conservative Government's Education Reform
Act of 1988 – part of the second wave of the Thatcher revolution – transformed the existing landscape by offering, under the
even then fashionable banner of 'choice', fresh opportunities of

self-determination to nearly all state secondary schools, including denominational ones. Whether by avowed political intent or as the result of an oversight on the part of the parliamentary draftsmen, the crucial 'opt-out' clause in the Bill – allowing schools of more than 300 pupils to apply to have control of their own budgets and, in effect, run their own affairs – applied just as much to 'voluntary aided' church schools as it did to those under the direct charge of a local education authority. Thus the status of being a 'grant maintained school' was as available to any secondary school founded (and until 1944 wholly funded in terms of its buildings) by the Catholic Church as it was to any institution paid for by the local ratepayers (generally represented by the county council, but in central London until the late 1980s by the Inner London Education Authority).

There was a clear anomaly here – not least in property rights over the buildings – and the Education Service of the Diocese of Westminster immediately went into action in defence of the historic claims of the faithful. Even as the Bill was going through Parliament, the Director of Education for the Westminster Archdiocese (a formidable woman graduate called Kathleen O'Gorman) was already heavily engaged in a lobbying campaign designed to remove Catholic schools from this particular enabling provision of the Bill. A contemporary circular letter sent out from the Education Service's headquarters and signed by Mrs O'Gorman reveals how seriously things were being taken even at that early stage:

> Many of you have already been able to arrange meetings for parents and governors, and the response has indicated the deep concern felt in the Catholic community at the threat contained in the Bill to the work of our schools. Thank you for your marvellous efforts.

The need to sustain activities is, however, acute. The Bill will shortly end its passage through the Standing Committee and return to the Commons for the Report Stage. Some amendments may emerge there. After that, it must be debated in the Lords. A list of Catholic members may be obtained from your area schools officer. Correspondence with them and others concerned for church schools, as well as with your own MP and directly with the Secretary of State, is extremely important.

This was a view clearly endorsed by Basil himself, for on three separate occasions meetings took place at Archbishop's House between the then Secretary of State for Education and Science, Kenneth Baker, and the Cardinal (who always took good care to be backed up by a powerful entourage of diocesan education officials). In his memoirs* Baker, at the time very much a rising star of the Government frontbench, leaves a vivid word picture of one of these encounters:

> I was conscious that I was not dealing merely with a local education authority, or merely a trade union, or even the British Cabinet, but rather with one of the great and enduring institutions of Western civilisation. The tall, stooping figure of its representative, Basil Hume, is well known. He conveys a sense of holiness, kindness and courtesy and it is not easy to argue with such a saintly man. But within that scarlet and purple apparition was the sinewy force of a prelate concerned with temporal as well as spiritual power.

Even given the politician's natural hyperbole in the last sentence, that evocative passage makes its point – for it was,

---

* Kenneth Baker, *The Turbulent Years: My Life in Politics*, Faber (1993), p. 218.

of course, the case that Basil saw himself as fighting for a principle. Church schools had always been regarded as an integral part of the Catholic worshipping community – indeed, it was for the sake of giving priority to the building of church schools that Cardinal Manning had deliberately held up the construction of Westminster Cathedral. Moreover, if one thing distinguished Catholic schools from their Anglican counterparts, it was the sense that a diocesan bishop's authority over them flowed not from any British institution but rather directly from the Pope in Rome and, therefore, indirectly, from God. With that as the background, it was always unlikely that there was going to be any meeting of minds between a secular emissary from Whitehall and the servant of a spiritual power. The negotiations between the Education Secretary and the Cardinal Archbishop broke down over the Government's refusal to exempt church schools from the new right of 'opt-out' contained in its Bill.

In itself, that plainly rated as a substantial defeat for the Cardinal and the British Catholic community. What, though, turned it into a disaster was a concurrent dispute that happened to be going on within the Westminster archdiocese itself. At least since the early 1980s, Basil had been planning that the six Catholic secondary schools in the Westminster central pastoral area should all give up their sixth forms so that a central sixth form college could be established with the widest possible range of subjects and specialities available to its pupils (who would mostly come from the existing six 'feeder' secondary schools). This was an educational innovation launched quite independently of the Government's proposed reintroduction of 'grant maintained' schools, but it inevitably became inextricably tangled up with it.

The sixth form college scheme had run into controversy right from the start. Two show-piece Catholic schools, The Oratory in West Brompton and The Cardinal Vaughan Memorial School in Kensington, had nailed their colours to the mast in outright opposition to the plan from the moment it was first floated by the Diocesan Education Service. Successful, self-confident institutions, they saw no reason why they should be required to sacrifice their respective sixth forms merely in order to benefit those attending weaker schools with under-subscribed sixth forms in the West London area.

There was, though, an important distinction between the two. By reason of its history, The Oratory was in much the stronger legal position. Founded in 1863 as an educational adjunct to the imposing, domed Oratory church on Brompton Road, it had never been legally accountable to the Archbishop of Westminster. Instead, its trusteeship was vested in the Fathers of the Oratory, and thus its supervision and guidance belonged to a Religious Order – an extension of the one that Newman had founded in Birmingham – and was not part of the normal educational chain-of-command within the diocese. This was the breast-plate that it successfully put on in order to exclude itself from the diocesan reorganisation scheme. As an act of what he saw as wilful disobedience, this had already caused considerable aggravation to Basil, who at one stage even prevailed upon a member of the Roman Curia (one Cardinal Baum) to send a letter to the Oratory Fathers designed to persuade them to put the wider needs of the diocese ahead of their own personal preferences – but all to no avail. In a considered reply that mixed deference with defiance in roughly equal proportions, the Fathers of the Oratory (through the skilful pen of their Provost) simply pointed out to Basil that, extensive as his writ might be, it did not apply to them. They would continue to run *their* school in the way that seemed to them to be right.

This was not so much a rebuff as a humiliation for Basil, and it may have had something to do with the unyielding mood in which he chose to approach the second stage of what was rapidly becoming both an emotive and a divisive conflict. The next target in the firing line was the 600-strong Cardinal Vaughan Memorial School, whose governors and parents had already made it abundantly clear that they wanted to retain their own sixth form and had no desire to co-operate in any educational reorganisation scheme that would involve their losing it. The final battle-lines in the controversy over The Cardinal Vaughan School had taken some time to draw up, but, by the time Kenneth Baker's new Act became part of the law of the land in July 1988, both sides were already in entrenched positions.

In fact, even before the Education Reform Act (1988) received the Royal Assent, the Archbishop had already removed two of the Cardinal Vaughan governors for failing to support him – and the angry response of the parents had been to vote by an overwhelming majority in favour of applying for opt-out status. That decision, however, could only be provisional for without a full quota of 'foundation governors' (who needed to be appointed by the Cardinal and his fellow diocesan trustees) no valid application could be made to become a grant maintained school under the terms of the Act – and it was this power of appointment that for months on end Basil refused to exercise, thereby stalling the Cardinal Vaughan parents' efforts to escape the net of the diocesan reorganisation plan.

It had not been an edifying spectacle on either side, but the loser in the public relations war was undeniably the Cardinal himself. He had a perfectly reasonable case to make in arguing that the Education Reform Act (1988) had never been intended as a means of enabling Catholic schools to free themselves from legitimate ecclesiastical authority, but neither that, nor his equally justifiable insistence that churches, unlike local authorities, could never simply walk away from schools that they had been responsible for bringing into being in the first place, cut any ice with the public. What popular opinion saw was a stubborn prelate adopting a dog-in-the-manager attitude – in effect, insisting that 'if I can't get my way, then you certainly won't get yours either'. It was not a permanently sustainable position and eventually (although not until Basil had unwisely intimated that he would be prepared to go to jail if the courts ruled against him) he and his advisers had the sense to see that they had no alternative but to back down.

The denouement came about in a rather unorthodox way. One of the governors whom Basil had sacked applied to the High Court for 'judicial review' and, although he failed at first instance, the Court of Appeal upheld his complaint. It also did more than that. It drew attention to a clause in the original Cardinal Vaughan trust deed that it clearly felt was lethal to the Cardinal's whole case. Most unusually – indeed probably uniquely for a Catholic secondary school in England and Wales – the trust deed establishing The Cardinal Vaughan School reserved to the governors specific powers. One of them laid down that the governors should 'have in their absolute management . . . the admission ages and attendances of scholars and generally all matters connected therewith'. Plainly, this could be said to include the governors' right to decide whether or not the school should run a sixth form. In the eyes of the Appeal Court this exceptional provision, laying out just how extensive the governors' powers were, undermined the archdiocese's entire position. This obviously applied not just to the action brought by the sacked governor but, more seriously, to the case that the Secretary of State for Education was threatening to bring. This would have required Basil and his fellow trustees to appoint new 'foundation governors' so that the application for grant maintained status could go ahead. It seems to have become the belated view of the Cardinal's legal advisers that he now had no hope of prevailing in such an action brought by the Secretary of State and, accordingly, the towel was thrown in virtually at the court room door. For Basil and the Westminster Diocesan Education Service it was undoubtedly a painful climb-down, but at least the last-minute decision in favour of cutting their losses left open the possibility of a clean end to the dispute, which was, in effect, what happened.

The Cardinal proceeded to the appointment of the necessary 'foundation governors'; The Cardinal Vaughan School successfully applied to be grant maintained; and a reduced but still substantial sixth form college went ahead on the site in St Charles Square, North Kensington, of what previously had been one of the diocese's less flourishing boys' secondary schools. Despite having lost its two main 'feeder' schools, the new sixth form college not only survived but actively prospered: St Charles in 1996 becoming what was then known as a 'beacon college' and one of the best (if not *the* best) further education institutions in London.

The whole episode had been a distinctly unhappy one, the blame for which in subsequent years tended to descend on the heads of the Cardinal's advisers. The question, though, still has to be asked as to how it was that Basil never sensed the danger or realised the unenviable nature of the position in which he had put himself. One answer, expressed even by some of those who were closest to him, is that he was often to be found at his most intransigent when he felt his will was being crossed or his wishes flouted. That kind of situation tended to bring out the autocrat in him, and those who tried to sound a warning note soon came to know the abbatial glare that could be called in aid whenever a dispute over one of his own decisions threatened. Yet it remains the lack of sensitivity to the vulnerability of his own position which provides the most puzzling aspect of the whole affair. How did he, for example, not foresee that his critics would be bound to raise the example of Ampleforth with him? What plausible answer could there be to the pointed question as to how his own alma mater would have felt if it suddenly discovered that it was to lose its own sixth form through some reorganisation scheme devised by the local diocesan, the Bishop of Middlesbrough? Certainly, the obvious riposte that Ampleforth, in its capacity as an independent, fee-paying school, fell into an entirely different category could hardly have been anything but self-destructive. For, even if defensively deployed, it was bound to lead to the far more damaging charge that, even in terms of Catholic education, there were two separate dispensations for parents – one for the rich and the other for the poor.*

Nor was the Archbishop entirely sure-footed in the tactics he chose to adopt. In public life it rarely does to huff and puff over the consequences of possible outcomes, especially when those outcomes are not in the end pursued. When Basil issued his veiled warning that it might well be that he would prefer to go to prison rather than submit to an adverse judgment of the courts, he merely raised the temperature of the debate without improving his own chances of winning it. There was never, in fact, much chance of his prevailing – least of all in the court of public opinion. A dispute which the press insisted on presenting as a conflict between 'parent power' on the one hand and the exercise of an episcopal veto on the other was predetermined in its likely result from the beginning. In his earlier, less authoritarian days Basil would surely have realised this.

Probably the best that can be said is that, once the matter was legally decided, Basil accepted his defeat with good grace. Since she had been so actively involved, it was probably inevitable that

---

* This point was pursued with some savagery by Piers Paul Read in an article in the *Spectator* of 3 June 1989 entitled 'Hume the Housemaster'.

within a year or two Mrs O'Gorman should have been forced out of her post as Director of the Diocesan Education Service (though the Cardinal insisted that she be retained as a 'personal consultant' to him). The attempts at reconciliation, however, went well beyond that. In particular, in addition to giving every possible encouragement to the new St Charles Sixth Form College, great efforts were made to rebuild bridges with The Cardinal Vaughan School – a process made easier by the notable magnanimity displayed by the clear victor in the contest. The individual who had led the campaign in defence of the school's sixth form was its Headmaster Tony Pellegrini (fifteen years later himself to be ordained as a Catholic priest). When Basil intimated that he would be prepared to let bygones be bygones and celebrate Mass for the school on its Founders' Day in 1991, he discovered to his delight that he was met more than halfway. This was the letter he received from the headmaster, even before the event took place:

Please forgive me for not writing sooner to thank you very sincerely for agreeing to celebrate Mass for the school on Founders' Day, 20 September 1991, at 2 p.m. We, all of us, greatly appreciate your kindness.

Would that one could put the clock back and undo the mistakes and sins of the past! I very greatly regret the distress that we caused you and I shall always do so. Given that I have also always thought of the Vaughan – perhaps foolishly – as one of the flagship schools in the diocese, desperately concerned to *teach* the faith and anxious to preserve valuable traditions, I am struck time and again by the irony that it should have been the Vaughan of all schools that should have caused you so much unhappiness . . .

It would have been difficult to put things more generously than that, and Basil's response to so disarming an act of contrition on the part of the man who had been for a year and more his principal antagonist was to scribble in his old schoolmaster's red ball-point pen on the top of the letter the single comment: 'Answered by giving kiss of peace at Mass on 20 September 1991.'*

Alas, not all the social policy challenges of the late twentieth century could be solved as easily and gracefully as that. There were other areas where Basil fought alone – and frequently with an equal lack of success. One of them involved his participation in the whole national debate over bio-ethics. It is easy today to overlook how rapid scientific progress in this field has been: the first IVF baby was not born until 1978, and until then society had had its hands full grappling with the ethical dilemmas provoked by artificial insemination (whether by husband or by donor).

These experiments, involving the use of embryos, had been going on, principally at a laboratory near Cambridge, since the mid-1970s, but it was not until Patrick Steptoe and Robert Edwards announced the creation of the first test-tube baby in July 1978 that the world sat up and took notice. Even then, there was a marked reluctance on the part of officialdom to rush to judgment. The appointment of a Whitehall Committee of Inquiry into Human Fertilisation and Embryology was not made until July 1982 and the Warnock Committee – as it came to be known after the name of its chairman, Dame Mary Warnock, then Mistress of Girton – did not publish its report until two years after that. So it seems safe to date Basil's

---

* Six years later, at the Vaughan's annual prizegiving in February 1997, Basil went a good deal further than that. He opened his speech with the announcement: 'Headmaster, you and I have had our differences in the past. I want to say that you were for the most part right and I was wrong.'

preoccupation with the ethical issues involved* to around that date.

No one, certainly none of the sixteen members of the committee (who anyway were divided 13–3 in favour of regarding experimentation on human embryos as permissible), was pretending that such moral questions were anything but complex – but this had the effect of making those who immediately came forward with simple, clearcut solutions look somewhat suspect. Unfortunately, one of these, as soon as the report was published, was Basil himself. He lost no time in seeking to make the position of the Church clear. Catholics, he announced, could not accept the majority Warnock recommendation that experimentations on human embryos should be allowed up to a time limit of fourteen days; nor could they acquiesce in the destruction of human embryos after that. In fact, the only two points at which the Church found itself in agreement with the Warnock Committee were over its proposals that surrogate motherhood agencies should be banned and that a licensing body should be established to control *in vitro* fertilisation.

Given the Catholic Church's traditional outlook on related topics such as artificial contraception, there was nothing perhaps too surprising about that – but what did tend to take people (including members of the Thatcher Government) by surprise was the ardour and enthusiasm with which Basil threw himself into the anti-Warnock parliamentary campaign. It so happened that in November 1984 Enoch Powell, then the Ulster Unionist MP for South Down, had seen his name come sufficiently high (fifth) in the annual ballot for Private Members' Bills for him

---

* Basil never felt entirely at ease with these. Monsignor Jim Curry, his last private secretary, recalls how, whenever a broadcast discussion or press conference on human reproduction threatened, the Archbishop would prepare himself for it by watching for the umpteenth time a TV cassette of an early Channel Four programme entitled *Where I Came From*.

to have a reasonable chance of getting any measure that he selected passed. To the consternation of the Government – who had hoped for a period of calm reflection to follow the publication of the Warnock Report – Powell at once announced that he would be introducing what he called the Unborn Children (Protection) Bill. Its emotive title said it all: designed to ban experiments on human embryos produced by *in vitro* fertilisation, it was deliberately aimed at pre-empting the whole Warnock debate. For Powell, as he made clear in a speech on the Second Reading, his stand was motivated not so much by religious principle (though he was a devout High Anglican) as by moral distaste. On first reading through the Warnock Report he had, he explained, undergone 'a sense of revulsion, deep and instinctive, towards the proposition that a thing, however it may be defined, of which the sole purpose or object is that it may be a human life, should be subjected to experiment to its destruction'.

It may have been an essentially aesthetic appeal, clothed in typical logician's language, but there was probably very little in the case that Powell made in the Commons that afternoon with which Basil would have disagreed. That was just as well – for on the very eve of the debate he had taken the unusual step of writing to every single one of the 650 Members of Parliament, asking them to give their support to the measure that the MP for South Down was hoping to get onto the Statute Book.

For a period it looked as if Basil's assistance had been of material help: on its Second Reading Powell's Private Member's Bill was carried by the decisive margin of 238 votes to 66. Eventually, however, as often happens with such backbench initiatives, Powell's Commons opponents outwitted him and his Bill was 'talked out', though not before it had reached its Report Stage. Eventually, in 1990, the Government introduced its own Human Fertilisation and Embryology Bill, broadly on the lines of the Warnock Report (down to and including the fourteen-day cut-off period for experiments on embryos), and, in protesting against it, the Cardinal found himself – in perhaps a more emphatic way than he may have foreseen – identified not so much with the quiet confidence of a 'silent majority' as with the noisiness of a vocal, if defeated, minority.

He certainly made no bones about what he felt to be the significance of what had been a very public defeat. Once the Government had got its own proposals through – passed in the same week in April 1990 as the Commons also approved both some widening and some narrowing amendments to David Steel's Abortion Act of 1967 – the Cardinal gave full vent to his sense of outrage and despair. Speaking on behalf of the Bishops' Conference, which happened to be meeting that week in Westminster, he roundly denounced what Parliament had done. Calling both decisions 'appalling', he went on to declare: 'What has emerged with stark clarity is the lack of a moral foundation for the formation of public policy in this most crucial area, that of human life and death.'

It is, of course, often the duty of a religious leader to swim against the tide – and the fact that a cause fails to prevail does not necessarily mean that it is wrong. The danger, though, for Basil was that, at least in this particular realm of public policy, he all too frequently appeared as being on the negative, restrictive side of the argument. This certainly became the popular perception as stem cell research progressed by leaps and bounds, and he and the Catholic Church (unlike, say, Nancy Reagan seeking a remedy for Alzheimer's) remained obstinately opposed to it. Much the same went for euthanasia where, as the public mood softened at least in the face of what came to be known as 'mercy killings', the Catholic Church stayed totally uncompromising in its condemnation of any death brought about, for whatever reasons of compassion, by another person.

Euthanasia was one area in which Basil never felt shy of taking the war into the enemy camp. In November 1997 he contributed a particularly trenchant article to *The Times*[*] in which he warned against what he took to be a dangerous drift of public opinion on the subject:

> Contemporary morality tends to elevate the right to choose above every other value. It finds offensive the traditional teaching on the sanctity of human life which has been part of common morality in Western societies. This outlook is having many profound effects. It has desensitised many people to the evil of abortion. It has also predisposed many to support euthanasia.
>
> Euthanasia aims at ending a life judged to be no longer worth living, either because of suffering or because of presumed 'poor' quality. The aim is accomplished either by a direct action, such as administering a lethal injection, or by depriving a person of medical treatment or of ordinary care in order to bring about death. An essential defining characteristic of euthanasia is the intention to end life, that is to kill.

As that short extract makes clear, Basil was no slouch when it came to polemical controversy – and to that extent the traditional impression of an essentially meek and mild public figure probably needs to be modified. But why did he not enjoy more success in fighting against what he rightly took to be the spirit of the age? One answer has to be that by temperament and instinct he was always a man who shrank from the vulgar but often effective populist gesture. When, for example, his brother Cardinal in Scotland, Thomas Winning, dramatically announced

---

[*] 'The Death of Trust', *The Times*, 27 November 1997.

just before the 1997 general election that his archdiocese of Glasgow would provide financial assistance to any woman 'irrespective of age, creed or colour' wishing to avoid having to undergo an abortion, Basil's reaction as delivered in public was noticeably low-key. It was, he told *The Times*, 'a good lead and one we should all consider carefully' – a classic example, as Winning instantly recognised ('What the hell does he mean by that?' he is reported to have asked) of someone seeking to damn with faint praise. In private Basil certainly worried about the expense that might prove to be involved if such a scheme were to be adopted nationally by the Catholic Church; but the real truth was that Winning's was not the kind of populist initiative that he could ever have imitated, since it simply did not represent his style. (In fact, he was heard by his private secretary, Jim Curry, to complain at the time that the 'cash for babies' policy that Winning was announcing with such a public flourish in Glasgow already went on in private in the archdiocese of Westminster, thanks to the devoted but discreet work of the Catholic Children's Society.)

There was perhaps another reason why even on abortion Basil never made much headway with either official or even popular opinion. The most vulnerable part of the Catholic Church's anti-abortion case is generally thought to be found in the attitude it takes towards a pregnancy brought about by rape – and even here Basil personally upheld the full rigour of Catholic doctrine. When a young woman who had been gang-raped in India was sent to see him by her well-meaning parents, in order to help her to recover from the ordeal, all went well until at the end of their talk she presumed to ask what the Cardinal would have advised if she had, in fact, turned out to be pregnant. 'Oh, my dear,' she found herself, almost unbelievingly, being told, 'in that case I should have had to say to you that you *must* have the baby.' With that one remark, according to her own account, any good that the rest of their meeting had done dissolved into thin air.

It was not Basil's fault but, especially in the field of social policy, the dice were heavily loaded against him, if only because by the end of the twentieth century people in Britain generally had ceased to believe in hard-and-fast rules. It was not just religious observance that had been relegated to the periphery of life; so also had the common acceptance of moral absolutes. In 1990, for example, according to one survey, 35 per cent of the population thought there were always clear guidelines as to what was right and what was wrong. Ten years later that figure had shrunk to 20 per cent, with 75 per cent of the public actually believing in the exact opposite – that there can never be universal standards as to what is right or wrong because such judgments must always depend on circumstances.*

This flexibility in public opinion was hardly fertile soil on which to seek to build a barrier against what became known as 'situation ethics'. Nor was Basil, or the Catholic Church, much helped by the example set by those who in the sphere of politics were just beginning to emerge in high places. Here Tony Blair, in particular, proved a great disappointment. Although, unlike Cardinal Winning, Basil never attacked the new Labour leader for claiming to be a personal opponent of abortion while supporting it with his vote in the Commons, he did – once Blair had become Prime Minister – feel compelled to administer a gentle rebuke. While appearing on GMTV's early morning programme a few months after Labour's landslide victory in 1997, this is what the Cardinal rather unusually had to say:

* 'The Soul of Britain' by Gordon Heald, the *Tablet*, 3 June 2000. The survey was undertaken by Opinion Research Business and formed the subject of nine BBC1 Sunday night programmes starting on 4 June 2000.

My message to Tony Blair would be this. You are an honest man and you see things clearly. I would have thought that you should give leadership within your party and try to convince them that abortion is wrong and that we ought, as a nation, to do something about it.

It was perhaps more of a reproach than a reprimand, and to those accustomed to the street-fighter ways of Basil's opposite number in Scotland, Cardinal Thomas Winning, it necessarily sounded rather namby-pamby toff's talk. But then it was never Basil's habit to seek confrontation and, as a mere matter of good manners, he, no doubt, recalled that in a personal note sent to him the previous October Blair had actually gone out of his way to praise the English and Welsh Bishops' pre-election statement *The Common Good*. (The cynical were probably entitled to point out that Labour's leader may well have done that precisely because it gave the appearance of soft-pedalling on the abortion issue, calling abortion on demand 'one of the greatest scandals of our time' but not going on to suggest that a candidate's attitude towards it should provide a litmus test for how a loyal Catholic should vote.)

Interestingly, Basil personally had not been too happy with *The Common Good*, believing that it would be viewed as altogether too much of a blanket endorsement of the aims and objectives of New Labour. His own relationship with Tony Blair before the 1997 election had been slightly complicated by the remonstrance he had felt compelled to deliver to the young Leader of the Opposition, telling him that he really must desist from taking Communion when he accompanied his wife and family to Sunday Mass at their local church of St Joan of Arc in Highbury, north London. (Blair himself was not a Catholic and the rules made by Rome on Inter-Communion were strict and clear: an Anglican or other recognised Christian might receive the Sacrament in a

Catholic church if no other religious option were available, but otherwise should participate in Holy Communion only according to the rites of his own denomination.*)

Apart, however, from that one spat – and the hovering in the background of such potentially contentious issues as genetics or (as many Catholics feared) eugenics – the relationship between Archbishop's House and the new Prime Minister in No 10 tended to be cordial, if not all that close. There is some evidence that Tony Blair (the fourth Prime Minister Basil had seen during the course of his already 21-year reign) toyed early on in his first term with the idea of reviving the proposal – originally made by two of his predecessors – that the Archbishop of Westminster should sit in the House of Lords. However, even though the inducement seems to have been added on this occasion that such an appointment could rank as that of a 'Lord Spiritual' rather than that of a 'Lord Temporal', Basil remained obdurately against it. That was probably only sensible, for membership of the House of Lords could only have propelled him further into the cockpit of secular controversy, something he never really relished, with every likelihood of his being expected to pronounce there upon such matters as Section 28, the age of consent, the sex offenders' register or whatever happened to be the fashionable, topical controversy of the moment.

If Basil needed to be persuaded of the fact that the role of being a national church was not necessarily an enviable one, he only had to look at the sad record of the Church of England throughout the 1980s and the 1990s. All too often – through debates in the General Synod and the occasional oratorical

---

* These rules were themselves toughened up by Pope John Paul II in April 2003 when, in the fourteenth encyclical of his papacy, he registered his displeasure at the practice. Strangely, however, when Tony Blair had visited the Vatican two months earlier, he was allowed to receive Communion in the Pope's own private chapel.

exertions of bishops in the House of Lords – the Established Church succeeded in giving the impression that it was obsessed with only one subject, sex. At least, through not having any equivalent body to the General Synod, and also through lacking any clerical representation in the House of Lords at Westminster, the Catholic Church avoided that fate. Moreover, Basil himself generally followed a policy of keeping his powder dry – intervening even in the field of faith and morals only when a film such as Martin Scorsese's *The Last Temptation of Christ* caused genuine offence (and then merely by advising the faithful to stay away), or by making a reasoned protest when a politician such as Neil Kinnock allowed his tongue to run away with him as when he described Margaret Thatcher as 'the immaculate misconception'. (Kinnock promptly expressed his regret if his choice of phrase had seemed insensitive.) Basil never aspired to join the ranks of the rent-a-quote Anglican bishops or archdeacons, and one reason why his public comments tended to have greater impact than those of many Anglican dignitaries was because he rationed them so carefully.

There was one area, of course, where he could never duck out – and that was in the face of misbehaviour by priests or even bishops within the Roman Catholic Church. On the whole Basil here was fortunate, there being no scandals during his watch over the English Church comparable to those of Bishop Roddy Wright in Scotland or even of Eamonn Casey, the former Bishop of Galway (and one-time chairman of Shelter) in Ireland. However, there was one case involving a well-known London priest that caused him considerable distress. Father Michael Hollings, whose name had originally been floated as a possible rival to his own for the archbishopric of Westminster,* had been

---

* See page 83. In 1976 Father Hollings was running the multi-ethnic parish of St Anselm's, Southall.

since 1977 parish priest of St Mary of the Angels, Bayswater (and before that had had a varied career as a decorated wartime Guards officer, Catholic chaplain to Oxford University and religious adviser to Thames Television). The truth, however, was that he and Basil had never really got on – indeed, it had fallen to the Archbishop to censure Hollings in 1983 when the latter agreed to hold a service of blessing following the divorcee David Frost's registry office wedding to Lady Carina Fitzalan-Howard, daughter of the Duke of Norfolk.

Always more radical than his Metropolitan, Hollings had never been one for rules and his own highly successful parish was run on far from traditional lines (with even the presbytery operating as an 'open door' refuge for down-and-outs). Yet while there may not have been much natural warmth between them, each respected the other's gifts – Basil, for example, despite an initial personal interest,* had long been content to leave it to Hollings to be the visible Catholic presence in the organisation of the annual Notting Hill Carnival. There could hardly, therefore, have been a graver blow than that which fell on 3 September 1995, when the *News of the World* sought to 'out' this particularly high-profile priest as a paedophile, if not a pederast.

The paper's evidence was flimsy – a statement from a 42-year-old man named John alleging that twenty-five years earlier Father Hollings had attempted to kiss and fondle him when he had been placed in his temporary care by a Southall probation officer. The *News of the World* had, however, managed to arrange some sort of confrontation between the accuser and the accused – and it was in these circumstances that the saintly, if also slightly innocent, Michael Hollings made it possible for the newspaper

---

* In 1977, his second year at Archbishop's House, and before Michael Hollings had settled in at Bayswater, Basil had made three incognito visits to the Notting Hill Carnival as well as laying on a Caribbean Mass in Westminster Cathedral.

to print the story by allegedly asking the now nearly middle-aged John to forgive him. Still, as clerical 'abuse' stories go, it did not add up to much and, but for one development, the *News of the World*'s contrived, grubby story would probably have died the death the Sunday it was published and never been taken any further.

But that development – a whole column in the following Friday's *Daily Telegraph* devoted to the dilemmas always involved for bishops in abuse cases – changed everything. Written by the paper's respected religious columnist, Clifford Longley, it was a measured and balanced piece of work, but, whether with the connivance of the Archbishop or not, the mere fact of its publication made it impossible for Basil not to act. A scandal sheet allegation was one thing: a reflective essay in a quality newspaper on the problems that such cases would always pose for the church authorities inevitably promoted the whole original attempted exposé to a sophisticated and more serious level.

Before the week was out, Hollings had abruptly left his presbytery in Bayswater, an announcement had been made by Archbishop's House that he was on 'administrative leave', and for the next six months his parishioners had not the slightest idea what had happened to their parish priest. (It later transpired that for at least part of the time he had found refuge at Arundel Castle as the guest of the Duke of Norfolk.) Basil himself had no direct personal contact with the priest he had been responsible for, in effect, placing under suspension, and ever afterwards greatly regretted it. However, that was not his fault: on the advice of his lawyers Father Hollings resolutely refused to speak to him – an unhappy situation that perhaps says something about the distance that had always existed between them.

Things were eventually to have a more cheerful outcome.

On 18 February 1996 the Cardinal arrived at St Mary of the Angels, just off Westbourne Grove, to celebrate Mass and before the service announced to the congregation that, as a consequence of the police having decided that there was no basis for any action to be taken, their parish priest would be returning to them 'with immediate effect'. His statement was loudly applauded, and only afterwards did some of the faithful begin to think it odd that Father Hollings himself had not been there to share in what was described by the Cardinal as 'a very happy day' (even if the use of that phrase did provoke a muttered 'No thanks to you, Your Eminence' from one aggrieved member of the congregation). The sad truth was that Hollings preferred not to be present, believing that the whole matter had been badly mishandled from the start and being in no mood for reconciliation with Basil. He also, of course, was aware that he had less than a year still to serve, being due to retire on his seventy-fifth birthday in December 1996. His health having given way (partly as a result of his ordeal), he barely made it till then. He died on 21 February 1997, almost the first anniversary to the day of his restoration to office at the hands of the Cardinal.

If this was an example of pastoral failure on Basil's part, at least it was a rare one. Generally he had the reputation of being a caring, compassionate pastor while being by no means unworldly (even as Abbot of Ampleforth he arranged for the monks there to have at their disposal the services of a sympathetic, Catholic psychiatrist who would visit the monastery two or three times a year). He enjoyed, too, the reputation within the Westminster archdiocese of being understanding of the difficulties experienced by homosexual Catholics, having written in 1992 and published in 1993 a document entitled 'Some Observations on the Catholic Church's Teaching Concerning Homosexual People'.

This document had a curious history. It came into being as a direct result of Basil's horror at a circular letter discreetly distributed – it apparently went out only to American and Italian bishops – by Cardinal Ratzinger's Congregation for the Doctrine of the Faith in June 1992. Specifically devoted to what turned out to be a highly incendiary issue, it was (slightly clumsily) entitled 'Some Considerations Concerning the Response to Legislative Proposals on the Non-Discrimination of Homosexual Persons'. Maybe the clumsiness was deliberate for, whatever might be true of the packaging, the content turned out to be dynamite. As the *Daily Telegraph* was the first to spot,* the core message of this Vatican document was that there existed areas where legal discrimination against homosexuals was not only prudent but fully justified as well. The spheres cited included adoption, teaching, military service and even the rights of landlords to select as tenants only those of whose way of life they approved. To add insult to injury, all Catholics simply of 'homosexual inclinations' found themselves roundly condemned as suffering from 'an objective disorder' (a technical term in Catholic moral theology, but no less hurtful for that).

It says a good deal for Basil's sense of fairness that his immediate resolve was that he should attempt to put together a considered response to the Vatican's own peculiarly strait-laced document. It took him over a year to do so, but by the autumn of 1993 he had completed it, and the letter he prepared to send accompanying it to Cardinal Ratzinger in Rome probably reveals more of his genuine anger than does the necessarily more measured language of what he publicly wrote arguing the case for notably more generous guidelines:

---

* *Daily Telegraph*, 24 July 1992: news story by Damian Thompson.

Archbishop's House,   25 September 1992
London SW1

Your Eminence,

I am sending you a copy of my reflections on the Church's teaching on homosexual persons The reason why I have had to prepare this document was because of the considerable distress, anger and misunderstanding which the document emanating recently from your Congregation has caused. I note that the document to which I am referring, entitled 'Some Considerations Concerning the Response to Legislative Proposals on the Non-Discrimination of Homosexual Persons' was not signed nor was it clear initially with what authority it had been issued.

I should emphasise that great distress has been caused by this latest document, and not only to homosexuals. Moreover, there are many homosexuals who would never think of acting in a militant manner who feel that the Church has abandoned them . . .

You will recall, I am sure, that on the occasion of my *Ad Limina* visit last March I stated when visiting your Congregation that I accepted fully the Church's teaching on the matter of homosexuality, but that I regretted the tone of the Congregation's Letter to the bishops of 1986.

This is a very difficult matter and I am sure you will be the first to appreciate and understand the very delicate pastoral situation in which bishops find themselves both as defenders of the faith and as shepherds of those who stray. We need your support.

The paper I am now sending you I have prepared after much thought and not without anxiety, concerned for those homosexuals who feel completely rejected by the Church and, therefore, by God.

I do appreciate that Your Eminence has a very difficult task and I would not wish to add to your burdens. But I do think we need to find a way of expressing the Church's teaching in a manner that is personally sensitive, and in a way that does not threaten the human dignity of homosexuals.

If it ever did reach the Vatican (the copy left in a file in the Westminster Diocesan Archives is marked in red ink 'Draft'), it can hardly have been the kind of letter that Cardinal Ratzinger was used to receiving – but then neither was the document that accompanied it. True, Basil at no point departed from the Church's teaching in condemning homosexual genital acts, but he was writing in a context of the Church being equally disapproving of heterosexual genital acts outside marriage. His aim throughout seems, in fact, to have been to drive home the message that, whatever may have been the case in the past, the Church no longer had any wish to differentiate between persons of homosexual or heterosexual inclination; in its eyes both were created in the image of God and, as such, were entitled to be regarded as heirs to eternal life.

For its time, that was a revolutionary attitude, and not one that would necessarily have been shared by all the English Catholic laity (let alone by such a stern Roman traditionalist as Cardinal Ratzinger). But it was a subject on which Basil had thought long and hard – and not without himself being the victim down the years of some militant tactics on the part of gay extremists. Hardly, for example, had he first published his own document (it was twice reissued, in 1995 and 1997) than an attempt was made to 'out' him on the BBC Radio Four programme, *The Moral Maze*. The circumstances appear to have been a bit confused but the allegation – at least according to the *Daily Telegraph* – was that the Cardinal had found his own name linked with what was called 'the disagreeable process of outing'. The matter was taken sufficiently seriously for the Catholic Media Office to issue a statement saying slightly pompously: 'This would appear to follow a pattern of recent statements about Anglican clergy and others. People should be very wary of believing such irresponsible and groundless insinuations.' Perhaps more to the point, Basil was the recipient of a grovelling letter of apology from the BBC's head of religious broadcasting (under whose aegis *The Moral Maze* goes out) expressing his personal regret for 'the considerable hurt and embarrassment' he must have been caused.

That was certainly more than he ever got from his next tormentor, an Australian gay activist called Nicholas Holloway who, having referred to himself in advance as 'an openly, publicly, actively homosexual person' – and wearing a rainbow sash as a badge of identity – challenged the Cardinal on 29 May 1997, the feast of Corpus Christi, to give him Communion at the altar rail of Westminster Cathedral. Forewarned, and feeling that the Sacrament was being exploited for publicity purposes, Basil offered Holloway a blessing instead and suggested that they had a talk. Such courteous conduct was not, however, enough to prevent the row from rumbling on long after its precipitator had returned to Australia. At least, however, on this occasion Basil got the support of the Roman Catholic caucus of the Gay and Lesbian Christian Movement, who appear to have looked upon the entire Holloway initiative as a stunt-too-far.

What was remarkable was the degree of understanding that Basil found he could count on from within such organisations as Stonewall, Quest* and, to some extent, from the militants enrolled in Peter Tatchell's organisation, OutRage. They must

---

* Basil, did, however, have a subsequent quarrel with Quest after insisting that a listing for it be removed from the official *Catholic Directory*.

presumably have recognised in him a figure who was well ahead of his time* – it was, after all, only a decade earlier, at the beginning of the 1980s, that even so liberal a churchman as Robert Runcie had publicly compared the lot of homosexuals with that of 'the handicapped'. Basil never made that sort of patronising mistake and, what is more, he remained remarkably steady on parade. When, for example, the bomb attack took place on the Admiral Duncan gay pub in Soho in April 1999, the Cardinal (though already mortally ill) was forthright on the BBC's *Today* programme in his denunciation of it as being typical of all vicious campaigns waged against minorities.

There were, of course, many Catholics who disagreed – seeing such episodes as equating more with the wrath of God – but this sort of homophobe correspondent tended to get particularly short shrift from Archbishop's House. Where Basil's patience never failed him was in dealing with those who wrote to tell him of the difficulties they experienced in trying to reconcile traditional Catholic teaching about homosexuality with the way they had been forced to lead their own lives. A typical letter sent out in September 1994, more than a year after he had completed his own riposte to Cardinal Ratzinger, read like this:

> Thank you for your letter. I do appreciate your sadness. It is true that documents that come out from the Vatican are not always couched in sympathetic language, even though the writers themselves may be persons full of understanding and compassion.
>
> I have tried to express the Church's thoughts on the matter of homosexuality. I am sending you a copy. If you wish to

---

* In a press release in 1993 Peter Tatchell hailed Basil's 'commitment to homosexual human rights' as representing 'an important first step in reversing centuries of Catholic homophobia'.

speak further on the matter, then perhaps we can arrange to meet. That would not really be possible until about November as I have several absences between now and then. But I would like to think that you will find the enclosed helpful.

Was Basil's attitude shaped at all by his awareness that some of the anxieties and worries individual lay Catholics brought to him must, on the law of averages alone, have been shared by a proportion of the 500 parochial clergy of his own archdiocese? Curiously, at least in the twenty-three years he spent in charge of it, the Westminster archdiocese was never much affected by homosexual scandal – though the subsequent history of abuses originating from that period has not been wholly reassuring. Of course, the Catholic Church did not then have in place the 'fail-safe system' that it was to acquire later at the hands of Lord Nolan – not that that (as lay Catholics in Kentish Town can bear witness) was to prove wholly effective.

It was not a matter on which Basil himself ever took much of a public lead, but then that was seldom his way. After he died, his old friend Adrian Hastings revealed how, when in 1976 he had gone to see him at Archbishop's House, they had fallen to talking about what his approach in pastoral terms ought to be towards homosexual priests. To his relief, Hastings found what the new Archbishop had to say 'quite surprisingly radical' and was taken aback when, virtually in the next breath, he found himself being warned that, if any word of what had just been said ever got out into the public domain, 'he would simply deny it'. While admitting that 'at the time this rather shocked me', Hastings went on to add that he later came to reflect that it illustrated rather well 'the difference Basil felt appropriate between public teaching and personal direction'.*

---

* 'Cardinal Basil Hume' by Adrian Hastings in *Priests & People*, June 2000.

The priests of the Westminster archdiocese must over seventeen years have had sufficient experience of Basil in the latter role not to have had to adjust too radically when, thanks largely to the insensitivity of Cardinal Ratzinger, their own Archbishop finally in 1993 felt confident enough to move from the personal guidance to the public teaching role. It was not a manoeuvre he managed to pull off on all issues, but on the question of the Christian attitude towards homosexuality Basil had the consolation of knowing that, at least in England, this was one vulnerable flank that he had successfully turned.

XIV

THE ROYAL CONNECTION

IT WAS ONLY A WEEK AFTER HE HAD BEEN INSTALLED AS Archbishop in March 1976 that Basil found himself, for the first time, the recipient of royal hospitality. He was bidden, or rather commanded by the Master of the Household, to 'dine and sleep' at Windsor Castle on Thursday 1 April – a rather intimidating invitation for April Fool's day, but still one that would have meant a great deal to so keen a royalist as the new Archbishop of Westminster. It also, as he would have been only too aware, marked a significant change in what had always been a slightly reserved and guarded attitude on the part of the Crown towards its Catholic subjects.

To find evidence for that, it is not necessary to go back to the days of Queen Anne, the Hanoverians or even Queen Victoria. As late as 1935 there had been a highly revealing episode. In May of that year Arthur Hinsley, the then freshly appointed Archbishop of Westminster in succession to Cardinal Bourne, attempted to present a Loyal Address to the Queen's grandfather, King George V, on the occasion of his Silver Jubilee. The message of greeting and congratulations, sent on behalf of the entire Catholic community of England and Wales, never officially reached its destination. Instead, it was stamped 'Unreceived' and briskly returned to Archbishop's House by the Home Office, which, by convention, acted as the Palace's agent in any matters involving church–state affairs.

Undeterred – and displaying a Christian capacity for turning the other cheek – Hinsley tried again. Writing this time direct to the King at Buckingham Palace, he spelt out politely but pointedly what he and his episcopal colleagues felt their dilemma to be:

> I and my brother Archbishops and Bishops are much concerned lest You should think that they and their people are not truly loyal to Your Majesty as their King for the reason that You did not receive an Address from them when You celebrated Your Jubilee. We beg to say that we sent a Loyal Address to Your Majesty on that occasion but we understand that, for some technical reasons, the Home Office would not allow this Address to be presented to You. May Your Majesty be pleased to accept our most sincere feelings of loyalty and devotion, and an assurance of our fervent prayers at all times.

That, one might have thought, represented a tactful and resourceful way around whatever the 'technical reasons' might have been that had prevented the monarch (presumably on the official advice of the Home Office) from accepting the original, more formal Address. However, to believe that would be badly to underestimate the traditionalism of the Crown and the sheer obstinacy and obduracy of its bureaucratic advisers in this area. For the second time, the Archbishop's felicitations were returned to him, accompanied on this occasion by a distinctly sniffy note signed by a junior Home Office functionary.*

All that – as Basil perhaps wryly recalled as he took his place at the long royal dining table – had happened only forty-one years earlier. So something had clearly changed. He can hardly have believed that he had been asked to dine and sleep purely on the strength of his own character and charm – any more than had the other guests (who included such heavyweight luminaries as the Chairman of the BBC, a retired Chief of the Defence Staff and a former Prime Minister of Canada). Like most social engagements in the royal calendar, this was essentially a representational occasion, and in breaking with tradition and treating the Archbishop of Westminster just as if he were the Moderator of the General Assembly of the Church of Scotland or even the Archbishop of Canterbury, the Palace was quite consciously signalling what it hoped would be – despite the Act of Settlement, the Royal Marriages Acts and all the other heirlooms of history – an entirely new era in the relationship between the Catholic Church and the House of Windsor.

It had been initiated, of course, well before Basil arrived at Westminster. The Queen had been granted an audience with Pope Pius XII in the Vatican while she was still Princess Elizabeth and, a decade later, in 1961, while on a State Visit to Italy, she had been received by John XXIII. (Her father, King George VI, by contrast, never visited the Vatican once.) There had been sounds of a certain amount of ice-breaking at home, too. Basil's first duty in Westminster Cathedral, even before his installation, was, as we have seen,† to attend the fund-raising

---

* According to a contemporary departmental memo, the grounds of rejection were the tendency of the Hierarchy to favour the term 'Catholic' over 'Roman Catholic', and the use on the part of some, though by no means all, Catholic dioceses of territorial titles properly belonging to the Church of England.
† See p. 107.

concert in March 1976 that launched the £1 million appeal for the cathedral's maintenance and repair. The guest of honour on that occasion had been Prince Philip, Duke of Edinburgh. If there had been any previous visit by a senior member of the Royal House to what has come increasingly to be seen as J. F. Bentley's architectural masterpiece, it would seem to have gone unrecorded: the Queen herself was not to see the inside of the cathedral until she attended a flower festival there, organised by the Duchess of Norfolk, in July 1979. Although nothing like as celebrated as her second visit – to hear Vespers sung there as part of the cathedral's centenary celebrations of 1995 – the occasion appears to have been a distinct success, producing an almost effusive letter of appreciation and thanks from her Private Secretary written on the afternoon of the same day that the visit took place.

A few weeks later a much sadder event occurred which appears to have placed the Cardinal's relationship with the Royal House on an altogether different footing. The murder of Earl Mountbatten of Burma in the Irish Republic on 27 August 1979, and the virtually simultaneous attack on a patrol of British soldiers at Warrenpoint in the North killing twenty men, came as a profound shock to the whole nation. Perhaps for the first time Basil displayed his capacity for capturing the mood of the moment and expressing it vividly, powerfully and uncompromisingly. Within twenty-four hours – when the news broke he was away on holiday – he had issued a statement that in its tone of toughness and outrage plainly struck a chord, particularly with Lord Mountbatten's relatives. It read:

The assassination of Earl Mountbatten and the murderous attack on the army patrol in Northern Ireland yesterday were evil and criminal acts. No claim to patriotism or political ideals can justify murder by self-appointed killers. Earl Mountbatten was an outstanding leader in peace and war. He was an imaginative patriot, a brave, humane man who harboured no bitterness and worked consistently for civilised solutions. The Catholic community in England and Wales mourns his cruel death, those of his companions and the loss of so many young lives in the County Down ambush. We extend our sympathy and support to all who have suffered the pain of bereavement. We shall offer prayers and Masses for those who have died.

Basil did not rest content with making a public statement. He also sent a telegram direct to the Queen at Balmoral, expressing the desire of the Roman Catholic community of England and Wales to share with her in mourning 'the death of one so close to yourself and so respected by all of us'.

Whether it was this or a follow-up personal letter that struck the spark we may never know, but Basil received a most unusual response. Instead of the normal typed reply from the Palace Private Secretary explaining that he had been asked to convey the monarch's gratitude, he got that rare example of genuine royal feeling, a hand-written, two-page letter from the Queen herself duly signed 'Elizabeth R'. It was a significant indication that what had begun as a purely official association – between the Supreme Governor of the Church of England and the leader of the second largest body of Christians within her realm – had moved up a notch. It might still be some years before the Queen would take to referring to Basil as 'my Cardinal' – rather as if the Reformation had never happened – but the foundations of the mutual respect and even affection that came to exist between them probably dated back to that black week in August 1979 when terrorism claimed its first victims from within the family of the House of Windsor.

The tragedy also introduced a new human element into the Cardinal's not always easy contacts with the Prince of Wales. The extraordinary speech in June 1978 that Prince Charles had decided to make on the same day that his cousin Prince Michael of Kent married his chosen bride Baroness Marie-Christine von Reibnitz (who had previously been the wife of a merchant banker called Tom Troubridge) still rankled in Catholic circles. The marriage had had to take place abroad because the terms of the Act of Settlement (1701) prevented a member of the Royal Family from marrying a Catholic (which the Baroness was) at home in England; but, even more offensively to the couple concerned, the venue had to be a Register Office rather than a Church for an entirely separate and distinct reason. Despite having granted the new Princess a decree of nullity rendering her first marriage void, the Vatican resolved at the last moment to withhold the necessary dispensation allowing her to marry her Protestant partner in a religious ceremony (the alleged ground being her unwillingness to undertake to bring up any children of the union in the Catholic faith, since such a promise would automatically have led to their losing their places in the line of succession to the throne).

Not to put too fine a point upon it, the entire story reflected little credit on anyone – least of all upon the papacy or the monarchy. But, instead of making a reasoned, temperate case against what looked uncommonly like restrictive religious practices, Prince Charles had chosen, on the day the wedding took place, to make a speech dismissing the whole place of dogma and doctrine within any faith. To make matters worse, his message had been delivered to an international congress of the Salvation Army, a body notorious for its distrust of the intellectual aspects of any religious belief. When, at Wembley Stadium, the Prince congratulated the Salvationists on being 'unfettered by theological or academic concerns for dogma or doctrine', and went on pointedly to say that he thought it 'worse than folly' that Christians should 'still be arguing about doctrinal matters that can only bring needless distress to a number of people', no one had the slightest doubt as to whom he had in mind. Indeed, the very fact that this haymaker of a speech was reported on the same day that the photographs of his cousin's wedding (loyally attended by Lord Mountbatten, Princess Anne and the bridegroom's brother, the Duke of Kent) appeared in all the newspapers made it inevitable that the intended connection should be made.

The Catholic counter-attack was not slow in coming. The next day the outspoken Archbishop of Glasgow, Thomas Winning, gave a newspaper interview in which he roundly proclaimed that the Prince's remarks would 'cause annoyance and anger to millions of the Queen's loyal subjects who care deeply about doctrine and principle'. By his reference to 'millions of the Queen's loyal subjects' the future Scottish Cardinal meant, of course, the Roman Catholic community within the British Isles and, as if to remove any doubt about it, he went on to attack the discriminatory provisions of the Act of Settlement designed to prevent anyone but a Protestant from succeeding to the throne.

It was a perfectly legitimate criticism for any Catholic prelate to make – indeed a spokesman for the Vatican had already called the Prince's speech 'sheer impertinence' – but, in contrast to his Scottish colleague, Basil decided that silence was the best policy and simply bit his lip. It was perhaps characteristic of his general attitude of respect towards the Royal Family that he never willingly entered into any controversy about them. In this instance it certainly stood him in good stead for, in little over a year, it meant that he was able to write a genuinely warm letter of sympathy to the Heir to the Throne on the murder in Ireland of his great-uncle, 'Dickie' Mountbatten.

Seldom can a letter from a relative stranger – they had met

barely more than once – have evoked so heartfelt a reply. In his own hand the Prince of Wales responded with ten manuscript pages ranging in material all the way from his own sense of loss, through his inability to comprehend the mind and character of those who had killed his uncle, to his total determination to see to it that he should not have died in vain. This last even involved the announcement of a half-intention on his part to write direct to the Pope, to discover whether His Holiness could be prevailed upon to intervene directly in the affairs of Northern Ireland – if only to attempt to end the centuries of bitterness and prejudice that had disfigured the relationship there between Protestants and Catholics. We do not know what the Cardinal's reaction to this somewhat naïve proposal was; but it must have been tactful, for within a matter of two or three months Basil had been invited, and had accepted, to serve as a trustee, under the Prince's chairmanship, of the Mountbatten Memorial Trust (a position he was to hold for the next six years). As for the Pope, it may or may not have been a coincidence that by the end of the following year the Queen should have received out of the blue an unsolicited letter from His Holiness asking permission 'to open my heart to Your Majesty regarding the situation in Northern Ireland'. It was an unusual communication to be sent from one Head of State to another, and presumably would not have come about unprompted (though whether by the Prince or the Cardinal can only be a matter for conjecture).

In an unusual mark of favour Basil found himself included in the robed ecclesiastical procession of clerics attending the Royal Marriage of the Prince of Wales to Lady Diana Spencer, held at St Paul's Cathedral on 29 July 1981. He took no part in the actual service, but the mere fact of his presence showed how far an ecumenical outlook had come to affect even the Royal House. (There had been no question of such an invitation being issued to Cardinal Griffin when the Queen herself had married Prince Philip in Westminster Abbey back in 1947.)

It was bad luck, therefore, that only three or four years after their marriage Prince Charles and his much younger wife should have provided the occasion for one of the more embarrassing episodes in Vatican-Buckingham Palace relations. The Pope's courtesy call on the Queen during his visit to Britain in May 1982 had gone reasonably well (though Basil himself continued to regret that his proposal that it should take the form of the Pope being a guest at a family lunch had not been taken up), and it was partly on the strength of this that arrangements were set in train for Charles and Diana to call on the Pope when they made their official visit to Italy in the spring of 1985. No one was in any doubt that the Vatican aspect of their trip to Rome might prove delicate, which was why the planning and preparation for it went on for eighteen months. Involved were the Prince of Wales at St James's Palace, the Archbishop of Canterbury at Lambeth Palace and the Cardinal at Archbishop's House – to say nothing of the Home Office in its traditional minder's role in Queen Anne's Gate. Originally the Prince, backed by both Archbishops, had favoured some form of special service being held in St Peter's Basilica to mark the first public act of reconciliation between the Roman Church and the British monarchy since the excommunication of Henry VIII in 1533. However, the Home Office, in particular, took fright at the prospect of the Heir to the Throne taking part in what would essentially be a Catholic religious ceremony. (Charles had been allowed to attend the service in Canterbury Cathedral when the Pope came to Britain in 1982 only in his capacity as a lay member of the Church of England, and not at all as a formal participant who one day himself would be the C of E's Supreme Governor.)

Eventually, after a good deal of negotiation between the various power centres, a compromise was reached. The Prince and

Princess of Wales *would* attend a Catholic Mass, but it would be held not in public but rather in the Pope's private chapel. There was only one fault to be found with this plan: with so many other interested parties involved, it had occurred to no one to inform the Queen or even Sir Philip Moore, her Private Secretary, of what was being proposed. The result, perhaps inevitably, was a nuclear explosion once the scheme came to light.

With only a fortnight to go before the service was due to take place, the whole idea of the royal couple attending (though not, of course, receiving Communion at) a Mass celebrated by the Pope was vetoed from Buckingham Palace. In a vain effort at damage limitation, the Palace Press Office even took it upon itself to make the new arrangements public via the gossip columnist of *The Times*. If anything, that only made matters worse. For the *Times*'s officially inspired version of events, which sought to pin the blame for the change of plan on what it somewhat curiously called 'the hierarchy of the Church of Scotland', soon backfired. Even more clumsy were the subsequent efforts of St James's Palace to pretend that the commitment to attend a papal Mass had been deleted from the Prince and Princess's schedule purely on the grounds of time – 'a logistical rather than an ecumenical decision', as Charles's own spokesman put it. Nobody accepted that for a moment, and the sceptics soon had the reassurance of knowing that they had the Vatican firmly on their side. 'Unattributable sources' there seized their chance to put it into the public domain that the decision had been taken by the Queen herself, and that an ordinary private audience with the Pope (such as she herself had enjoyed with John XXIII in 1961 and would do so again, this time with John Paul II, in the Year of the Millennium) was all she was prepared to sanction in the case of her son.

Never were Basil's own royalist credentials put to a sterner test and he emerged from it with flying colours. At the height of the inevitable hubbub he was to be heard earnestly assuring anyone who would listen:

> I think it is wonderful that Prince Charles has been to visit the Pope and very significant that he should do so. I would be very sad if that visit were to be marred by any controversy about attending Mass. The Mass should never be anything controversial. I, for my part, and I think I speak for a great number of Catholics, would not feel that this is a kind of snub to the Catholic community. I regret it if there are people who are a bit sensitive about Prince Charles attending Mass. I regret that but I respect their views.

No courtier could have put matters more tactfully, and there seems little doubt that the Cardinal's efforts to pour oil on troubled waters – the Archbishop of Canterbury was lucky enough to be away in Australia and, therefore, was able to avoid saying anything – did his standing nothing but good with the Palace. There was, however, one oddity in his statement, and that was its failure to mention at all that the visit to the Vatican and the accompanying 45-minute audience with the Pope had been a joint enterprise which the Prince had undertaken with his wife.

The failure to make any reference to Diana – though she (dressed entirely in black and wearing a veil) inevitably dominated the photographs – had a fairly simple explanation. At that stage the Cardinal had never met the Princess, whose first three years of married life had been very much taken up with producing her two sons (Prince William being born in June 1982, just eleven months after the Royal Wedding, and Prince Harry in October 1984, a mere six months before the Vatican visit). As the boys grew up, this was an omission, however, that was soon repaired. The Cardinal remained on perfectly cordial terms with the Prince of Wales – the work of the Mountbatten Trust bringing them intermittently together – but, as their correspondence shows, it was Diana who brought warmth into the relationship.

That came about partly because their interests rather neatly coincided. One of the first things Basil had done on arriving at Westminster had been to try to tackle the problem of the homeless and in particular of the 'night sleepers' who thronged the cathedral piazza. The result had been the establishment of the Cardinal Hume Centre in Horseferry Road, and the setting up of both the Passage and the Night Passage centres virtually next door to the cathedral. They were the kind of humanitarian refuges guaranteed to attract the sympathy and support of the Princess of Wales. She visited the three centres on a number of occasions, invariably writing to the Cardinal afterwards to say how much she had learnt from her visit, and not hesitating to contrast her own good fortune with the lot of those to whom she had talked (even confiding after her first tour of the Night Shelter that she had not found it easy to sleep in the comfort of her own bed once she got home to Kensington Palace). To the delight of the staff – she had taken a particular liking to a nun called Sister Bridie – she was at least once, in 1994 after her separation from her husband, accompanied on a visit to the Passage by her two sons, William being then twelve and Harry nine.

By the time the royal divorce loomed, it was hard to think of the Cardinal as being anything else but a fully paid-up member of the 'Princess's Party' (he kept a photograph of her on his desk and continued to do so even after her death). While his correspondence with the Prince of Wales had rather petered out, he appears to have gone out of his way to keep in regular touch with Diana. He wrote to her in 1991 to offer his sympathy when Prince William had his accident with a golf club at his prep school, and again later the same year to pass on a message from Mother Teresa. He was in contact again the next year, 1992, writing a note of sympathy on the death of the Princess's father, Earl Spencer, in April and – perhaps more strikingly – a couple of months later sending a morale-building letter to the Princess at the height of her own troubles over the *Sunday Times*'s serialisation of the Andrew Morton book, *Diana: The True Story*. His reward on this latter occasion was to be told that his support had always been 'of great value – and never more so than now'.

By then, of course, Basil had had a good deal of experience in handling the distaff side of the Royal Family. From the moment that the Pope had refused to relent over the 'mixed marriage' of Prince Michael of Kent and his Austrian bride in 1978, Archbishop's House had found itself bombarded with correspondence from Princess Michael ('an impetuous soul' as Basil called her), protesting at the manifest injustice of what had been done. This was more a matter for canon lawyers than for an Archbishop of Westminster, but it was the fate of Basil to bear the brunt of the attack. It, therefore, says much for both his patience and his persistence that by 1983 he was able to inform the aggrieved Princess that Rome had changed its mind and was prepared to 'validate' her by now five-year-old marriage. The justification given was that the Vatican had taken note of all she had done to try to make sure that her children were made aware of the tenets of the Catholic faith – but, since her son was only four and her daughter two, that sounded a pretty threadbare excuse for what may well have been simply a reversal of a bureaucratic Vatican decision.

Not that Basil thought it politic to accept any overt responsibility for it. When the moment came for the marriage validating ceremony to take place, he may have lent his own private chapel for the service but, pleading prior holiday plans, studiously avoided taking part. (In the additional absence, in his case through illness, of the Apostolic pro-Nuncio, Archbishop Bruno Heim, the ceremony was left in the hands of Basil's Vicar-General, Monsignor Ralph Brown.)

As coincidence would have it, the private chapel in Archbishop's House would a decade later also provide the setting for a similar, though by no means identical, service involving another female member of the same branch of the Royal Family: the Duchess of Kent. Katharine Worsley, as she had been before her marriage to the Duke in 1961, had first been to see the Cardinal while in some distress in 1990, and, after three or four years of regular meetings with him (including her help with a young people's concert held in the cathedral), made the decision that she wished to be received into the Roman Catholic Church. It was inevitably a matter of some constitutional sensitivity – if only because there was no record of anyone belonging to the Royal Family (even if only through marriage) having converted from the Church of England to the Church of Rome at least since the seventeenth century. Nor, in the climate of the times, were things made any easier by there having already been some high-profile conversions in the world of politics – notably of two ministers in the Major Government, John Gummer and Ann Widdecombe.*

All in all, it was probably just as well that the news had not yet broken of an in some ways even more celebrated conversion – that of Frances Shand Kydd, Princess Diana's mother, which took place in Scotland that same year. The reception of the Duchess of Kent into the Church was a model of tact and discretion. The ceremony took place in the Archbishop's private chapel on 14 January 1994, and everyone from the Buckingham

---

* The latter's conversion and reception was attended by such publicity that it prompted the Cardinal to mutter: 'I thought she was being received into the Catholic Church, not into the media.'

Palace press office to the Archbishop of Canterbury at Lambeth Palace seems to have been primed to say the right, graceful things. In response, the Catholic Church rigorously excluded any note of triumphalism, the Cardinal in his own statement even noting the Duchess's 'great affection for the Church of England'. It was a very far cry indeed from the days of the Oxford Movement and John Henry Newman.

Of course, the one thing Basil knew he must not do was allow a short-term publicity coup to imperil his long-term strategy. He was also, no doubt, aware of the importance the Royal Family (and especially the Queen) attached to reticence. Moreover, good manners alone would have dictated – especially after her *annus horribilis* of 1992 – that nothing should be done which could embarrass the monarch (whose permission to convert the Duchess, of course, had had to seek).

In any event, though Basil may not have realised it at the beginning of 1994, the hour of vindication for the royalist policy he had pursued ever since arriving at Westminster in 1976 was only just round the corner. The year 1995 had been chosen as marking the centenary of the building of Westminster Cathedral, though, in fact, it commemorated little more than the laying of the foundation stone. Basil had known from the beginning what public symbol he most wanted as marking the event. Somehow or other the Sovereign must be persuaded to come to the cathedral – not merely to attend a concert, a flower-show or anything like that, but rather to take part in an ordinary act of worship. After all the hassle over the Mass in the Pope's private chapel which the Prince and Princess of Wales had been banned from a full decade earlier it was realised at Archbishop's House that it would be no good proposing any service involving the sacrament. But why should the Queen not come for a non-sacramental act of devotion? And what better for that purpose than a Sung Vespers – the same plainsong

Office as had been heard at Westminster Abbey all those years ago on the day Basil first became Archbishop? The only difference would be that on this occasion it would be taking place in a Catholic place of worship rather than an Anglican one.

To considerable accompanying nervousness the proposal was put to the Palace – the days had long since gone when all such business had to be shunted through the Home Office – and, to the Archbishop's delight, he got a letter from the Queen's Private Secretary, Sir Robert Fellowes, on 25 April 1995 intimating that his invitation had been accepted. The only condition was that no one was to breathe a word about it until the public announcement was made. The Palace disclosed the Queen's intention to join in the cathedral centenary celebrations on 10 July, when an official press statement was issued to the newspapers. It was perhaps more notable for what it did not say than for what it did (there was, for instance, no mention of the fact that the occasion would mark the first participation by a reigning monarch in a Roman Catholic religious service since the sixteenth century). Perhaps lacking a sense of history, the royal and religious correspondents accepted what they were told (it being prudently explained to them that no Mass would be involved), if not wholly with indifference, then at least without consternation. It was exactly the reaction for which Basil had hoped.

When the afternoon arrived for the Queen to take her place in Westminster Cathedral amid a predominantly Catholic congregation – it was 30 November (St Andrew's Day) 1995 – someone was rash enough to mention within the Cardinal's hearing that it was gratifying that there had not been more of a popular protest or even populist-inspired backlash. (All there had been was a bit of ultra-Protestant shouting out on the piazza.) This expression of wonder and relief was met with an exasperated (and perhaps slightly indiscreet) murmur from the head of the Catholic Church in England and Wales: 'What do they think I have been working for all these years?'

Taken by itself, that was an unbalanced assessment of the objective towards which Basil had striven ever since coming to Westminster in 1976. Certainly, he had brought the Catholic Church in from the cold so far as the light of royal favour was concerned – but that had never been his sole aim and there had, indeed, been moments when he had deliberately put it at risk. That was certainly true, for example, of his stubborn loyalty to Princess Diana (even after she had been stripped of the title of Her Royal Highness and had had her name deleted from the official prayers offered on behalf of the Royal Family in Anglican churches every Sunday). What the Cardinal's own views were of these twin callous acts of official disavowal can only be a matter for surmise, but there was at least one occasion when the action he took spoke far louder than any words.

When Diana was killed in the Paris car crash on the morning of Sunday 31 August 1997, one of the first things the Cardinal did was to arrange for a Requiem Mass to be held in Westminster Cathedral for the repose of her soul. It was a bold move to make. Although there had been recurrent rumours of her intention to convert, Diana had not died a Catholic, and at the time he took the decision Basil already knew that proposals were well advanced for her official funeral to take place in Westminster Abbey on Saturday 6 September. However, the Cardinal was not to be deterred and, in consultation with her Catholic convert mother (though not with any other member of Diana's family), he pressed ahead with his plan for the Catholic community to pay its own separate tribute to the memory of the dead Princess on the evening before the Abbey service was due to take place.

In terms of public opinion the Requiem Mass, which was

carried 'live' on network television just an hour or two after the Queen's own broadcast to the nation, had an extraordinary impact. In part, no doubt, this was due to its essentially unofficial nature: no seats were reserved or anything like that, and people simply came into the eventually packed cathedral off the main thoroughfare of Victoria Street. In his homily the Cardinal himself chose to address Diana directly (rather as the Princess's brother, Earl Spencer, was to do in the Abbey the next day). It could hardly have sounded more intimate or informal – more the testimony of a friend than the panegyric of a Prince of the Church:

> Diana, you are now on your way to the vision of God, to a happiness this world cannot give, where true peace is to be found. Tell us: did you, early on Sunday morning, suddenly find yourself in the Presence of God, realising then, as we all must, that none of us is worthy to be in that Presence, face to face, until ready to be so . . .
>
> I know that you will not mind my saying that you were like the rest of us frail, imperfect, flawed but we loved you still . . .

It was manna from Heaven for the popular newspapers ('"Diana No Saint" Says Cardinal'), but it brought a predictable load of reproach down on Basil's head. Some of his correspondents took the view that he had been altogether too indulgent towards 'a self-confessed and apparently unrepentant adulteress', while others, offended by his reference to the Princess having possessed a 'flawed' personality, took the fundamentally opposite tack:

> Perhaps you will agree with me that it is customary (and perhaps even Christian) to refrain from remarks concerning

the personal deficiencies of the deceased at a moment of what is intended to be tender feeling. Instead, you chose crassly to blunder in with tasteless and tactless comments. One comfort I take is that you will not be comforting *me* at a time of bereavement . . .

Basil, however, proved more than capable of looking after himself, even replying to one correspondent (not the one quoted above, whom he wisely ignored) with a vigorous defence of his choice of language. To a woman protester from Manchester he wrote:

One reason for my reminding people that they must pray for Diana was that she was, indeed, 'flawed'. She knew it, too. There was a tendency in some parts of the world to turn her into a saint. She was not – she was a fine girl, loveable, who did a great deal of good.

There was probably, however, only one letter that really mattered to Basil, and that was the one that he had to wait for from Diana's mother, Frances Shand Kydd. For no doubt understandable reasons she took her time in sending her thanks to the Cardinal, but when her letter eventually came, he could hardly have asked for more:

Callanish, Isle of Seil,
By Oban, Argyll   2nd October 1997

Your Eminence:
    I feel guilty – and should feel so – that I have taken an age to write and thank you for your kindness to me. I shall always remember the comfort and goodness and nourishment of the Requiem Mass in the Cathedral. It

'warmed me up' and made Westminster Abbey less frightening. Thank you enormously for helping us so consol-
ingly.

Yours sincerely,
Frances
(Shand Kydd)

For his part, Basil did his best to preserve the proprieties
elsewhere, sending the Prince of Wales a letter two days after
the accident, typewritten but one that came clearly from the
heart:

Archbishop's House,
Westminster SW1   2nd September 1997

Your Royal Highness:
    I am sure you will not mind my writing to you in this
manner but my handwriting declines almost every day. I
just wanted to let you know that you are much in my
thoughts and prayers these days. I believe you are carrying
a very heavy burden. It would be lovely if some of us could
help carrying it with you.
    Many things are not clear and simple in our lives. We
have to live with muddle and difficulty. I have always
believed that we see only the messy side of life, forgetting
that it is God who sees the whole picture, which is the other
side.
    I hope you won't mind this rather personal note.
    Yours sincerely,
    Basil Hume

Whether Charles minded it or not, he made a distinctly less
than forthcoming response. Six days later a *pro forma* letter

arrived by the usual royal special delivery at Archbishop's House. It consisted of just three lines and had no sort of personal message attached to it – but by then, the Requiem Mass over which he presided having already taken place, Basil must have realised that he had put down his marker rather too publicly for there to be much likelihood of the kind of relationship that he had briefly enjoyed with the Heir to the Throne after the death of Lord Mountbatten eighteen years earlier being at all easily resumed.

There was no similar shadow, however, over his continuing cordial contacts with Buckingham Palace. The Queen had appreciated the discreet and private way in which he had handled the separate problems of Princess Michael and the Duchess of Kent, and had come to regard the Cardinal as a valued counsellor (possibly more of a natural confidant than George Carey, who had taken Robert Runcie's place at Lambeth in 1991). As its Supreme Governor she also felt grateful for the general restraint he had shown in face of the whole storm that had enveloped the Church of England over the issue of women priests. The two of them may not have met all that frequently – the Cardinal, as we have seen, tended to keep away from formal Royal occasions such as the annual Remembrance Day ceremony at the Cenotaph – but, when they did meet, it was increasingly with reciprocated warmth and affection. In a sense, no doubt, the presence of the one tended to reassure the other: in a changing world in which politicians and officials change and move on all the time, a Cardinal Archbishop of twenty years' standing becomes almost as much a symbol of continuity as the Crown itself.

There is every reason to believe, therefore, that when the Queen heard in April 1999 of Basil's personally announced battle with cancer, she felt as affected as anyone. The only difference was that, unlike the majority of her subjects, she was in a position at least to make a public gesture of gratitude and appreciation. However, although its timing was undeniably accelerated by it, there is no evidence (indeed, rather the reverse) to show that the royal decision to appoint Basil to the Order of Merit was prompted by his final illness. The proposal, originally thought of to coincide with his retirement, had, in fact, been in the pipeline for some time. A file headed 'Order of Merit', logging all the recent appointments that had been made to it had been in existence at Archbishop's House ever since 1996*, and one of the more revealing documents included in it is a distinctly elliptical reply from Sir Robert Fellowes, the Queen's Private Secretary, to a letter from the Duke of Norfolk dated 30 January 1998. (That does not, of course, imply that Basil himself knew anything at all about what was being mooted on his behalf: the same file includes a formal application, complete with a full *curriculum vitae*, for him to be awarded the 1998 American Templeton Foundation Prize† – an initiative on the part of his staff to which he would certainly never have given his blessing.)

In the case of the Order of Merit – the sole honour, apart from the Garter, the Thistle and the Royal Victorian Order, in the exclusive gift of the Crown – there is anyway conclusive proof that Basil had not the slightest idea of what was going on. When the first letter intimating the Queen's wish to appoint him an O.M. arrived on 1 May 1999 – just a fortnight after Basil had announced his mortal illness – he was clearly totally taken aback. So much so, indeed, that he felt compelled to reply to the new Palace Private Secretary, Robin Janvrin, with

---

* This was the same year that Derek Worlock, the Archbishop of Liverpool, was made a Companion of Honour, thereby blocking off – so far as Basil's friends were concerned – that particular Honours route.

† The prize, given for (in a fine American phrase) 'progress in religion', was awarded that year to Basil's devoted Jewish admirer, Sir Sigmund Sternberg.

what was a characteristically modest but also emotionally confused letter:

Archbishop's House,
Westminster, SW1   7 May 1999

Dear Sir Robin,

I must thank you for your letter of 30 April. I just do not know how to react to the kind suggestion of Her Majesty. On the one hand, I am not at all anxious for anything personal. After all, I have done no more than my job, and not always well. And I dread publicity.

On the other hand, I appreciate that being appointed a member of the Order of Merit is a singular honour and a personal gift of the Sovereign. My great esteem and admiration for Her Majesty makes it very hard for me to decline such a generous gesture on her part. If I were to accept, then I would like to think that it is in some manner an honour for the loyal Catholic subjects of Her Majesty.

I suspect that this is not a very helpful letter. I am as much looking to you for advice as anything else. First of all, I must ask: how long can I go on dithering? Or is dithering a form of *lèse majesté*? Let me know.

With kindest regards,
Yours sincerely,
Basil Hume

Private Secretaries at the Palace, like their opposite numbers at Downing Street, cannot have much experience of receiving diffident letters of this kind – and it is, no doubt, a tribute to his earlier diplomatic training (Sir Robin had been recruited from the Foreign Office to the service of the Palace only in 1987) that the relatively new Private Secretary to the Queen was able to lay Basil's doubts and hesitations to rest. Ten days later, on 18 May, Basil wrote to the Queen herself in an altogether more positive vein:

Archbishop's House,
Westminster, SW1   18 May 1999

Your Majesty,
   You have very kindly invited me to be a member of the Order of Merit. I am much honoured by this kind gesture on the part of Your Majesty. I am happy to accept.
   I am happy, too, to think that this honour will strengthen the ties between your Catholic subjects and Your Majesty.
                                        Yours respectfully,
                                              Basil Hume

To Robin Janvrin he wrote on the same day in rather less formal terms, pointing out that 'health-wise I have not been in very good shape this past week' and suggesting that this might be something that they would need to discuss. If that was a slightly ominous hint, the Palace obviously took it. The Cardinal's appointment to the Order of Merit was announced on 26 May and simultaneously the date for the audience with the Queen, at which it would be personally conferred, was fixed for only a week later, Wednesday 2 June. However, by then Basil was already back in hospital and it was from the St John and St Elizabeth Hospital in St John's Wood that he made the trip to the Palace.

He spent more than half an hour with the Queen, and that evening, tired but triumphant back in his hospital bed, he was asked by his confessor what they had talked about. 'Oh,' he replied airily, 'death, suffering, the after life – that sort of thing.'

The number of occasions on which any reigning monarch experiences that kind of conversation with a subject cannot be all that many. It must have left its imprint on the Queen's memory and may even help to explain why, well after his death, she would still habitually refer to him as 'my Cardinal' – a use of the royal possessive that would have gratified no one more than Basil himself.

XV

THE LAST DAYS

SOME TIME IN THE 1930S – OR SO THE BENEDICTINE legend has it – the renowned Headmaster of Ampleforth, Father Paul Nevill, found himself attending the annual September meeting of the Headmasters' Conference. One of his independent school colleagues was burbling away about all they sought to achieve for the pupils at *his* school. 'What we try to do,' he eventually declared with an impressive rallentando, 'is to equip our boys for life.' *Sotto voce*, Father Nevill was heard to murmur: 'How fascinating! You see, at Ampleforth we always seek to prepare our boys for death.'

This exchange may have predated Basil's own schooldays, but the riposte attributed (in various forms) to Paul Nevill has come to owe a good deal of its resonance to the example of a Christian death that the ninth Archbishop of Westminster provided at the very end of the twentieth century. For two months he endured the process of dying very much in public, but he managed to do so with a dignity and restraint, untainted by any Victorian mawkishness, that commanded respect well beyond the borders of his own faith. Yet it remained, in its way, a surprising ending.

Throughout his twenty-three years at Archbishop's House Basil had consistently been a reasonably fit man – even at the age of seventy-five and beyond he insisted on taking at least three two-mile walks a week – and the fact that was broken to him in mid-April 1999 that he had incurable cancer seems to have gone unsuspected by anyone. Although he had recently been showing signs of slowing down, his health generally – at least for a septuagenarian – had been good (although a niece who came to see him in March 1999 from Norway was shocked at how ill he looked). He had come through one hip replacement operation in 1983 and another one on the same left hip ten years later. Both operations inevitably tended to restrict his mobility. After the first one he gave up playing squash and (quite unnecessarily) simultaneously abandoned the swim in the club pool with which he used to accompany his visits to the squash court at the Royal Automobile Club in Pall Mall. However, to compensate for this reduction in physical activity, he arranged for a mini-gymnasium to be installed next to his 'cell' on the top floor of Archbishop's House, where he regularly exercised with weights – though he was always careful to explain that he did this as much for the relaxation of tension as for any Atlas-like attempt to build up muscles.

The only other physical mishap Basil suffered once he got into his seventies was the breaking of his wrist in a fall at Archbishop's House. This happened in the autumn of 1997; but, despite briefly having to wear a cast, it proved no serious impediment. Since it was his left wrist that he broke, it did not even affect his fishing, which, with other recreational options closed to him, was something in which he had come to take increasing pleasure. He spent three successive holidays fishing the Derwent in Cumbria as the guest of Lady Egremont of Cockermouth Castle – the first two visits in the company of the local parish priest at Workington Priory, Father John Macauley, whom he had known since they were schoolboys and fellow monks together at Ampleforth. Once Father Macauley moved on to be parish priest at Easingwold,

North Yorkshire, Basil went to Cockermouth for one last time alone – and disaster almost struck when he toppled over standing in the river in his waders and had to be rescued by his hostess.*

Most holidays, however, were spent at Hare Street in Hertfordshire – the country retreat left under the will of the Edwardian writer and convert, R. H. Benson, as a kind of Chequers for use in perpetuity by the Archbishop of Westminster. Here Basil always claimed to be so exhausted by the time he arrived that he did little else but sleep – though this, as we shall see, was not strictly true.†

As required by canon law, Basil had submitted his resignation to the Pope well in advance of his seventy-fifth birthday due on 2 March 1998 – only to see it refused in early February and to find himself required to stay at his post *donec aliter providetur* (until other arrangements are made). If the decision had been one for him alone, would he have chosen retirement? The evidence here is sketchy and inconclusive. Although he had already made disapproving noises about the minimal role religion was assigned in the Blair Government's Millennium Dome project, there was a side to him that wanted to be still in office to see the Millennium (or the Holy Year, as he preferred to put it) come in. Left to his own devices, his preference would probably have been to serve on as Archbishop of Westminster until Pentecost 2000, and then

---

* With no other male staying, he also had to be dressed in dry clothes belonging to Lady Egremont. She fortunately turned out to possess a particularly lengthy sweater. The rod and waders Basil used that day are still kept at Cockermouth Castle and are occasionally loaned out to privileged guests.

† It did, however, serve as a defence mechanism for warding off unwanted attentions. Hence perhaps Basil's 1987 letter to the local Anglican vicar: 'I am afraid all I do when I get here is to collapse.'

to insist at the age of seventy-seven that Pope John Paul II (inconveniently by then eighty himself) should respect his wish to retire. In any event, in 1998 he appears to have made remarkably little provision for the contingency of his resignation being accepted – no doubt feeling, as he was entitled to do, that the position he had won for himself both nationally and internationally made it highly unlikely that the Pope would ask him to step down.

He must, though, equally have been aware that, in the view of some, he had become a thorn in the flesh of the Vatican. Nor was that a reputation from which he necessarily shrank. He undeniably took a number of risks. An earlier chapter* has examined the almost unilateral stand he took on the subject of homosexuality, and there had been other challenges to Rome's authority in addition to that one. Not content with putting out the hand of friendship to the banned Catholic theologian Hans Küng (whom he actually invited to tea in Archbishop's House), he had also at the beginning of the 1990s effectively blocked the Vatican's desire to appoint a member of Opus Dei to the Catholic diocese of Northampton (even, or so it was said, threatening to resign himself if the nomination went ahead). The last of the three Papal pro-Nuncios of Basil's reign, Archbishop Pablo Puente, was widely believed to feel intimidated in the Cardinal's presence and certainly things were not always made easy for the Pope's own diplomatic representative in London.†

One reason for this lay in Basil's decision in the last full year of his life to take up the cudgels on behalf of an independent-

---

* See Chapter XIII.
† After Basil's death, Archbishop Pablo Puente, in his capacity as Nuncio (as the pro-Nuncio in London had by then become), was to say to the Bishops' Conference: 'I want to thank you all for your unswerving support of the Cardinal because I know at times how costly this has been for some of you.'

minded nun, Sister Lavinia Byrne of the IBVM,* whose 1994 book in favour of female priests, *Woman at the Altar*, had attracted severe condemnation in Rome. Basil's decision to intervene and champion her cause resulted in perhaps the most public and forthright campaign he had ever mounted against the Vatican. It was not motivated on his part by any sense of support for the arguments that this well-known writer, broadcaster and nun had tried to put forward (if the topic of women priests sometimes sounded like a subject on which Basil's own attitude was a trifle ambivalent, it was certainly not an issue on which he felt passionately). Rather was it the case that he had convinced himself that in her treatment by Rome – and particularly in the light of the almost medieval demand for her publicly to recant, originating with the Congregation for the Doctrine of the Faith – this daughter of the Church had received rather less than justice. The Vatican's conduct towards her had represented just the kind of repressive behaviour guaranteed to summon the Cardinal to battle, and, in terms of forcefulness and fearlessness, the letter Basil eventually sent to Archbishop Tarcisio Bertone, the secretary of the Congregation for the Doctrine of the Faith in Rome, could hardly have been bettered:

Archbishop's House,   18 September 1998
Westminster, SW1

Your Excellency,
    On Monday 14 September I met with Sr Lavinia Byrne, IBVM, and her Provincial, Sr Cecilia Goodman. The purpose of our meeting was to discuss the aftermath of the publication of Sr Lavinia's book, *Woman at the Altar*. I explained

---

* In 2004 the Institute of the Blessed Virgin Mary changed its name to the Congregation of Jesus.

to the two sisters that I had no mandate to interfere in the affairs of their religious Institute. I also said that, whereas I had to make certain that the teaching of the Church was known and accepted by the Catholics of England and Wales, at the same time I had to ensure that no harm would come to the Church. I, too, had to be concerned that every individual be treated with justice and charity.

Having considered the present matter carefully, having spoken with Sr Lavinia and her Superior, taking also into account the sensitivities of people in our country and abroad, I have concluded that I must advise, and strongly, that no further action be taken by the Congregation in the matter of Sr Lavinia's book . . .

She is a much respected person in this country, and not only in the Catholic Church. She has done much good and will continue to do so. I am sure the Congregation will act wisely and with prudence, and now leave the matter to rest. Any other policy will be harmful for the Church in this country.

Please accept my advice,

Yours devotedly,

Basil Hume

The reaction of the Congregation to receiving such a letter has not, alas, been recorded, but it had the desired effect. The demands for Sister Lavinia to repent publicly of the words she had written ceased to be heard – and, although she ultimately (after Basil's death) felt compelled to leave her Order, she did so as a Catholic in good standing who continued to write and broadcast about her faith. It was a very different outcome from the exemplary one on which Rome had originally seemed to set its sights.

There is reason to believe, though, that the episode took its toll on Basil. Whether through the strain this clash imposed upon him or not, he began frequently to complain of feeling tired – with the staff at Archbishop's House noticing that he began to go up to his 'cell' earlier and earlier until sometimes, when he had no evening engagements, he would take himself off at 8.30 p.m. No one thought, of course, that he was going straight to sleep: a monk to the end, he had always tried to fit in time for prayer and meditation before bed. There did appear, however, to be a decline in the relish that he showed for ordinary life, and yet he remained determined to fulfil all his obligations. One of these (long agreed) was to go to the United States in the summer of 1999 in order to deliver two important lectures: one to the Conference of American Bishops[*] on the topic of 'collegiality' and the other, in memory of a friend, the late Archbishop of Chicago, Cardinal Joseph Bernardin, to what was known at the time as the 'Catholic Common Ground Initiative'.

These were commitments (both scheduled to take place within a single week in June) that Basil took very seriously. Despite feeling distinctly under the weather – he even complained to his doctor[†] just before Christmas of loss of appetite and occasional feelings of nausea – he never seems to have contemplated trying to get out of either engagement. Indeed, that January he devoted his post-Christmas break at Hare Street to working on draft manuscripts for each address. This task – in which he had the help of a young priest, Father Liam Kelly, whom he had

---

[*] Basil had last addressed this body in 1982 when his talk was widely remembered and considered a great success.
[†] Basil's GP throughout his time at Archbishop's House was Martin Scurr, who already looked after the staff and boys of the Choir School. Once Basil arrived in London from Ampleforth, Doctor Scurr took him under his care as well, becoming not just his medical adviser but also a friend.

first met at the English College in Rome* and whom he had recently brought into the secretariat of the Bishops' Conference – seems to have done him a power of good. Certainly, by the end of January he was reporting to his doctor, who meanwhile had arranged for blood tests which showed nothing wrong, that he was feeling much better and that there was no further need for concern.

It proved, however, to be only a temporary respite. By the end of March the old symptoms had returned and arrangements were set in train for Basil to have a more comprehensive medical examination via an ultrasound scan. Easter fell relatively early in 1999 – on 4 April – and accordingly it was not until Holy Week was over that the hospital tests began.

There was one disadvantage to this timetable. The Bishops' Conference of England and Wales traditionally meets during Low Week (that is, during the first full week after Easter Sunday) and Basil's absence was bound to attract attention, if only because, as its President, he had been such an assiduous attender in the past. The impression seems to have been given that he was undergoing some routine medical checks (in themselves no cause for alarm) and that he would be back at work from St John and St Elizabeth Hospital before anyone but the bishops had even noticed that he had been away. In fact, though, by the time the conference got properly started, he had already undergone a biopsy and the results of it when they came in could hardly have been more gloomy. He was found to be suffering from hepatic metastases (or, in layman's language, cancer of the liver), normally the quickest form of cancer to bring about

---

* In Rome, whenever the Cardinal was staying at the English College, it fell to Liam Kelly, a student there who also worked part-time at Vatican Radio, to bring him the Saturday night football scores, including the result of any match in which Newcastle United had been involved.

death. He then underwent a colonoscopy at the London Clinic, as a result of which it was revealed that the primary cancer was in the large intestine.

Basil himself was told of his terminal condition on Tuesday 13 April, the second day of the Bishops' Conference, at which he had managed to put in only an initial token appearance. His immediate reaction was to go to the hospital chapel to pray, and after that the first person to whom he confided the news (in the course of a telephone call) was his private secretary, Father Jim Curry. Together they decided that the Bishops' Conference should not be informed, and its members only discovered the truth once they had all gone home. They learned of it in exactly the same way as the rest of the nation, via a letter to the priests of his diocese that Basil had composed once he got back to Archbishop's House. It remains a remarkable document:

Archbishop's House,   16 April 1999
London, SW1.

Dear Father,

You may have heard that I have recently been in hospital for tests. The result: I have cancer and it is not in its early stages.

I have received two wonderful graces. First, I have been given time to prepare for a new future. Secondly, I find myself – uncharacteristically – calm and at peace.

I intend to carry on working as much and as long as I can. I have no intention of being an invalid until I have to submit to the illness. But, nevertheless, I shall be a bit limited in what I can do. Above all, no fuss. The future is in God's hands. I am determined to see the Holy Year in.

This is an opportunity for me to thank you all for your friendship, your patience and, not least, your good humour.

I know that the diocese has a great future. The Gospel must live again in our society. May that grace be given to us all in the Holy Year. You, dear Fathers, have a key role to play in that.

Please pray for,

Yours devotedly,

Basil Hume

Having sent off more than 500 such letters (a similar one went to his colleagues in the Conference of Bishops), Basil had next to resolve how the news should be communicated to the public. He was determined that his priests should hear direct from him first, but at the same time he did not welcome the prospect of an avalanche of media inquiries overwhelming Archbishop's House. Accordingly, that Saturday morning – after (in those days) the post would have arrived at most presbyteries – a copy of the letter was released to both the Press Association and the BBC. The story led the BBC Saturday TV lunchtime news, watched by the Cardinal himself. He even risked the wry comment that he would now never be forgiven by those from whom he had accepted congratulations on looking so much better. Entering into the mood of black humour his private secretary promptly replied that, if that was the case, he had better make sure that he died pretty quickly. Unprovoked, Basil then remarked that the last thing he wanted to be was 'a celebrity invalid' and settled down, as was his habit, to watch the 'Football Focus' section of the BBC's Saturday afternoon sports programme, *Grandstand.*

On the Monday following his return from hospital, he presided over the Memorial Mass in Westminster Cathedral for the former Bishop of Brentwood, Patrick Casey, without referring once to his own illness. Then for three weeks and more he continued to go about his duties in the normal way, until the moment came for him to return to the London Clinic for chemotherapy treatment. He had never been keen on this, but felt that he owed it to fellow sufferers from the same condition not, as it were, to be seen to be 'throwing in the towel'. His last pastoral visit was made on 9 May to the church of St Mary Magdalene, Willesden Green, in north-west London, where he celebrated a commemorative Mass marking the sixtieth anniversary of its foundation. At a reception held afterwards he mingled and chatted with the parishioners just as if he had not a care in the world. He showed much the same sang-froid two days later when, although looking disturbingly gaunt, he received the Dalai Lama at Archbishop's House and joked with him in front of the photographers.

More and more, however, his longer-term engagements were having to be reconsidered, and thought frequently had to be given to finding alternative arrangements by which they might be fulfilled. A top priority here was his scheduled visit to the United States to address the Conference of American Bishops. Eventually – and in reluctant recognition of the fact that he would hardly be likely to be in any shape to fly the 6,000 miles there and back – the decision was taken that he should instead transfer what he intended to say to a video-cassette which could then itself be flown to America and played before the assembled bishops. With invaluable help from the BBC, a thoroughly professional cassette was duly made of Basil talking from his desk in Archbishop's House and doing so with notable charm; he even included an elegant, if elliptical, introductory passage in which he apologised for not being present in person: 'I'm very sorry indeed that I'm not with you today but, as you well know, we're not always in control of the circumstances of our lives.' In the event, and adding even greater poignancy to the occasion, the video was played to the conference on the day after he died. That circumstance alone ensured that it attracted a good deal of attention – 'Hume Attacks Vatican from beyond the Grave' ran one typical British newspaper headline – and the tone of his remarks was, it has to be conceded, strikingly more forthright than anything he had previously said. The cause of his impatience is perhaps best reflected in a single paragraph:

> If I now proceed to sound a note of criticism, it is out of fraternal charity and love of the Church. For instance, some of us have been surprised by the form and tone of some letters from Curial offices. There are concerns about the manner of some episcopal appointments and the length of time taken to make them. Not all appointments have been satisfactory. There is often unease about the way in which theologians and their writings have been investigated. There can be a sense of frustration at not having been consulted on issues which are important to us as local bishops.

This last note of irritation Basil then went on to transform into a formal call for John Paul II to meet – at least once every two years – with the heads of all the various national bishops' conferences 'so that he can hear directly from them their collegiate advice'. That was not just a clearcut advocacy of 'collegiality' on the old John XXIII model: it was also an open assault on the power of the Curia, which possibly explains why the proposal was never taken up by the Vatican (already accused by Basil in the same speech of sometimes having 'made me feel like a naughty schoolboy doing something unacceptable').

Nor did the American Church's British guest show himself to be much more emollient in what he planned to say to the Catholic Common Ground Initiative conference held in Washington, DC, a week later (the day that his funeral took place in London). On this occasion his script was read for him by the Most Reverend Oscar Lipscomb, the Archbishop of

Mobile, Alabama, who had issued the original invitation. Once again his central message was captured in a single passage:

It is important always to be strict concerning principles and endlessly compassionate and understanding of persons. It does happen that a person or group may take up a position on some issue against the teaching of the Church. How should the pastor act? A first instinct may be to exclude from the community those who dissent. We must rather keep them within the community and work – sometimes very hard – to lead them to take up positions consistent with the Church's teaching.

Knowing what we now do about the origins of both those addresses, we are surely entitled to assume that Basil saw and seized the opportunity to get important things said that he had long wanted to get off his chest. He had for long, after all, been a 'collegiality' man who, as he showed in his second speech, was tempted to see diversity as the other side of the coin to unity. If during his lifetime his monk's vow of obedience had prevented him from blurting out such insights before, is it not possible that the reality of illness and the prospect of death released him from such inhibitions?

Even to suggest this as an interpretation is, of course, to challenge the conventional wisdom that Basil became more conservative as he grew older, but, like many things that are widely believed, it is by no means self-evident that this was the case. His battle with Rome during the last full year of his life in defence of the rights of Sister Lavinia Byrne hardly supports such a proposition. Nor, for that matter, does his attitude to secular politics – in his last years and long after Margaret Thatcher had left No 10, he would regularly chant 'Maggie out, Maggie out!' whenever he found himself driving past Downing

Street. The piece of evidence most regularly cited in support of Basil's general drift in an authoritarian direction lies in his growing hostility to the Tridentine Mass* – which, it was once claimed in the *Daily Telegraph*, ended up by surpassing even that of Rome. Leaving aside the question of whether this should not more properly be classified as an example of liberal intolerance, the truth is that from the beginning Basil harboured his own doubts about the wisdom of the ban on the Latin Mass – a ban which successive Popes had enforced. As early as 1977, in only his second year at Westminster, he was to be found writing to one correspondent (admittedly an old Amplefordian): 'Rome has not handled the question of the Tridentine Mass very cleverly – I have felt for a long time that the new rite should have been introduced, allowing the old rite to continue. We should have been spared a great deal of trouble had this been done.' That hardly sounds like the battle-cry of an old-fashioned ultramontane.†

The truth probably is that in his attitude to Rome Basil always represented a bit of a mixture. As his friend Adrian Hastings was to argue in a highly perceptive essay written a year after his death,‡ Basil's difficulties in relation to Rome derived from an incompatibility between two separate strands of feeling that he held: on the one hand, the belief in the monarchical papacy on which he had been brought up and, on the other, the post-Vatican II version of collegial papal leadership for which, at least during the second half of his life, he tended to yearn. If that

---

* After Vatican II the Tridentine Latin Mass, which had represented the world-wide Eucharistic liturgy for 400 years, was (with very few exceptions) swept away to make way for the use of the vernacular in Catholic worship.

† This remains, however, the field in which Basil was most frequently criticised, even after his death. See 'A Secular Beatification' by Michael McMahon, former Chairman of the Latin Mass Society, in the *Spectator*, 3 July 1999.

‡ 'Cardinal Basil Hume' by Adrian Hastings, *Priests & People*, July 2000.

dilemma was never quite resolved, at least the two viewpoints came as near to being expressed alongside each other as they ever did in those two highly revealing posthumous lectures delivered in America.

Meanwhile, the routine of life at Archbishop's House had to go on. In his separate letters to his fellow bishops and to the clergy of his own diocese Basil had sentenced himself to a very public form of death – and it was understandable that some steps should have been taken to protect his privacy. No publicity, for example, was ever given to the fact that, on the advice of a cancer specialist, Maurice Slevin, he was undergoing chemotherapy treatment – it was anyway abandoned at the patient's request after two cycles – nor was the nature of his cancer ever identified. He seemed relieved once he got back to St John and St Elizabeth (he had never liked the London Clinic much, and the nature of the chemotherapy treatment he endured there made him dislike it all the more). It was thus from the Catholic hospital in St John's Wood that he set off on 2 June to go to the Palace for the conferment at the hands of the Queen of the Order of Merit. (It had been indicated by Robin Janvrin, the Queen's Private Secretary, that, if the Cardinal did not feel up to it, a royal representative would come to the hospital and invest him with the insignia there, but neither Basil nor his advisers were having that.) Accordingly, pumped up as he was with drugs – 'I know what you're up to,' he is alleged to have said as he was prepared for the trip – he set out on his last journey. His condition did not, however, stop him from insisting on dropping in at Archbishop's House both on the way out (in order to change) and then also on the way back (to say his goodbyes).

What, however, surprised him – and perhaps pleased him – most was the sight of his extended family assembled in considerable strength as the car drove past the gates into the forecourt of Buckingham Palace. That evening, having made his farewells both to the staff at Archbishop's House and to those working at the nearby Passage day centre for the homeless, he returned to the hospital room at St John and St Elizabeth which he was never to leave again. To the outside world, though, appearances had to be kept up. As we have seen, in his clergy letter of just six weeks earlier his overall instruction had been 'Above all, no fuss', and to those who worked for him 'Business as usual' seemed to be as good a translation of that as any. (That also went for Basil himself – it was almost casually that he remarked to his confessor, who was also one of his own auxiliary bishops, 'I think the time may have come for a review of life.'*) The last press release, supposedly emanating from the Archbishop himself, was issued on 14 June, just three days before he died. In it he expressed his regret at not being able to take part in 'the human chain' along the banks of the Thames designed to back the Jubilee 2000 campaign for the cancellation of Third World debt. This was a cause Basil had fully endorsed ever since he first wrote to the Pope about it in 1993 and then presided over a London conference which pressed the case for it in 1996.†

The first unofficial intimation of just how gravely ill he was had come a week earlier when Archbishop Couve de Murville of Birmingham stepped in at the last moment to take the Cardinal's place at a Sunday Mass commemorating the centenary of the St John and St Elizabeth Hospital, held in its own chapel. Basil had fully intended to preside at it, if only in recognition of all the care he had been given, and it was a measure of just how much the Buckingham Palace trip had taken out of him that he simply was not up to even attending. The congre-

---

* The confessional procedure that all Benedictines are supposed to go through before death.

† After Basil's death Gordon Brown, as Chancellor of the Exchequer, paid full tribute to the crucial part he had played in the success of this campaign.

gation was said, when the Mass was over, to have melted away in tears.

By now, the whole weight of the medical effort was going into conserving Basil's energies so that he could still receive visitors. Most of these tended to be very old friends – contemporaries from school and, in particular, those surviving from the 1939–41 Ampleforth Rugby XVs (most of whom he had last met at a dinner held on his seventy-fifth birthday), novices and monks with whom he had served in the monastery, as well as members of his own family (his three sisters survived, though his younger brother, John, had died some five years earlier after a succession of strokes and a prolonged battle against ill-health). To this general pattern there was however, one exception. Early in June a telephone call had been put through to Archbishop's House from No 10 Downing Street saying that the Prime Minister and his wife would very much like to come and see the Cardinal in hospital. The message was received with some surprise – relations with Tony Blair, after the run-in with the Cardinal over his receiving Communion at Mass, had never been particularly close and, while Basil admired the charitable aspects of Cherie Booth's work, he had never come to know her in the same way that he had, for example, Diana Princess of Wales.

The news of the Prime Minister's message was conveyed to Basil and, if with a faint air of resignation – 'It's not a question of what I *want* to do, it's a question of what I *ought* to do' – the necessary assent was forthcoming. The Blairs duly came, were alone with the Cardinal for twenty minutes (or twice their allotted time) and, to their credit, made no attempt at all to exploit the visit for publicity purposes. In this they certainly showed tact: on the day they came the Cardinal was in a slightly cast-down state, telling another visitor, the Dominican leader Timothy Radcliffe that, while when he first learned he was mortally ill 'the veil had parted and I found myself in the presence of God', things had subsequently become much tougher.

As a general rule, all visitors were rationed to five minutes each and the time limit was rigorously enforced by Father Jim Curry, the Archbishop's private secretary, who by now was virtually living at the hospital. Although he tried to be a model patient, Basil at times grew frustrated, exclaiming: 'Why doesn't God take me?' or 'Why is He keeping me waiting?' For the most part, in these last days he said his prayers through a sense of touch, keeping a crucifix in his hand and feeling Christ's wounds with his fingers. This was something he had started doing during an earlier phase of his illness: one day, noticing a young priest passing his study door at Archbishop's House, he had summoned him in and, with simplicity and humility, explained to his much younger colleague that he could no longer either read or pray and had to be content with simply holding the crucifix and reflecting on Christ's suffering. Later, in hospital, Basil would sometimes talk of 'a curtain' having come down between himself and God – but at least, as his oldest friend, Father Martin Haigh observed, it was no more than a curtain and, having come down, would certainly go up again. Basil, he felt sure, was quite confident of that.

Spiritual confidence was, in fact, to mark the very last day of his life. By Thursday 17 June Basil was slipping in and out of consciousness and Jim Curry, sensing that the end could not now be far away, offered either to celebrate Mass or simply to offer him Communion. To his surprise, both offers were rejected, with the dying man murmuring: 'God will show His love to me in other ways.' That afternoon his condition deteriorated still further and at around 5.15 p.m. Father Curry anointed him. He died – in the presence of his private secretary, another priest, Father Liam Kelly, one of his nephews and a nurse – just minutes later.

His death was not, of course, a shock. Just as he had prepared himself for it, so – as he had intended – other people were not taken aback by it. There could hardly have been a greater contrast with the chorus of horror and disbelief that had attended the abrupt ending of the life of the Princess of Wales only two years earlier (a far nearer analogy was with the death of Mother Teresa, which had taken place only days after that of the Princess). However, that did not imply there was no sense of national loss. Rupert Murdoch's *Sun* reflected the public mood in one of its more surprising headlines – 'Farewell our Beloved Basil: Friend who touched all our hearts'.

Over the next few days millions of words must have been written about the monk who had also served as Archbishop of Westminster for so long. The extraordinary thing was that there was hardly a carping, or even a critical, note among them. Tributes poured in from the Pope, the Queen, the Prime Minister, the Leader of the Opposition, a host of fellow religious leaders (to say nothing of the Newcastle United football team).

There would, it was announced, be a lying-in-state of the Cardinal's body in the Hall of Westminster Cathedral from the morning of Monday 21 June through to noon on Thursday 24 June, when the coffin would be formally received into the Cathedral itself. More than 30,000 mourners streamed past the plain catafalque, decorated only with a white linen cloth marked by a cross at its centre, and with the Cardinal's biretta (presented to Basil by Pope Paul VI) standing next to it. Chelsea Pensioners, Knights and Dames of Malta, together with Knights of the Holy Sepulchre and of St Columba took turns in keeping vigil over the coffin, within which, according to his own instructions, Basil's body was dressed in a simple black Benedictine habit and hood.

The funeral Mass took place on Friday 25 June, just a week and a day after the Cardinal's death. Celebrated by the Pope's

Special Envoy, the Australian Cardinal Edward Cassidy, who served in Rome as President of the Pontifical Council for the Promotion of Christian Unity, it drew a packed congregation of 2,500, with many more listening to the service on loudspeakers outside in the Cathedral piazza. Both the British Prime Minister and the Irish Taoiseach attended, interrupting their talks on Northern Ireland in order to be present, as were political leaders from across the party spectrum at Westminster together with leaders of other Churches from the length and breadth of the United Kingdom. If there was a source of disappointment, it arose from a perception on the part of some that it might have been appropriate for there to have been royal representation at a rather higher level than that of the Duchess of Kent or Princess Michael (both of whom happened to be Catholics anyway).

Although it was generally accepted that the Queen herself did not attend funerals – unless they were State ones or involved very special circumstances of close personal friendship – even newspapers normally as far apart as the *Independent* and the *Daily Mail* found it hard to understand why the Prince of Wales could not have been there. In particular, the official explanation offered that he had 'private engagements' that morning which prevented his attendance appears to have satisfied no one.*

If that was interpreted as 'a royal snub', Basil would have been the last person to recognise it as such. As he had demonstrated over his reaction to the cancellation of the private papal Mass for the Prince and Princess of Wales back in 1985, that was not the way he ever allowed himself to look at such things. Nor, to be fair, did the bulk of the Catholic community. What

---

* In the end, the inadequacy of this excuse appears to have registered even with St James's Palace. When a subsequent Memorial Mass was held for Cardinal Hume in Westminster Cathedral just over three months later, on 6 October 1999, the Prince of Wales was on parade as the representative of both the Queen and the Duke of Edinburgh.

the faithful were concentrating on that Friday was the memory of an exceptional Christian life. They also had an even rarer phenomenon to celebrate, a thoroughly Christian death.

It may have been 350 years since Bishop Jeremy Taylor had written his classic work *Holy Dying*, but a much less naturally reverent generation had just been given a glimpse of that process in action. It is one thing, after all, to set an example of a Christian life: it is quite another to leave behind a similar lesson in the Christian way of meeting death. In addition to achieving the first, Basil had brought off the second – thereby doing as much as anyone to vindicate the claim once made on behalf of the boys of Ampleforth (and quoted at the beginning of this chapter).

XVI

EPILOGUE

URING THE LAST QUARTER OF THE PAST CENTURY THE decline in the number of practising Roman Catholics in Britain was remarkable and remorseless. The Republic of Ireland may have been harder hit, but even on the mainland the record was hardly a cheerful one. Vocations dwindled until they almost died away, attendance at Mass went down by nearly a half and the Hierarchy lost most of the public policy battles (including those on stem cell research and *in vitro* fertilisation) in which it engaged. Admittedly, the Catholic Church in England and Wales more or less escaped the grosser scandals involving sexual abuse that were to threaten to engulf the Catholic community in both Ireland and the United States, but even in the United Kingdom there was always the sense of an institution living on the edge of a precipice.

It is all the more striking, therefore, that the individual who presided over the fortunes of English Catholicism during this period of disillusionment should continue to be seen as one of the most remarkable spiritual leaders Britain has ever seen. How did such a paradox occur and in what way is it possible to reconcile the diminished appeal of the Catholic Church with the distinguished reputation still enjoyed by the man who led it from 1976 to 1999?

This apparent contradiction is, no doubt, partially to be explained by the distinctive approach adopted by Cardinal Basil Hume. In the first place, he never shied away from admitting that he, too, was no stranger to the kingdom of doubt. That was what made him so effective an ambassador to a largely irreligious world. Far from coming across as a merchant of moral certainties, he always gave the impression that, like most other people, he was a searcher after truth. It was no coincidence that his first and best-known book was called *Searching for God*.

There has, though, to be more to it than that – and in terms of personal impact there is: Basil Hume also performed the even more difficult feat of persuading a predominantly unbelieving public that it was perfectly possible to be a convinced Christian without being in any sense a crank. Here, one might have thought, the cards were stacked against him, for he was not merely a priest but that far greater twentieth-century curiosity, a monk as well. Before emerging onto the national stage he had spent the first thirty-five years of his adult life abiding by the Rule of St Benedict behind a monastery wall.

Fortunately, at least in the world's view, there were some compensating factors. In his tastes and interests – fishing, squash, football – he was the epitome of normality. He could never be accused – as a near-contemporary Archbishop of Canterbury once was – of being 'proud, prelatical and pompous'.* Nor did he ever assume – while talking about God more freely than most clerics – that exaggerated tone of piety which, however well intentioned, seldom succeeds in doing anything but putting other people off. In that respect he was typically English. He

* In showing off his archiepiscopal portrait to a brother Anglican bishop, Cosmo Gordon Lang (Archbishop of Canterbury from 1928 to 1942) is said to have complained that 'they say it makes me look proud, prelatical and pompous' – only to be stopped in his tracks by the silky riposte, 'And may I know to which of those epithets your Grace takes exception?'

loathed the 'touchy-feely' side of modern religion and, noticeably, at first had difficulty at Mass even with the kiss of peace.

He was, of course, born a 'Geordie' and few things would have pleased him more than that the first sight confronting any rail traveller today, on coming out of Newcastle upon Tyne railway station, is a rather fine statue, the work of Nigel Boonham, of the Tyneside boy who rose to be Cardinal Archbishop of Westminster.

None of his predecessors had had their lives celebrated by such a memorial (initiated, incidentally, by the city council) and it is a fitting tribute – if only because Basil was easily the most recognisably English of the six successive Archbishops of Westminster appointed during the twentieth century. For him nationality was as much a matter of aesthetic style as of historical record. Kate Adie, the BBC broadcaster and war correspondent, tells a revealing story of what happened when she once met Hume by appointment for an interview in Rome. Being pre-eminently good-mannered, he started off by complimenting her on the hat she was wearing. Touched but slightly embarrassed, she explained that she did not normally wear hats at all. 'Then why', came the inevitable question, 'are you wearing one today?' 'Well,' she heard herself saying, 'I suppose I took the view that when in Rome . . .' and her voice trailed away just as the interruption came: 'Oh no, my dear, you must *never* feel that. Always remember that you are English, it's a very proud thing to be.'

Interestingly, Basil himself could be described as 'English' only on a very loose definition of the term. His mother was French and his father was half-Scottish, but that never prevented him from personifying through his bearing and demeanour the very quintessence of Englishness. This set him apart from most of his predecessors. At least since Henry Manning's successor, Herbert Vaughan (who came from an old Herefordshire recusant family), was appointed in 1892, Archbishops of Westminster, either from birth or assimilation, had generally come to share a common identity with the flock to whom they ministered. If the out-dated jibe about the English Catholic Church representing 'an Italian mission to the Irish' could still occasionally be heard during the dozen years Basil's predecessor, John Carmel Heenan, spent at Westminster, it had ceased to have any plausibility at all by the time of his own death.

It is sometimes claimed that during his near-record twenty-three-year reign – his only modern rival in terms of length of service being the first twentieth-century Archbishop, Francis Bourne, who remained at Westminster for a remarkable thirty-one years – Basil, in effect, annexed the English Catholic Church to the British Establishment. Although it is true that there were areas where he changed everything, he was in no sense the pioneer of the process. He merely symbolised the culmination of a gradual development that had gone on throughout the second half of the twentieth century. In fact, by the time Basil appeared on the national scene his own Roman Catholic brother-in-law, Sir John Hunt, was already Secretary of the Cabinet, both the Director-General of the BBC and the Editor of *The Times* belonged to the same faith, and a Bill was just going through Parliament allowing even the Lord Chancellor to be a Catholic (leaving only the roles of monarch, consort and the heir to the throne out of reach for anyone but a Protestant).

Of course, the air of the patrician Englishman that Basil carried around with him did make a difference. It helped to set the seal on a concordat between the Catholic Church and the British State that could never afterwards be dismantled. When, at New Year 2001, Basil's successor, Cardinal Cormac Murphy-O'Connor, was summoned to Sandringham to preach before the Royal Family, this unprecedented mark of royal favour may have gone to the man who was the tenth Archbishop, but the responsibility for making the whole thing possible belonged firmly to his predecessor.

Inevitably, this public *rapprochement* between the Roman Catholic Church and the English social and political power structure had repercussions elsewhere, and nearly all of them were beneficial. So long as Catholics, or Papists as they were sometimes still called at the start of the twentieth century, were discriminated against (or simply regarded as living upon some special tribal reservation of their own), it was all too likely that they would come to think of themselves as 'outsiders'. Robert Runcie, one of the three Archbishops of Canterbury whose tenure overlapped with Basil's at Westminster, often used to say how much he loathed it when someone to whom he had only just been introduced would feel compelled to start off by saying: 'I'm terribly sorry, but in fairness I ought to tell you that I'm a left-footer.' If one of the legacies of Basil's reign at Westminster has been to banish all such coy self-abasement from our national dialogue, then so much the better for Catholics and non-Catholics alike.

Yet by 'Anglicising' his Church – at least to the point of putting it on virtually an equal footing with the Church of England in our national life – Basil could claim to have done more than that. He also presented it with the chance for an entirely new type of independence and self-determination. Of course, as a monk, Basil believed implicitly in obedience, and in his various utterances on moral or ethical issues he would constantly emphasise that he saw himself as being 'a man under authority'. Yet, simply by being who he was, he also built up his own reserves of that self-same quality, at least to the point that Rome itself – and in particular powerful figures within the Curia – could sometimes betray signs of being slightly apprehensive of him. Certainly, in such fields as episcopal appointments, while operating strictly through first the Apostolic

Delegate, then (after 1982) the pro-Nuncio, and finally (after 1995) the Nuncio, he appears to have been granted virtually a free hand in a way that his Continental opposite numbers (whether in Germany, The Netherlands or Austria) could only envy. Ethical issues posed an altogether more delicate question, but even here – for instance on homosexuality or birth control – it sometimes appeared as if the English Church was conceded a licence of interpretation that was by no means universally available.

It is not an analogy that should be pushed too far, but it is almost as if, having spent a dozen years of his life as a schoolmaster, Basil had a model in his mind for the English Church's relationship with Rome. He saw himself as what he had once been – an experienced housemaster who, provided he kept his own house in order and under control, did not need (and certainly would not welcome) interference from the headmaster in the papal apartments, still less from any administrative body within the Roman Curia.

There could have been no more vivid illustration of the position he had established for himself than the way in which the Vatican reacted to the crisis precipitated by the General Synod of the Church of England's vote in favour of women priests in the autumn of 1992. The fall-out from that decision – and, in particular, the handling of the few hundred Anglican clergy it provoked to leave the C of E and join the Church of Rome – could easily have put at risk all the progress that had been made in inter-Church relationships over the previous thirty years. There would have been a real danger of that happening had the reactive strategy been made the responsibility of the authorities in Rome. By persuading the Vatican that the whole question of the proper response should be left exclusively to him, Basil may not have avoided every pitfall, but he did pull off one of the most delicate exercises ever in ecclesiastical diplomacy. Even today it is impossible not to marvel at the ease with which the English Catholic Church has come to terms with the clear anomaly of maintaining, on the one hand, the rule of celibacy while, on the other, welcoming into the priesthood former Anglican clergy with both wives and children.

Inevitably, in following the strategy that he did, Basil could not avoid riding roughshod over those Catholics, by no means all of them traditionalists, who had hoped for an altogether more rigorous line to be taken. Some of his own colleagues in the Hierarchy belonged in this company, and it was at around this time that criticisms began to be heard about the autocratic way in which Basil ran not only the Conference of Bishops but the whole English Catholic Church. He certainly could be imperious, especially in face of criticism, but that was hardly surprising. Before coming to Westminster, he had, after all, been an abbot for thirteen years – and an abbot is far more of an absolute monarch than a diocesan bishop who often has to find a solution to problems by calculating the weight of the relative pressures operating on the faithful.

Yet there were also advantages in his having had the experience of running a monastery. If he tended, as a monk, to exaggerate the duty of obedience that he owed to the Holy Father (even, after 1978, to such a conservative one as Pope John Paul II), it was equally true that he was not inclined to dismiss the obedience that, as the Ampleforth monks had once done, the bishops, priests and laity of the English Church owed to him. He may not have set out to create a national church, but he did leave behind him a semi-autonomous one – and he could never have done that without possessing at least some of the qualities of 'a benign despot'.

Always, however, alongside the tendency towards autocracy went an overwhelming personal charm – a quality, since it worked particularly with women, that some were even tempted to equate with 'sexual attraction'. (For a celibate priest, he had a remarkable number of close women friends.) There are too many witnesses among both men and women of his ability to put people totally at their ease for it to be possible to attempt any assessment of Basil's record at Westminster without taking this element of personal magnetism into account.

It worked just as much with strangers as with those he had already got to know. After the unfortunate start, in his first full TV interview with Ludovic Kennedy, he soon learned how to get even the media eating out of his hand. Interviewers as detached from organised religion as Jean Rook, who at the time proudly wore the title of 'the first lady of Fleet Street', or John Mortimer, the creator of *Rumpole*, may have come to scoff, but they stayed, if not to pray, then at least to praise a man whom they obviously found a mysteriously compulsive figure.

It helped enormously, of course, that he looked the part. Tall, lean and with an ascetic face crowned by a halo of white hair, his very presence suggested someone who could have stepped straight out of a medieval stained glass window. To the most hardened journalistic cases he managed to convey spirituality in a way that no other Church leader of the twentieth century had ever done, and not only to journalists either – it was the celebrated agnostic intellectual, Noël Annan,* who once paid him this unsolicited tribute: 'If I may say so, you have a wonderful gift for conveying what the spiritual life means; and that is why your influence is so wide and why so many feel in your debt.'

Partly, it was probably a matter of innate simplicity. In contrast to his predecessor, who was very conscious of his dignity as a Prince of the Church, Basil's favourite garb, even when receiving

---

* Provost of King's College, Cambridge, 1956–66, Provost of University College London, 1966–78, Vice-Chancellor, University of London 1978–81. The tribute came in a private 1981 letter from Annan after Basil had taken an ecumenical service for those who had just graduated from London University.

visitors at Archbishop's House, was an old pair of dark trousers and a somewhat shabby woollen sweater with holes in it.* He could, on the other hand, be vain. A former private secretary, Father Pat Browne, has never forgotten how, when they were swimming together in Australia in 1988, they both got into difficulties. Once they had made it back to the shore and were lying exhausted on the beach, something about the Cardinal suddenly attracted his attention. Without the normal grooming of his hair and the spreading of it carefully across his scalp, there was a large, normally invisible bald patch. It remained a secret that both of them managed to keep from the world.

Generally, though, there was never any pretence – or pretentiousness. It was typical of Basil that he always refused to sign any letters he wrote with the episcopal cross that normally precedes a bishop's signature. It was the kind of embellishment with which he never really came to terms – and maybe for a very personal reason. When once asked what was the besetting sin of Benedictines – for Jesuits it has traditionally been said to be arrogance – he replied, without missing a beat, 'smugness'. Although always very much a monk, he was rarely anything but an unusually clear-sighted one.

There was, however, one other reason for the undoubted impact that the Cardinal made. Unlike most clerics, he fully understood the need to ration his interventions, at least in the realm of public affairs, and to use his influence extremely sparingly. Not long after he became Archbishop, he remarked to an old Ampleforth friend that he had come to the conclusion that he was not a bad politician. When asked what he

---

* He could, of course, take this hair-shirt side of himself too far. When a favourite niece, having noticed while he was convalescing after his first hip operation how threadbare his dressing-gown was, went out and bought a new one for him, he got very cross and insisted she take it back immediately to the shop. She, understandably, felt a little hurt.

meant, he simply replied: 'Well, you see, I think I know when to speak and, more importantly, I know when not to speak.' At Westminster this self-denying ordinance became the lode-star governing all his public utterances.*

That was particularly true of Ireland. More than any other Church leader within the United Kingdom, Basil – belonging, as he did, to what was the majority denomination in Ireland as a whole – understood the bewilderment caused to the rest of the world by the repressive policy the British Government was sometimes seen, however unfairly, as pursuing. By character and instinct far too much of a patriot to want to sound any public note of dissent, Hume nevertheless worked tirelessly behind the scenes to try to remove those factors which led to a sense of injustice. His most celebrated campaign was that on behalf of the Maguire Seven (which led directly also to the release of the Guildford Four) but that was merely a symptom of a whole range of activities he put in – largely behind the scenes.

What made this all the more remarkable was that it was a highly delicate area for any Westminster Archbishop to get involved in since, as a Catholic country, Ireland had its own Hierarchy presided over by the Primate of All Ireland, the Archbishop of Armagh. For thirteen of the twenty-three years that Hume spent at Westminster, the Irishman who held this post was Cardinal Tomàs O'Fiaich, thought by the British Government to be altogether too nationalist in his sympathies. There was even a *canard* officially floated that Basil, at the instigation of the Northern Ireland Office, had tried to prevent O'Fiaich's appointment as a Cardinal. There was no foundation

---

* There was no doubt that his reluctance to sound off on each and every topic paid off. In 1986 John Biffen, then Tory Leader of the House of Commons, was troubled in his conscience over the American bombing of Libya. Although not a Roman Catholic, his immediate instinct was to approach the Cardinal for moral guidance.

for that particular piece of government-inspired propaganda, although it was certainly the case that there was a divergence of view between the two Cardinals – Basil tending to be much more forthright than O'Fiaich in his condemnation of such overt political actions as the hunger strike undertaken by Bobby Sands and other IRA members in the Maze Prison in the spring of 1981. Yet, if Basil (to the relief of Margaret Thatcher) was never a soft-sword, he was also someone who believed that the blade of justice must always be unstained and unsullied. This was the reason behind his twelve-year fight with the Home Office to secure the overturning of the convictions obtained back in the mid-1970s against both the wrongly convicted 'bomb-manu-facturing' Maguires and the falsely accused Guildford 'bombers'.

What struck those – by no means all of them Catholics – who worked with him on both these campaigns was the ease with which he could master what was often a fairly intricate brief. Intellectually, he liked to claim that he 'belonged in the third division', but whatever might have been true theologically (and it is possible that his various devotional books* did not do him full justice), that was certainly not the case in any wider, more worldly sense. Here he usually displayed a firm grasp and a sure touch, as politicians who risked taking him on gradually came to realise.

In the public arena there was perhaps one aspect of Basil's personality that involved some element of contradiction. When he first learned of his appointment as Archbishop of Westminster he liked to claim that he was both 'shattered and distressed'. But can this really have been true of someone whose last (admittedly jocular) words to one of his sisters on the day

---

* Eight of these were published, culminating (posthumously) with *The Mystery of the Incarnation* in 1999, but they tended to be merely edited transcripts of addresses Basil had already delivered.

he joined the monastery were 'Pope or bust!'* and who, later, repeated the same phrase to his fellow novices as he rammed the abbot's mitre on his head in the sacristy of Ampleforth Abbey?

In his notorious essay on Manning in *Eminent Victorians*, Lytton Strachey quoted a fellow priest as saying of Cardinal Wiseman, the first Archbishop of Westminster, that there was 'a lobster salad side to his nature' – and it may be, if in a less literal sense, that something of the same sort was true of Basil Hume.

Certainly, in the light of his career, it is hard to believe that he lacked any element of ambition in his make-up. To find yourself elected an abbot just after you have turned forty hardly argues a shrinking, diffident character. Moreover, the description most often used about him by those who knew him as a young man always tended to be that he was 'a natural leader'. So, despite his own careful propagation of it, the theory that the very notion of leaving Ampleforth for Archbishop's House, Westminster, filled him with dread is probably best treated with a measure of scepticism – as is his claim (this time privately made) that the prospect of becoming a Cardinal simply 'depressed' him.

Why, then, did he insist on saying such things? The obvious answer has to be that he knew what was expected of him. Just as, long after the event, he publicly questioned whether he should not have joined the Army rather than entering the monastery in 1941, so, on getting to Westminster in 1976, he realised that it would be politic to appear as if he was totally overwhelmed by all that had happened to him. In both instances he may have

---

* 'Pope or Bust' was also the message scribbled on a piece of cardboard and left on his pillow by the two sons of the house in which he was staying on the eve of his departure for the second conclave in Rome in 1978. This suggests that by then the use of the original phrase had achieved a certain notoriety.

been forced to shave the truth a little; on the other hand, he had certainly displayed a shrewd, instinctive understanding of the English character.

In the last resort, that was precisely the appropriate qualification necessary for becoming Archbishop of Westminster in the last quarter of the twentieth century. What the Church needed was not merely someone who would symbolise Christian values in an increasingly sceptical society. It equally required a leader who would identify English Catholicism with English culture. Whatever he may have failed in – and what he called 'the marginalisation of the Church' during his lifetime was certainly his greatest grief – no one could question Basil Hume's success in attaining both those objectives.

ACKNOWLEDGEMENTS

I N MOST CASES THIS SECTION OF ANY BOOK CONSISTS OF a roll-call of the names of the various individuals that the author has interviewed, together with a slightly *pro forma* record of the permissions that have been granted for the reproduction of copyright material. I have no wish to shirk my obligations in either respect. Yet that sort of conventional formality has increasingly struck me as having become rather a routine, empty exercise. I hope, therefore, that I shall be forgiven if I waive the traditional custom on this occasion and merely reiterate my gratitude to the hundred or so friends and contemporaries of Basil Hume who talked to me, and simultaneously express my appreciation to the much smaller number of those who – whether directly or through their literary executors – have authorised me to quote from letters that were written to the Cardinal.

To all rules there are, however, exceptions. At least the earlier part of this book could never have been written had not the Cardinal's own literary executors, Liam Kelly and Charles Wookey, made a far-sighted move very early on. Within a year of the Cardinal's death in 1999, they travelled together to Ampleforth in order to interview those monks who had not merely known their former Abbot well but in many cases had actually grown up with him. The two of them recorded (and later transcribed) all ten of those interviews, which thus became invaluable witness statements for the early part of my narrative. I subsequently supplemented what I came to call the 'depositions' with interviews of my own, but the challenge of evoking Ampleforth both as a school and as a monastery would have been infinitely more daunting without that timely, preliminary groundwork. I am much in their debt.

There are four or five other individuals whom I must single out for special mention. Simon Hoggart, my one-time colleague on the *Observer*, Ian Brunskill, my successor as obituaries editor on *The Times* and Liam Kelly, secretary to the Abbot at Ampleforth, all devotedly (to borrow a favourite word of the Cardinal) read the text, saving me from any number of egregious errors and stylistic inelegancies. Father Ian Dickie, the Westminster diocesan archivist, was a tower of strength throughout. The ready access that he granted me to the 600 boxes covering Basil Hume's archiepiscopal career – held at the Parish Centre of the Church of Our Lady of Victories in Kensington – greatly speeded up the progress that I was able to make.

Sister Clement and Mary McGhee, secretary to Cardinal Cormac Murphy-O'Connor, were equally helpful in guiding me through that section of the documentary material pertaining to Basil Hume's twenty-three years at Westminster which is still retained at Archbishop's House.

When I started out, there was in addition a substantial cache of more personal correspondence preserved at Ampleforth and, though that has now been added to the official archive in Kensington, it has not yet been catalogued. Accordingly, I thought it wiser not to offer specific source references (apart from those that surface in the text itself) and I ask the forbearance of any scholarly readers in this respect. That and all other shortcomings are entirely my responsibility.

INDEX

Note: BH denotes Basil Hume (Basil is preferred to George for entries prior to 1941 in order to avoid confusion). Subheadings are in chronological order. The letter *n* appended to a page number denotes a footnote.

BACKING INTO THE LIMELIGHT

ALEXANDER GAMES

'Games has done an excellent job . . . this is an affectionate, dryly funny and shrewd overview'
Daily Express

He was always the shy, retiring one, seemingly dismissive of his gifts. Yet Alan Bennett, who came to prominence in the mould-breaking 1960 revue *Beyond the Fringe*, has slowly but surely become one of Britain's best-loved national figures, acclaimed for his work on TV, stage and screen. Running parallel with Bennett's evolution as an author, actor and celebrity is the story of his love-hate relationship with the media, a remarkable and at times farcical tale of trust mislaid, and eventually lost.

In this, the first full biography of Alan Bennett, Alexander Games tracks the writer's life from childhood in Leeds through his formative years at Oxford and onward as he stepped reluctantly into the limelight. The result is a penetrating, often hilarious and sometimes harrowing journey which attempts to unravel the multi-faceted life of the man behind *Forty Years On*, *A Private Function*, *Talking Heads*, *Writing Home*, *The Lady in the Van* and many other triumphs.

NON-FICTION / BIOGRAPHY 0 7472 6661 1

Now you can buy any of these other bestselling non-fiction titles from your bookshop or *direct from the publisher*.

FREE P&P AND UK DELIVERY
(Overseas and Ireland £3.50 per book)

| *Emma Darwin* | Edna Healey | £7.99 |

A beautifully researched and elegantly written portrayal of the wife of one of science's greatest geniuses.

| *The Tiger Ladies* | Sudha Koul | £10.99 |

This remarkable book is an enchanting account of the author's life growing up in a beautiful, remote valley in Kashmir, set against the troubles of the region.

| *The Celebrated Captain Barclay* | Peter Radford | £7.99 |

This extraordinary and unique story maps one of the greatest sporting challenges ever: 'to walk a thousand miles in a thousand hours for a thousand guineas'.

| *Cane River* | Lalita Tademy | £6.99 |

The compelling tale of the lives and relationships of a family of slaves in the American deep south, and of their ultimate emancipation.

| *Hildegard of Bingen* | Fiona Maddocks | £6.99 |

A fascinating insight into the life and social times of this incredible medieval abbess and composer who was later made a saint.

TO ORDER SIMPLY CALL THIS NUMBER

01235 400 414

or visit our website: www.madaboutbooks.com

Prices and availability subject to change without notice.